REMEMBERING SOCRATES

Remembering Socrates

Philosophical Essays

Edited by
LINDSAY JUDSON
and
VASSILIS KARASMANIS

CLARENDON PRESS · OXFORD

OXFORD
UNIVERSITY PRESS

Great Clarendon Street, Oxford OX2 6DP

Oxford University Press is a department of the University of Oxford.
It furthers the University's objective of excellence in research, scholarship,
and education by publishing worldwide in

Oxford New York

Auckland Cape Town Dar es Salaam Hong Kong Karachi
Kuala Lumpur Madrid Melbourne Mexico City Nairobi
New Delhi Shanghai Taipei Toronto

With offices in

Argentina Austria Brazil Chile Czech Republic France Greece
Guatemala Hungary Italy Japan Poland Portugal Singapore
South Korea Switzerland Thailand Turkey Ukraine Vietnam

Oxford is a registered trade mark of Oxford University Press
in the UK and in certain other countries

Published in the United States
by Oxford University Press Inc., New York

© the several contributors 2006

The moral rights of the authors have been asserted
Database right Oxford University Press (maker)

First published 2006

All rights reserved. No part of this publication may be reproduced,
stored in a retrieval system, or transmitted, in any form or by any means,
without the prior permission in writing of Oxford University Press,
or as expressly permitted by law, or under terms agreed with the appropriate
reprographics rights organization. Enquiries concerning reproduction
outside the scope of the above should be sent to the Rights Department,
Oxford University Press, at the address above

You must not circulate this book in any other binding or cover
and you must impose the same condition on any acquirer

British Library Cataloguing in Publication Data

Data available

Library of Congress Cataloging in Publication Data

Data available

Typeset by SPI Publisher Services, Pondicherry, India
Printed in Great Britain
on acid-free paper by
Biddles Ltd., King's Lynn, Norfolk

ISBN 978-0-19-927613-4

Contents

	Notes on Contributors and Editors	vii
	Introduction	1
1.	Socrates' Dialectic in Xenophon's *Memorabilia* *Carlo Natali*	3
2.	If you Know What is Best, you Do it: Socratic Intellectualism in Xenophon and Plato *Gerhard Seel*	20
3.	Socrates and Hedonism *Charles H. Kahn*	50
4.	Socrates and Euthyphro: The Argument and its Revival *Terence Irwin*	58
5.	Did Socrates Agree to Obey the Laws of Athens? *Lesley Brown*	72
6.	*Aporia* and Searching in the Early Plato *Vasilis Politis*	88
7.	Types of Definition in the *Meno* *David Charles*	110
8.	Definition in Plato's *Meno* *Vassilis Karasmanis*	129
9.	Sharing a Property *Theodore Scaltsas*	142
10.	Socrates the Sophist *C. C. W. Taylor*	157
11.	Arcesilaus: Socratic and Sceptic *John M. Cooper*	169
12.	The Early Christian Reception of Socrates *Michael Frede*	188
	Index	203

Notes on the Contributors and Editors

Lesley Brown is Centenary Fellow in Philosophy at Somerville College, Oxford, and the author of numerous articles and book chapters on Plato and Aristotle.

David Charles is Fellow and Tutor in Philosophy at Oriel College, Oxford. He is the author of *Aristotle's Philosophy of Action* (London, 1984), *Aristotle on Meaning and Essence* (Oxford, 2000), and a variety of articles on topics in ancient and contemporary philosophy.

John M. Cooper is Stuart Professor of Philosophy and Director of the Program in Classical Philosophy at Princeton University. His books include *Reason and Human Good in Aristotle* (Cambridge, Mass., and London, 1975), *Seneca: Moral and Political Essays* (co-edited with J. F. Procopé, Cambridge, 1995), *Plato: Complete Works* (edited with D.S. Hutchinson, Indianapolis and Cambridge, 1997), *Reason and Emotion: Essays on Ancient Moral Psychology and Ethical Theory* (Princeton, 1999), and *Knowledge, Nature, and the Good: Essays on Ancient Philosophy* (Princeton, 2004).

Michael Frede is Emeritus Professor of the History of Philosophy, Oxford University. His publications include *Galen: Three Treatises on the Nature of Science* (with Richard Walzer, Indianapolis, 1985), *Essays in Ancient Philosophy* (Oxford, 1987), *Aristoteles* Metaphysik Z (with Günther Patzig, Munich, 1988), and *The Original Sceptics: A Controversy* (with Myles Burnyeat, Indianapolis and Cambridge, 1997).

Terence Irwin is Susan Linn Sage Professor of Philosophy and Humane Letters, Cornell University. His books include *Aristotle's First Principles* (Oxford, 1988), *Classical Thought* (Oxford, 1989), *Plato's Ethics* (Oxford, 1995), and *Aristotle's* Nicomachean Ethics (2nd edn, Indianapolis and Cambridge, 1999).

Lindsay Judson is Official Student and Tutor in Philosophy, Christ Church, Oxford. He is the author of a variety of articles on ancient philosophy, and is the Editor of the *Clarendon Aristotle Series* and Co-editor (with Julia Annas) of *Oxford Aristotle Studies*.

Charles H. Kahn is Professor of Philosophy, University of Pennsylvania. He is the author of *Anaximander and the Origins of Greek Cosmology* (New York, 1960), *The Art and Thought of Heraclitus* (Cambridge, 1979), *Plato and the Socratic Dialogue* (Cambridge, 1996), and *Pythagoras and the Pythagoreans* (Indianapolis and Cambridge, 2001), *The Verb 'Be' in Ancient Greek* (2nd edn, Indianapolis and Cambridge, 2002).

Vassilis Karasmanis is Professor of Philosophy, Technical University of Athens. He is the author of numerous articles on ancient philosophy and ancient mathematics. He was Director of the European Cultural Centre of Delphi from 1994 to 2004.

Carlo Natali is Professor of Philosophy, Universita' di Venezia. His books include *The Wisdom of Aristotle* (Albany, 2001), *L'action efficace. Etudes de la théorie de l'action d'Aristote* (Louvain-la-Neuve, 2004), and *Aristotle's Life and the Organisation of his School* (Princeton, 2006). He is Co-editor (with Lloyd Gerson and Gerhard Seel) of *International Aristotle Studies*.

Vasilis Politis is Lecturer in Philosophy, Trinity College, Dublin. His publications include *Aristotle and the* Metaphysics (London, 2004) and a translation of Paul Natorp, *Plato's Theory of Ideas* (with John Connolly, Berlin, 2004).

Theodore Scaltsas is Professor of Ancient Philosophy, University of Edinburgh. His books include *Substances and Universals in Aristotle's Metaphysics* (Ithaca, 1994) and *Unity, Identity and Explanation in Aristotle's* Metaphysics (co-edited with David Charles and Mary Louise Gill, Oxford, 1994). His most recent publications are on the topics of plural subjects, relations, and ontological composition. He is the Director of *Project Archelogos*.

Gerhard Seel is Professor of Philosophy and Director of the Institute for Philosophy, University of Bern. His publications include *Sartres Dialektik* (Bonn 1971), *Die Aristotelische Modaltheorie* (Berlin and New York, 1982), and *Ammonius and the Sea Battle* (with J-P. Schneider and D. Schulthess, Berlin, 2001). He is Secretary General of the International Academy for Philosophy of Art and Co-editor (with Lloyd Gerson and Carlo Natali) of *International Aristotle Studies*.

C. C. W. Taylor is Emeritus Professor of Philosophy, Oxford University, and an Emeritus Fellow of Corpus Christi College. He is author of *The Greeks on Pleasure* (with J. C. B. Gosling, Oxford, 1982), *Plato,* Protagoras (2nd edn, Oxford, 1991), *Socrates* (Oxford, 1998), and *The Atomists: Leucippus and Democritus* (Toronto, 1999). He was Editor of *Oxford Studies in Ancient Philosophy* from 1993 to 1998.

Introduction

Socrates died in Athens in 399 BC by drinking hemlock, condemned to death by his fellow citizens. In 2001 the European Cultural Centre of Delphi, with the support of the Greek Ministry of Culture, organized a number of activities and events to commemorate the 2,400th anniversary of Socrates' death. One of these was an international conference on Socrates, held in Athens and Delphi: in this volume, with the permission of the European Cultural Centre of Delphi, we publish some of the papers presented at this conference. For the selection of the papers the editors were assisted by David Charles and Michael Frede.

The essays in this collection pursue in various ways Socrates' most famous saying 'The unexamined life is not a life worth living for a human being' (*Apology* 38a). One theme is Socrates' own methods of examination. Socrates enquires by question and answer, argument and counterargument, with a variety of interlocutors, an approach which some writers called 'dialectic', and which had among its offspring Platonic and Aristotelian dialectic. Carlo Natali discusses Socratic dialectic as portrayed by Xenophon. Vasilis Politis focuses on another key ingredient of Socrates' examinations—*aporia*, puzzlement—in which some of Socrates' conversations begin and many end. Socrates linked the idea of the examined life to the good life in at least two ways. First, his enquiries often focus on the need to arrive at *definitions* of notions central to living well, such as courage, piety, or friendship: David Charles and Vasilis Karasmanis explore the development of this idea of definition in Plato's *Meno*. Second, Socrates embraced the idea that coming to know the truth about living well—enquiries of the type he engaged in being one, if not the only, way to achieve this—was enough to guarantee that one did indeed live well. Gerhard Seel and Charles Kahn explore different aspects of this difficult and challenging doctrine. Three further papers are concerned with particular sets of arguments in Platonic dialogues. Terence Irwin and Lesley Brown consider famous and much-discussed arguments associated with Socrates' trial and execution, in Plato's *Euthyphro* and *Crito* respectively, while Theodore Scaltsas looks at a more neglected one in the *Hippias Major*, in which Socrates is represented as exhibiting a somewhat less characteristic interest in metaphysics. The final theme is that of the life lived: though he disavowed all knowledge of how to live, the manner of Socrates's own life—his unwavering dedication to philosophical enquiry, his austere uprightness and his uncompromising resolution in the face of death—proved a profound inspiration both to contemporaries and to later generations. Christopher Taylor examines Plato's reflections in the *Sophist* and other dialogues on the figure of Socrates and his own portrayals of him as a genuine philosopher in contrast to the Sophists; John Cooper traces the influence of his example on the Academic sceptic Arcesilaus; and Michael Frede traces the complexities of the early Christian reception of the figure of Socrates. We hope that the essays in this collection demonstrate the vitality as well as the diversity of Socratic studies at the start of the twenty-first century, 2,400 years after Socrates' death.

We would like to thank all the scholars who contributed their papers for the volume, and to the two anonymous referees who commented on the papers. We are also grateful to those at the European Cultural Centre of Delphi and Oxford University Press who helped with the publication of this volume.

Lindsay Judson
Vassilis Karasmanis

1

Socrates' Dialectic in Xenophon's *Memorabilia*

Carlo Natali

In recent years there has been a tendency to revise the harsh judgement given on Xenophon by philologists of the nineteenth century and the first part of the twentieth century. Some contemporary scholars maintain that it is interesting to study Xenophon's Socratic writings, even if it is not possible to find in them a historically accurate image of Socrates. Also the tendency to find in Xenophon the remains of all the literature written by the Minor Socratics is not as strong as it was previously. The analysis of the structure and the arguments of the *Memorabilia* as a complete and uniform whole, without referring immediately one passage or the other to some other philosopher, but rather trying to interpret it in the light of the rest of the work, has helped interpreters to arrive at a better understanding of Xenophon's theses.

In this article I will not retrace the history of the interpretations of Xenophon's Socratic writings, from the great appreciation typical of the early nineteenth century to the complete depreciation of the following decades, and to the new stream of studies written in defence of Xenophon's work by reputable scholars like Erbse, Cooper, Dorion, Morrison, Gray, and others.[1]

My aim is more limited. I think that a way to arrive at a more balanced evaluation of the work is to examine some key concepts, to see if there is some coherence in the way they are employed. For this reason I will analyse some passages of the text in order to establish if it is possible to trace in the *Memorabilia*

---

[1] Cf. H. Erbse, 'Die Arkitektonik im Aufbau von Xenophon. Memorabilien', *Hermes*, 89 (1961), 257–87; D. R. Morrison, 'Xenophon's Socrates as Teacher', in P. A. Vander Waerdt (ed.), *The Socratic Movement* (Ithaca, NY, and London, 1994), 181–207; id. 'Justice et legalité selon le Socrate de Xenophon', in G. Romeyer Dherbey and J. B. Gourinat (eds.), *Socrate et les socratiques* (Paris, 2001), 48–70; V. J. Gray, *The Framing of Socrates* (Stuttgart, 1998); J. M. Cooper, *Reason and Emotion* (Princeton, 1999), ch. 1: 'Notes on Xenophon's Socrates', 3–28; L. A. Dorion, 'Introduction', in *Xénophon*, Mémorables, ed. M. Bandini and tr. Dorion (Paris, 2000). One could add also the essays by C. Viano, 'La Cosmologie de Socrate dans les *Mémorables* de Xénophon', in Romeyer Dherbey and Gourinat (eds.), *Socrate*, 97–119; and by C. Natali, 'Socrate dans l'*Economique* de Xénophon', ibid. 263–88.

a coherent theory of a couple of central concepts such as *dialegesthai* and *dialektikos*.

Xenophon speaks about dialogue and dialectics mainly at the beginning of book 1, when presenting his intentions, and in book 4, where he describes the logical aspect of Socrates' teaching. The two groups of passages are consistent with each other. In 1. 3. 1, after the end of the section dedicated to the defence of Socrates in the proper sense of the word, Xenophon begins the long section devoted to the description of his life and of how he benefited Athenian people. He says: 'I will tell you how he benefited his companions alike by actions that revealed his own character, and by his conversation (*dialegomenos*), as far as I remember it' (1. 3. 1. 1–4).[2] Here the participle *dialegomenos* indicates in general the philosophical and ethical training Socrates gave to his disciples, and not some particular technique, such as the *elenchos* or the definition.[3] More indications on what this 'conversation' consists in can be found in two passages, one which precedes 1. 3. 1 and one which follows it.

In 1. 1. 16 Xenophon tells us about the content of Socrates' *dialegesthai*:

He always discussed about human things, examining what is godly and what is ungodly, what is beautiful and what is ugly, what is just and what is unjust, what is prudence and what is madness, what is courage and what is cowardice, what is a city, what is a statesman, what is government upon men, what is to be a governor; and also the other thing the knowledge of which he esteemed to be typical of a gentleman, while people ignorant of those matters are rightly called 'slaves'. (1. 1. 16. 2–9)[4]

In this passage there is a tendency to divide the subject of the inquiry into pairs of different headings, one positive and one negative: godly/ungodly, beautiful/ugly and so on. However, the technique is not followed consistently: at the end of the passage we have the pairs city/statesman, government/governor in which there is no opposition, but derivation of one term from the other.

In some of the following chapters we will find, indeed, definitions of the beautiful/the ugly (3. 8. 4–7), the just/the unjust (3. 9. 5; 4. 4), the prudent/the unwise (3. 9. 4), the courageous/the coward (4. 6. 10–11). But there are also definitions which describe only the positive part and do not make explicit the contrary, as the definition of the pious (4. 6. 2–4), the just (4. 6. 5–6), the beautiful (4. 6. 9).

In another chapter, 1. 4, Xenophon gives us more indications on his method in *dialegesthai*:

---

[2] Ὡς δὲ δὴ καὶ ὠφελεῖν ἐδόκει μοι τοὺς συνόντας τὰ μὲν ἔργῳ δεικνύων ἑαυτὸν οἷος ἦν, τὰ δὲ καὶ διαλεγόμενος, τούτων δὴ γράψω ὁπόσα ἂν διαμνημονεύσω.

[3] Dorion, 'Introduction', 124; Gray, *Framing*, 105; cf. L. Strauss, *Xenophon's Socrates* (Ithaca, NY, and London 1972), 19.

[4] αὐτὸς δὲ περὶ τῶν ἀνθρωπείων ἀεὶ διελέγετο σκοπῶν τί εὐσεβές, τί ἀσεβές, τί καλόν, τί αἰσχρόν, τί δίκαιον, τί ἄδικον, τί σωφροσύνη, τί μανία, τί ἀνδρεία, τί δειλία, τί πόλις, τί πολιτικός, τί ἀρχὴ ἀνθρώπων, τί ἀρχικὸς ἀνθρώπων, καὶ περὶ τῶν ἄλλων, ἃ τοὺς μὲν εἰδότας ἡγεῖτο καλοὺς κἀγαθοὺς εἶναι, τοὺς δ' ἀγνοοῦντας ἀνδραποδώδεις ἂν δικαίως κεκλῆσθαι.

If anybody has the opinion, based on what some authors write and say about him, that though [Socrates] was very able in exhorting men to virtue, he was unable to lead them to it, let him examine if Socrates was able of improving his companions. They should take account not only of the refutations based on questions, to which Socrates submitted those who thought themselves omniscient, in order to chastise them, but also of the things he used to say in everyday conversations to his companions. (1. 4. 1–2)[5]

Here Xenophon attacks the idea that Socrates concentrated only on the refutations of other people's theories and had nothing to teach his disciples. It is a familiar picture, which emerges also from the dialogues belonging to the first stage of Plato's evolution. Xenophon does not like this picture, and in the rest of the *Memorabilia* tries to show that Socrates had many positive bits of advice to give to his friends—unfortunately, the examples he gives us of those pieces of advice are not very satisfactory from a philosophical point of view, and the modern reader tends to think that some of them are commonplace and rather dull.[6]

Anyway, Xenophon's *Memorabilia* are the main testimony for a non-refutative dialectic in Socrates, a dialectic which has the aim of arriving at positive determinations, and definitions of the moral good and of human virtue. In the only passage in which an attitude of 'Socratic ignorance' is attributed to Socrates this is put into the mouth of an opponent of Socrates, the sophist Hippias (4. 4. 9).[7] It is clear that Xenophon does not subscribe to this image and thinks that a more positive description of Socrates' philosophy is needed in order to defend him from his detractors and to show that he was a useful companion and a good citizen.

In the passage quoted above, the function of exhorting (*protrepsasthai*) is *exemplified* by the use of the refutation (*elenchein*),[8] and the function of leading

---

[5] Εἰ δέ τινες Σωκράτην νομίζουσιν, ὡς ἔνιοι γράφουσί τε καὶ λέγουσι περὶ αὐτοῦ τεκμαιρόμενοι, προτρέψασθαι μὲν ἀνθρώπους ἐπ' ἀρετὴν κράτιστον γεγονέναι, προαγαγεῖν δ' ἐπ' αὐτὴν οὐχ ἱκανόν, σκεψάμενοι μὴ μόνον ἃ ἐκεῖνος κολαστηρίου ἕνεκα τοὺς πάντ' οἰομένους εἰδέναι ἐρωτῶν ἤλεγχεν, ἀλλὰ καὶ ἃ λέγων συνημέρευε τοῖς συνδιατρίβουσι, δοκιμαζόντων εἰ ἱκανὸς ἦν βελτίους ποιεῖν τοὺς συνόντας.

[6] The idea that Socrates' dialectic was always refutative and never arrived at positive answers is one of the most widely accepted in the scholarship. Cf. for instance H. Maier, *Socrate*, Italian tr., 2 vols. (Florence, 1944); G. Giannantoni, *Cosa ha veramente detto Socrate* (Rome, 1971); a more complex position in G. Vlastos, *Socrate: Il filosofo dell'ironia complessa*, Italian tr. (Florence, 1998). O. Gigon, *Kommentar zur ersten Buch von Xenophon Memorabilien.* (Basle, 1953), 121–2 rightly notes that Xenophon wants to contrast the idea of the Socratic Ignorance.

[7] Vlastos, *Socrate*, 136–40, does not take account of the fact that Xenophon is explicit in his intention to criticize the philosophers who attribute to Socrates the Socratic Ignorance, and does not realize that this single passage in the *Memorabilia*, where this position is attributed to Socrates, is put on the mouth of an adversary, as an unjust reproach. In general Vlastos's account of Xenophon's position is unsympathetic and does not do justice to what Xenophon actually says.

[8] Is the *elenchos* identical to the function of *protrepsasthai*? K. Joël, *Der echte und der Xenophontische Sokrates* (Berlin, 1893–1901), i. 383; Gray, *Framing*, 75–6 and Dorion, 'Introduction', cxxvi–cxxxiii, with further bibliography, think so. Gigon, *Kommentar*, 119 and Strauss, *Xenophon's Socrates*, 21, think that it is impossible to identify them. We will see later that Xenophon's Socrates uses also other forms of exhorting, all intended to make the interlocutor dislike his present intellectual condition. The *elenchos*, in the technical meaning of the term, is one example of exhortation, among others. See later the discussion of 4. 1. 3–5.

to virtue is *identified* with the everyday conversations (*ha legôn sunêmereue*) with disciples and friends.

In what remains of book 1, and in books 2–3, Xenophon describes the Socratic virtues, tells us how Socrates benefited his friends by helping them to acquire all the virtues, and how he gave them good advice on relationships with their family, friends, and fellow citizens. There is no more discussion of *elenchos* or dialectic in those pages. Only in the last part of book 3, chapters 8–14, which look like a depository of unconnected essays and texts, do we find some definitions and discussions by Socrates which are similar to the definition alluded to in 1. 1. 16 quoted previously.[9]

The question of dialectics, on contrary, is at the centre of the last book of the *Memorabilia*. Here Xenophon starts again from the idea that Socrates benefited his friends very much, and shows how he was effective by describing a series of encounters with a young and beautiful Athenian, Euthydemus (4. 2–3 and 5–6), and with a Sophist, Hippias (4. 4). The chapters which describe the encounters between Socrates and Euthydemus form a complete course of Socrates' pedagogy. The final part of book 4, on the contrary, is composed of two chapters on how he advised his companions to study the different sciences (4. 7), and a general recapitulation of the entire work (4. 8). My research will concentrate on chapters 2, 5 and 6.

At the beginning of 4. 1, Xenophon describes again how useful Socrates was to his friends, and how in particular he was eager to help the young people he felt in love with. The erotic subtone of the Socratic teaching is clearly indicated, but Xenophon specifies that Socrates always felt in love with people 'whose souls excelled in goodness' (4. 1. 2. 1–3) and not only with good-looking youngsters. He was always eager to awake the well-born souls to virtue, friendship, and dialectic.[10]

Xenophon tells us one more time that Socrates used different methods towards different types of disciples: 'He did not use the same method with everybody', he says (4. 1. 3. 1–2). There were some people who did not think they needed education, either because of their natural gifts or their wealth. With them Socrates used a protreptical attitude, pointing out (*epideiknuôn*) and admonishing them (*ephrenou legôn*) that some sort of *paideia* was necessary even for people gifted like them (4. 1. 3–5). This is a sort of protreptical speech, different from the *elenchos* but, like *elenchos*, not very flattering for the people to whom it was addressed.

There were also people 'who thought they had received the best education and prided themselves on wisdom' (4. 2. 1. 1–3). To make them change their mind Socrates used the *elenchos*, which is described in 4. 2. In this chapter Euthydemus

---

[9] On the structure of the *Memorabilia*, cf. Dorion, 'Introduction', clxxxiii–ccxl.
[10] Cf. Joël, *Der echte*, i. 376 and 540–1; R. R. Wellmann, 'Socratic Method in Xenophon', *Journal of History of Ideas*, 37 (1976), 307.

is refuted by Socrates and reduced to admitting that he is as ignorant as a slave. At this point Xenophon reiterates the indication given in 1. 4. 1:

> Well, many people who were brought to this point by Socrates never went to see him again, and he judged them mere blockheads. But Euthydemus ... never left him and even began to adopt some of his habits. Socrates, seeing Euthydemus' attitude towards him, ceased to embarrass him and began to explain in a very plain and clear way the things he thought to be most important to know and the behavior he judged most important to adopt.[11] (4. 2. 40)

We are told again that Socratic *dialegein* and dialectics are not identical to the *elenchos*, but that the *elenchos* was a preliminary technique to be used only with some people who needed to be converted.

A progression towards a more complete understanding of Xenophon's idea of dialectic is made in the following chapters. In 4. 3 Xenophon says that, before acquiring the capacity of speech and efficiency and skill in affairs, his disciples needed to acquire *sôphrosunê*. This is again a way to show that Socrates wasn't only concerned with refutation but had also some positive indications to give to his disciples.[12] Here *sôphrosunê* is not only a virtue of the irrational part of the soul, like in Aristotle, but has also some propositional content. *Sôphrosunê* towards gods is piety (*eusebeia*), Socrates tells us. To make the disciples *sôphronas peri theous*, 'prudent towards the gods', Socrates teaches them some theories about how the gods provide and care for us.

In the 4. 5, again, it is said that the possession of *enkrateia* is necessary in order to become more capable of acting (*praktikôterous*). According to Xenophon, *enkrateia* is the foundation and a necessary condition of all virtue and of reflection on ethical matters (*aretês krêpis*, 1. 5. 4. 5).[13]

I cannot go in depth here into the question of the concept of *enkrateia* in the *Memorabilia* and its relationship to the Socratic intellectualism. I will simply say that there is evidence that Xenophon endorsed both the idea that, according to Socrates, training and moderation were necessary to defeat bodily pleasures and to act virtuously (e.g. 1. 2. 23) and the idea that justice and every other form of virtue is wisdom (*hê allê pasa aretê sophia esti*, 3. 9. 5). The two positions may seem incompatible to a reader familiar with Plato's *Gorgias* and book 7 of the *Nicomachean Ethics*. However, Xenophon seems to have something to say which

---

[11] πολλοὶ μὲν οὖν τῶν οὕτω διατεθέντων ὑπὸ Σωκράτους οὐκέτι αὐτῷ προσῇσαν, οὓς καὶ βλακοτέρους ἐνόμιζεν ὁ δὲ Εὐθύδημος (...) οὐκ ἀπελείπετο ἔτι αὐτοῦ, εἰ μή τι ἀναγκαῖον εἴη· ἔνια δὲ καὶ ἐμιμεῖτο ὧν ἐκεῖνος ἐπετήδευεν. ὁ δ', ὡς ἔγνω αὐτὸν οὕτως ἔχοντα, ἥκιστα μὲν διετάραττεν. ἁπλούστατα δὲ καὶ σαφέστατα ἐξηγεῖτο ἅ τε ἐνόμιζεν εἰδέναι δεῖν καὶ ἐπιτηδεύειν κράτιστα εἶναι.

[12] Joël, *Der echte*, i. 62 and 335; M. Treu, 'Xenophon von Athens', *Paulys Realencyclopädie*, (Stuttgart, 1867), col. 1828. Treu thinks that *sôphrosunê* can be identified to *sophia* and *aretê*.

[13] Joël, *Der echte*, i. 561 ff. and many others think that this idea derives from Antisthenes; the same opinion in the recent book by A. Brancacci, *Oikeios logos. La filosofia del linguaggio di Antistene* (Naples, 1990), ch. 4. On contrary, Gigon, *Kommentar*, 192, and Dorion, 'Introduction', 149, think that it is an original position. I will discuss this problem again in the following pages.

is both original and different from the accounts given by Plato and Aristotle.[14] He wants to emphasize the importance of self-control, but not at the expense of Socratic intellectualism. For Xenophon, as is clear from *Mem.* 3. 9. 4–5, lack of self-control destroys knowledge:

> When asked further whether he thought that people who know what they should do and yet do the opposite, were at the same time wise and lacking self-control,[15] he answered: 'I think that they are nothing more than both unwise and lacking in self-control.[16] For I think all men choose and put into practice, between various possible courses, the one which they think is most conducive to their advantage. Therefore I hold that those who follow the wrong course are neither wise nor prudent. (3. 9. 4. 4–9)[17]

Xenophon's Socrates denies that someone can be wise and lack self-control, but identifies the self-controlled man with the wise. His position is similar to one of the *endoxa* listed by Aristotle at the beginning of *NE* 7: 'The self-controlled person seems the same as one who abides by his rational calculation' (1145b 10–11).

The argument is: *ta kala* = *ha dei prattein* = *ta sumpherotata*. What is morally good is what is to be done; and what is to be done is what is most useful; this implies that people who choose what is base go against their own advantage. But people who do that are unwise. In conclusion, one cannot do base things if one is wise.[18] *Enkrateia* and *akrasia*, according to Xenophon, are about what Aristotle would call the first premise of the practical syllogism, and about the moral principles.

Xenophon's Socrates admits that there are vicious desires which can divert us from virtuous actions, but he doesn't admit that people who are slaves of them possess knowledge. In this way he manages to connect his appreciation of *enkrateia* and Socratic intellectualism. His position is different from Plato's because he gives more importance to bodily desires and to the capacity to

---

[14] Cooper, *Reason*, 27, thinks that Plato chooses not to stress the ascetic aspect of Socrates' teaching in order to emphasize the importance of the Socratic Paradox.

[15] I read here *akrateis* instead of *enkrateis*, with A. Delatte, *Le Troisième Livre des souvenirs socratiques de Xénophon* (Liège and Paris, 1933), 115, and R. A. Gauthier and J. Y. Jolif, *Aristote: L'Ethique à Nicomaque*, introd. tr. and comm. (Paris, 1970), 2nd edn., ii. 591, *contra* the modern edns. by Marchant (Oxford, 1901) and Hude (Stuttgart, 1934).

[16] Delatte, *Troisième Livre*, 116, suggests *Ouden mallon ... hê asophous kai enkrateis*, and translates 'Pas plus qu'il ne sont pas sages et temperants'. It seems unnecessary, because the answer doesn't maintain the opposition of the qualities, but connects in the same man the two negative ones. Here *Ouden ge mallon ... hê* doesn't mean 'Just as little as' (Delatte), but 'Not so much that, as' (Marchant, Santoni; Strauss, *Xenophon's Socrates*, 79, combines the two explanations). Gauthier, ii. 592, has another interpretation: there are no people both wise and incontinent, and it is indifferent to call them wise or unwise. All the interpretations, however, arrive at the same conclusion.

[17] προσερωτώμενος δὲ εἰ τοὺς ἐπισταμένους μὲν ἃ δεῖ πράττειν, ποιοῦντας δὲ τἀναντία σοφούς τε καὶ ἀκρατεῖς εἶναι νομίζοι, Οὐδέν γε μᾶλλον, ἔφη, ἢ ἀσόφους τε καὶ ἀκρατεῖς ·πάντας γὰρ οἶμαι προαιρουμένους ἐκ τῶν ἐνδεχομένων ἃ οἴονται συμφορώτατα αὑτοῖς εἶναι, ταῦτα πράττειν νομίζω οὖν τοὺς μὴ ὀρθῶς πράττοντας οὔτε σοφοὺς οὔτε σώφρονας εἶναι.

[18] Cf. Joël, *Der echte*, i. 335; *Troisième Livre*, 116–17.

withstand them.[19] But Xenophon never gives up Socrates' intellectualism. He says:

[Socrates] said also: 'Justice and every other form of virtue is wisdom. For just actions and all forms of virtuous activity are beautiful and good. He who knows the beautiful and good will never choose anything else, he who is ignorant of them cannot do them, and even if he tries, will fail ... Therefore since just actions and all other forms of beautiful and good activity are virtuous actions, it is clear that justice and every other form of virtue is wisdom. (3. 9. 5)

The wisdom described by Socrates is twofold: the virtuous man should know which are good actions and which are vicious, in order to practise virtue and avoid vice.[20] *Enkrateia* has been connected with *sophia*, via *sōprosune*, as a necessary condition of moral knowledge. This position is completely consistent with what has been said in book 1.

The idea in 4. 5 is very much the same. At one point of his celebration of the *enkrateia* (4. 5. 9) Xenophon's Socrates expresses the rather commonsense view that it is necessary to suffer hunger, thirst, and fatigue to some degree in order to taste fully the pleasures of food, drinking, and rest. Food is much more pleasant after a short fast, and rest is much more welcome after a long walk, as everybody who does trekking in the mountains can tell. A certain degree of endurance makes pleasures all the more pleasant, he says (4. 5. 9. 8–18). This implies a sort of calculation, as in Plato's *Protagoras* (355e–357e), and *enkrateia* appears as the basis of a rational choice among pleasures.

In the following paragraph (4. 5. 10) *enkrateia* is connected with learning, and putting into practice, the ability to rule over oneself, over a household and a city, to win war, and so on. This ability and self-control leads to much greater pleasures than the immediate pleasures in which people without self-control indulge. This idea, of different kinds of pleasure, will be picked up by Aristotle in his discussion of *NE* 10. 1–5, while the connection of self-control with the ability to rule is at the heart of Xenophon's *Oeconomicus*.

Socrates adds that people unable to control themselves are no better than wild beasts, and look only for the most pleasant things (4. 5. 11. 4–5). And he concludes: 'Only those who are self-controlled have the power to consider the things that matter most, and, sorting them by kind by word and deed, are able to choose the good and reject the evil'[21] (4. 5. 11. 7–9). This passage in the *Memorabilia* is one of the most discussed. But if we look at it from the point of view of what precedes, it seems clear that Socrates says that *enkrateia* enables men to make the right choice between different pleasures, i.e. to prefer the

---

[19] Cf. J. J. Walsh, '*The Socratic Denial of Akrasia*', in G. Vlastos (ed.), *The Philosophy of Socrates* (New York, 1971; repr. Notre Dame, 1980), 236–41; Cooper, *Reason*, 25–7; Strauss, *Xenophon's Socrates*, 79.

[20] Cf. 3. 9. 4. 1–4; but the text is difficult, see Delatte, *Troisième Livre*, 113–15.

[21] τοῖς ἐγκρατέσι μόνοις ἔξεστι σκοπεῖν τὰ κράτιστα τῶν πραγμάτων, καὶ λόγῳ καὶ ἔργῳ διαλέγοντας κατὰ γένη τὰ μὲν ἀγαθὰ προαιρεῖσθαι, τῶν δὲ κακῶν ἀπέχεσθαι.

pleasures that need some kind of suffering to those which are immediate (*tas engutatố hedonas*, 4. 5. 10. 11–12).

The choice Socrates is speaking about is done on the basis of reasoning and action. It is a practical choice, not an intellectual exercise. The expression *kata gene* which appears here (4. 5. 11. 9) means nothing more than 'good and bad', as is made clear immediately after (*ta ... agatha/tôn kakôn*).[22]

Now it is necessary to make a digression. I have already said that some contemporary scholars have tried to revive the old theory according to which this idea of dialectics comes from Antisthenes and is not Xenophon's own position. But, since the objects of the choice and of the distinction in kinds are *ta pragmata*, as Xenophon repeats twice (4. 5. 11. 9 and 12. 5), it seems that this very fact rules out the possibility of connecting this passage to Antisthenes' *episkepsis tôn onomatôn*. Epictetus suggested this connection, according to received opinion, in antiquity; it has been repeated many times in modern scholarship.[23] It is however not completely certain that Epictetus refers to this passage of the *Memorabilia* (4. 5. 12–4. 6. 1), when he says:

> Who says that? Only Chrysippus, Zeno and Cleanthes? And does Antisthenes not say the same, when he affirms 'The beginning of education is the examination of terms'? And does not Socrates say the same? About whom Xenophon said that *he began from the examination of names*, to understand what they could mean. (*Diss*. 1. 17. 11–12 test. v A 160 Giannantoni, my emphasis)[24]

In the text of book 4 there is no reference to 'names' but only to *pragmata*. It is much more likely that the reference is to *Mem*. 3 14. 2, a passage in which Socrates' *zêtêsis* is about names and their meaning: 'He observed on one occasion that one of the company at dinner stopped taking bread, and ate the meat by itself. Since *the talk was about names*, to which activity every name was properly applied, he said: "We could say, gentlemen..." '[25] (3. 14. 2. 1–4, my emphasis).

---

[22] On this point I agree with Joël, Erbse, Brancacci, and others, contra Maier and S. Novo. *Ricerche sulle interpolazioni nei 'Memorabili' di Senofonte* (Turin, 1960), 44, who translates: 'distinguere le cose e raggrupparle secondo i loro principi logici'. *Genê* here has no metaphysical meaning, but indicates a moral evaluation.

[23] Cf. Joël, *Der echte*, i. 354 ff. Interesting are the acrobatics of p. 355, where Joël tries to show that the very fact that here Xenophon speaks of *ta onta* and never of *onomata* demonstrates that the *episkepsis* is about *onomata*. The same position is held in Wellmann, 'Socratic Method' 310, Brancacci, *Oikeios logos*, 119–29, etc.

[24] τίς λέγει ταῦτα; μόνος Χρύσιππος καὶ Ζήνων καὶ Κλεάνθης; 'Ἀντισθένης δ' οὐ λέγει; καὶ τίς ἐστιν ὁ γεγραφὼς ὅτι 'ἀρχὴ παιδεύσεως ἡ τῶν ὀνομάτων ἐπίσκεψις'; Σωκράτης δ' οὐ λέγει; καὶ περὶ τίνος γράφει Ξενοφῶν ὅτι ἤρχετο ἀπὸ τῆς τῶν ὀνομάτων ἐπισκέψεως, τί σημαίνει ἕκαστον.

It is not even necessary to read in the text the idea that Epictetus wanted to make a direct connection between Antisthenes and Xenophon's Socrates, as Joël (*Der echte*, i. 354) and others think. One can understand Epictetus saying only that both Antisthenes and Xenophon's Socrates said the same as Chrysippus and the others. If I say that A and B did the same as C, I establish a connection A = C and B = C; but not necessarily a connection between A and B.

[25] Καταμαθὼν δέ ποτε τῶν συνδειπνούντων τινὰ τοῦ μὲν σίτου πεπαυμένον, τὸ δὲ ὄψον αὐτὸ καθ' αὑτὸ ἐσθίοντα, λόγου ὄντος περὶ ὀνομάτων, ἐφ' οἵῳ ἔργῳ ἕκαστον εἴη, Ἔχοιμεν ἄν, ἔφη, ὦ ἄνδρες, εἰπεῖν ... .

If this is true, Epictetus' testimony can be eliminated and a connection between *Memorabilia* 4. 5–6 and Antisthenes remains only the hypothesis of modern critics.

Let's go back to Xenophon. The phrase at the end of 4. 5 I have discussed so far is the conclusion of the dialogue between Socrates and Euthydemus. To this, Xenophon adds a general statement, expressed by Socrates on another occasion, but intended to conclude the narration and to clarify the last lines: 'And thus, he said, men become excellent, supremely happy and extremely strong in discussion?' (4. 5. 12. 1–3).[26] The word *houtôs*, 'thus', must be referred to the entire discussion which precedes and means 'by acquiring and exercising self-control'. Self-control enables people to become better, happier, and *dialektikóteroi*. It is unlikely, as Joël maintains, that 'thus' refers only to the last lines and that it means 'by sorting *pragmata* by kind by word and deed'. It is not the sorting which makes people happy and excellent, but it is self-control, which enables people to make good choices; and, in turn, good choices are the way to become happy and excellent.[27]

But why does self-control enable one to become stronger in dialectics? This is explained by another remark by Xenophon, added as an afterthought:

He said that 'to discuss' (*to dialegesthai*) owes its name to the practice of meeting together for a common deliberation, sorting out the *pragmata* by kind (*dialegontas kata genê*); and therefore one should be ready and fully prepared for this, and be zealous for it, because from this activity derive men superior to others, very able to dominate, and strong in discussion.[28] (4. 5. 12. 3–9)

The etymology is original, and not attested in other authors. Xenophon wants to separate 'dialectics' from the idea of *elenchos* and from mere refutation, as Aristotle will do later. He tries to connect it to a more positive endeavour, relating it to the active form of the verb *dialegein*, which means 'to select, pick up'. It is an original position, which has no predecessors and, as far as we know, no followers either.[29] The idea seems to be that, in order to become better men, the disciples should gather together and deliberate which *pragmata* are good and

---

[26] καὶ οὕτως ἔφη ἀρίστους τε καὶ εὐδαιμονεστάτους ἄνδρας γίγνεσθαι καὶ διαλέγεσθαι δυνατωτάτους.

[27] Cf Joël, *Der echte*, i. 334; on the structure of the passage, see Erbse, 'Arkitektonik', 256–7.

[28] ἔφη δὲ καὶ τὸ διαλέγεσθαι ὀνομασθῆναι ἐκ τοῦ συνιόντας κοινῇ βουλεύεσθαι διαλέγοντας κατὰ γένη τὰ πράγματα δεῖν οὖν πειρᾶσθαι ὅτι μάλιστα πρὸς τοῦτο ἑαυτὸν ἕτοιμον παρασκευάζειν καὶ τούτου μάλιστα ἐπιμελεῖσθαι· ἐκ τούτου γὰρ γίγνεσθαι ἄνδρας ἀρίστους τε καὶ ἡγεμονικωτάτους καὶ διαλεκτικωτάτους.

[29] Maier, *Socrate*, 60–4 and 98–103, has tried to find an ancestor of this position in the *Phaedrus* (265e, 266b) and in the *Politicus* (285d–287a), and a reprise of the same idea in Aristotle, *Metaph.* M 4. 1078^{b}17–32. Both the identifications are far from convincing. In the Platonic dialogues there is a description of *diairesis* as the ability to distinguish the different realities of the world according to their nature, which is different from the simple distinction of *pragmata* in *kala* and *aiskra* to which Xenophon alludes here. Joël, *Der echte*, i. 334, has understood Xenophon's text much better than Maier here. On Aristotle's passage, see T. Deman, *Le Témoignage d'Aristote sur Socrate* (Paris, 1942), 71–80: Aristotle distinguishes the dialectic of the first Platonic dialogues from the more refined

which are bad. The ability to distinguish between good and bad deeds makes men *eudaimonestatous, dunatôtatous dialegesthai, aristous*, and *hegemonikôtatous*. Some commentators have tried to connect this passage to texts in which Xenophon says that a good general should know rhetoric,[30] but this is far from convincing. The element Xenophon wants to stress here is the activity of sorting out things by kind, not the moment of deliberation (*bouleusasthai*, 4. 5. 12. 4). This implies *enkrateia* as a necessary condition and, when repeated with insistence and eagerness, makes the disciples better.

An example of the 'sorting out' Xenophon is alluding to can be found in the context of an *elenchos*, in *Mem*. 4. 2. 13. Here Socrates wants to test the *paideia* of Euthydemus, and to see if he can distinguish the just actions (*dikaiosunês erga*, 4. 2. 12. 8) from the unjust ones. He says to Euthydemus: Do you agree, that we write here J and there U, and proceed to place the just actions under the "J" and the unjust actions under the "U"? (4. 2. 13. 1–5). This is, I think, a clear example of *dialegein kata genê*. It is true that here Euthydemus immediately shows he is unable to do it properly. But the same procedure can be used, outside the *elenchos*, by a disciple who wants to progress in virtue and happiness.

In conclusion, the two last paragraphs of 4. 5 are well connected to the rest of the chapter and expand an idea already present in what precedes. It is not true that the only justification of this reference to dialectics is that it provides a link to the next chapter, 4. 6, as many interpreters maintain. The passage makes a necessary conclusion to 4. 5.

In 4. 6 we will find a rather different, but not incompatible, idea of dialectic; this makes it unlikely that the indications given here in connection with the idea of *dialegein kata genê* could be applied directly to the different dialectic of the following chapter. In 4. 6 Xenophon wants to describe how Socrates made his disciples *dialektikôterous*. As I have already said, this conception of dialectics is somehow different from the description we have seen in 4. 5. Here, in fact, the idea of sorting *pragmata* by kind isn't present anymore, and a new aspect of dialectics is now at the centre of Xenophon's attention. But it is still a positive procedure, not a refutation. He says that dialectics enables men to grasp the nature of things: 'Socrates held that those who know what any given thing is, can also expound it to others; on the other hand, it is not strange that those who do not know are misled themselves and mislead others'[31] (4. 6. 1. 2–7).

The two aspects of dialectic, described in 4. 5 and 4. 6, are not incompatible. We have already seen that in 1. 1. 16. 2–9, Socrates is described as examining

---

dialectic of later dialogues such as the *Parmenides* and the *Sophistes*. There is no connection to Xenophon's position.

[30] Cf. Joël, *Der echte*, i. 334 and Novo, *Ricerche*, 45, both referring to 3. 3. 10. 11.

[31] Σωκράτης γὰρ τοὺς μὲν εἰδότας τί ἕκαστον εἴη τῶν ὄντων ἐνόμιζε καὶ τοῖς ἄλλοις ἂν ἐξηγεῖσθαι δύνασθαι· τοὺς δὲ μὴ εἰδότας οὐδὲν ἔφη θαυμαστὸν εἶναι αὐτούς τε σφάλλεσθαι καὶ ἄλλους σφάλλειν.

what a virtue is, and which is the connected vice. That passage has already connected on one side the search for *ti estin*, and on the other the division in two different kinds, good and bad, of different realities: moral activities, people, and so on. In 4. 5, because of the connection to the *enkrateia*, Xenophon wanted to stress the practical side of dialectics and connected it to the division in kind and to the choice.

In 4. 6, on the contrary, Xenophon wants to concentrate on the logical aspect of dialectical training. He will give us a description by examples: 'It would be an arduous task to go through all his definitions; but I will say only enough to indicate the method of the research' (4. 6. 1. 10–12).[32]

There are two questions which need to be settled immediately. First, in the preceding chapter it has been said that *enkrateia* is a necessary condition of dialectics. But there is the need for a more active cause, and here the cause is present: it is Socrates' teaching method.

Secondly, many earlier interpreters, and some contemporary ones, have held that here *dialektikôterous* means 'skilled in rhetoric'.[33] It is evident, on the contrary, that here dialectics is an intellectual activity, a practical science leading to action. In fact the description we find here is very similar to Aristotle's well-known statement that Socrates 'was seeking the universal and fixed thought for the first time in definition' (*Metaph.* A 6. 987^b 1–6). There is a difference, however. Aristotle's testimony can be constructed in a way that doesn't contradict Plato's Socratic Dialogues and the theory of the Socratic ignorance we find there. We could understand Aristotle's statement in the sense that Socrates was always 'seeking (*zêtountos*)' the definition and the universal, but never arrived at a definitive formula.[34] The statement we find in the *Elenchi sophistici* confirms this: 'Socrates used to ask questions and not answer them—for he used to confess he did not know' (34. 183^{b}6–8). If it is connected to Xenophon's *Memorabilia*, Aristotle's testimony assumes a more positive meaning: Socrates was seeking definitions of moral activities and virtues, and was able to find them.

Let's go back to Xenophon. He says that he will present some examples of the procedure by which Socrates defined things. The examples are many because Socrates used different methods of definition in different circumstances. I do not have now enough time to examine fully all the examples: I will describe very briefly the less important cases (4. 6. 10–15) and I will concentrate on the passages in which a more interesting procedure is exemplified (4. 6. 2–6).

In 4. 6. 10–11 there is an analysis of courage, based on the distinction between cases of good behaviour and cases of cowardice. The method of analysis is similar to the method of paragraphs 2–6, which I will discuss later. The text is interesting

---

[32] πάντα μὲν οὖν ᾗ διωρίζετο πολὺ ἔργον ἂν εἴη διεξελθεῖν· ἐν ὅσοις δὲ τὸν τρόπον τῆς ἐπισκέψεως δηλώσειν οἶμαι, τοσαῦτα λέξω.

[33] Hartman and Schenkl, quoted by Novo, *Ricerche*, 43; Strauss, *Xenophon's Socrates*, 116–17. For a contrary opinion see Joël, *Der echte*, ii. 593.

[34] Cf. Deman, *Le Témoignage*, 63–5 and 77–80.

because of the opposition between positive and negative aspects of behaviour, which corresponds to the *dialegein kata genê* described in 4. 5. 12.[35] It is, however, the only definition which respects the indications of the preceding chapter.

In 4. 6. 12, there is a résumé of Socrates' theory of regimes, without any argument in support. It is difficult to understand how this can be useful in indicating the method of the research, even if Xenophon says that he wants to concentrate on this point. It is true, however, that in the corresponding passage of book 1, 1. 16. 2–9, there were questions about 'what is a city, what is a statesman, what is government upon men, what is to be a governor'. Those questions, as we saw before, were presented without any reference to the distinction of good cases and bad cases.

In 4. 6. 13–14 a dialectic procedure is described. It is a kind of *elenchos*, to be sure, because it is applied to people who have only apparent wisdom. But the characteristics are unusual:

Whenever anyone argued with him (*antilegoi*) without having anything clear to say, but asserting without any proof that so and so was wiser, or a better politician, or braver, or possessing some other virtue, he would lead the discussion up to the assumption.[36] (4. 6.13)

It seems, despite the unusual wording, that we are considering a bona-fide *elenchos*, as the following example shows clearly (4. 6.14). The *antilogia* consists in the choice between two citizens. Socrates says that the first citizen is the better, his opponent maintains the reverse position. The *antilogia* is solved by finding the definition of a good citizen, and showing, in relation to the definition, which man was the better: 'By this process of leading back the arguments to the definition, even his opponent came to see clearly the truth'[37] (4. 6. 14. 19–20).

About paragraph 4. 6. 15 there is a disagreement among the interpreters. Let us see first what the text says: 'Whenever he himself discussed fully some theme he advanced by steps that gained general assent, holding this to be the only sure method'[38] (4. 6. 15. 1–3). Some think that here Xenophon alludes to long speeches *ex cathedra* by Socrates.[39] This seems unlikely: Socrates never delivers long speeches to his disciples, in either Xenophon or Plato. The allusion here is to the dialogues between Socrates and his disciples when Socrates tries to gain the assent from the hearers using what later Aristotle will call the *endoxa*. The aim

---

[35] Cf. Brancacci, *Oikeios logos*, 133–4.
[36] Εἰ δέ τις αὐτῷ περί του ἀντιλέγοι μηδὲν ἔχων σαφὲς λέγειν, ἀλλ' ἄνευ ἀποδείξεως ἤτοι σοφώτερον φάσκων εἶναι ὃν αὐτὸς λέγοι ἢ πολιτικώτερον ἢ ἀνδρειότερον ἢ ἄλλο τι τῶν τοιούτων, ἐπὶ τὴν ὑπόθεσιν ἐπανῆγεν ἂν πάντα τὸν λόγον.
[37] οὕτω δὲ τῶν λόγων ἐπαναγομένων καὶ τοῖς ἀντιλέγουσιν αὐτοῖς φανερὸν ἐγίγνετο τἀληθές.
[38] ὁπότε δὲ αὐτός τι τῷ λόγῳ διεξίοι, διὰ τῶν μάλιστα ὁμολογουμένων ἐπορεύετο, νομίζων ταύτην τὴν ἀσφάλειαν εἶναι λόγου.
[39] Strauss, *Xenophon's Socrates*, 122; Novo, *Ricerche*, 46. For a contrary opinion, see Maier, *Socrate*, ii. 82 and Wellmann, 'Socratic Method', 310.

seems to be similar to the aim of Aristotle's *Topics*: 'To find a method whereby we shall be able to reason from reputable opinions about any subject presented to us, and also shall ourselves, when putting forward an argument, avoid saying anything contrary to it' (100^a18–21, cf. 104^a3–8).

The proof can be found in 4. 6 itself. Here we find dialogues in which Socrates argues with Euthydemus about the definition of piety, justice, courage, etc., and he always proceeds step by step, granting the assent of the disciple to every passage, and even letting him contribute positively to the discussion. Let's see an example:

—Tell me, Euthydemus, what sort of thing is Piety, in your opinion?
—A very excellent thing, by Jove, (he said)
—Can you say what sort of man is pious?
—He who worships the Gods, I think
—May a man worship the gods according to his will and pleasure?
—No, there are laws to be observed in worshipping the gods, etc. (4. 6. 2).

The procedure is dialectical and the passage from one proposition to another is granted by the assent of the respondent. At the end of the procedure we find the definition we are looking for:

Shall we therefore rightly define the pious man as one who knows what is lawful concerning the Gods?
—At any rate I think so (4. 6. 4. 9–11).

The procedure described in 4. 6. 15 is applied in 4. 6. 2–4 and 5–6.

I would like, now, to examine more closely the first two speeches (4. 6. 2–4 and 5–6), about Piety and Justice. If we eliminate the dialogical structure already described, and we analyse only the logical progression from the first question to the final definition, we find a schema more or less similar to what follows:

FIRST EXAMPLE

(*) Piety is a very excellent thing (4. 6. 2. 1–3).
(1a) Pious is the man who worships the gods.
(1b) The gods must be worshipped according to the laws (2. 3–3. 1).
(2) The man who knows the laws in general knows how to behave properly (3. 1–3).
(3) The man who behaves properly does not think that he should do otherwise (3. 3–5).
(4) The man who does not think that he should do otherwise does not do otherwise (i.e. he behaves according to the laws) (3. 5–4. 1).

Then (from 1–4)

(5) The man who knows the laws about the gods behaves lawfully (4. 1–3).

(6) The man who behaves lawfully behaves properly towards the gods (4. 4–5).
(7) The man who behaves properly towards the gods is pious (4. 6–7).

In conclusion (from 5–7)

(8) 'The man who knows the laws about the gods' is the right definition of 'pious' (4. 9–11).

The knowledge of the laws about the gods implies pious behavior. This result derives from a series of identifications: 'to know the laws' = 'to know how behave properly' = 'not to think that one should do otherwise' = 'not doing otherwise' = 'to behave according to the laws'.

Steps (1)–(4) posit the identifications; steps (5)–(7) recapitulate the procedure and apply to the special case of the gods. From this specification, the definition (8) clearly derives.

SECOND EXAMPLE

The case of the justice is more complicated. It can be summarized as follows:

(*) There are laws also about how to behave towards men (5. 1–2).

This is not part of the argument, but just a connection to the preceding discussion of 'piety'.

(1) Observing (*chrômenoi*) the laws towards men is behaving properly (5. 2–5).
(2) Behaving properly is behaving well (5. 5–6).
(3) Behaving well is acting well (2. 7–8).
(1') Obeying (*chrômenoi*) the laws towards men is doing what is just (5. 8–9).
(2') Just are the actions that the laws[40] command (6. 1–2).
(3') The man who does what the laws command does what is just (6. 2–4).

So (from 1'–3')

(4') The man who does what is just is a just man (6. 4–5).
(1") The man who obeys (*peithomenoi*)[41] the laws knows what the laws say (6. 5–7).

---

[40] Xenophon at every step repeats that we are speaking of the laws towards men. I will not repeat this specification from here onwards.
[41] Here the change from *chrômenoi* to *peithomenoi* has no relevance for the argument, it is just a literary *variatio*.

(2″) To know what the laws say is to know the things proper to do [implicit].
(3″) To know what are the things proper to do is not to have the opinion of doing otherwise (6. 7–8).
(4″) Not having the opinion of doing otherwise is having the opinion of doing what one has to do [implicit].
(5″) Having the opinion of doing what one has to do implies doing it and not something else (6. 8–10).

So (from 1″–5″):

(6″) To know what the laws say implies to do just actions (6. 10–11).

But (from 4′)

(7″) Doing just actions is to be just (6. 11–13)

In conclusion (from 1″–7″):

(8″) 'To know the lawful actions towards men' is the definition of 'being just' (6. 15–17).

Despite some abbreviation, the arguments (1′–4′) and (1″–7″) form an unity, from which derives the definition of 'being just'.[42] It is a Socratic definition, as is the preceding one, because in both cases the knowledge implies a just behavior. This use of dialectic is very similar to the idea we will find in Aristotle's *Topics*, according to which dialectic is 'a process of criticism wherein lies the path to the principles of all enquiries' (101^b3–4). The result derives from a series of identifications:

(A) 'obeying the laws' = 'doing what is just' = 'doing what the laws command' = 'being just'
(B) 'obeying the laws' = 'knowing what the laws say' = ['knowing what is proper to do'] = 'not having the opinion of doing otherwise' = ['having the opinion of doing what one has to do'] = 'doing it and not something else' = 'doing what is just'.

In the *Oeconomicus* we find a similar series of identifications. In the first chapter Socrates makes h is respondent accept the following series *oikos* = *ktêmata agatha* = *ta ophelounta* = *chrêmata agatha*, to demonstrate that even money is not a good if it is not used well.[43]

What are the reasons, besides the acceptance of the respondent, which grant the possibility of those identifications? Taragna Novo thinks that Socrates starts from an unclear and obscure definition and arrives at a more precise formulation of the same definition; Brancacci thinks that Socrates derives, in an analytical

---
[42] We are not sure, however, what the role of argument (1–3) is. It is not a part of the procedure needed to arrive at the conclusion.
[43] Cf. Natali, 'Socrate', 277.

way, all the notions from the first definition[44]. Both analyses are beside the point, in our opinion.

The passage from theses like 'not to think that one should do otherwise' to 'not doing otherwise', or from 'having the opinion of doing what one has to do' to 'doing it and not something else' are not analytic nor evident, but are typical of Socratic intellectualism. They can be accepted only by somebody who is an enthusiastic follower of Socrates, and would be refuted, e.g. by a follower of Aristotle's theory of *akrasia*. If the passage from 'knowing what the laws say' to 'knowing what is proper to do' implies the thesis, typical of Xenophon's Socrates, that the right is identical to the lawful,[45] the assent of the respondent is not enough to grant the necessity of the passage. The consequence is not proved, even though it is possible that Xenophon thought that the passages were endoxastic enough to gain the assent of every reader.

I would like to add a last remark: the series of identifications we find in *Mem.* 4. 6 strongly reminds us of a couple of Stoic arguments reported by Alexander of Aphrodisias in his *De fato* 35 and 37.[46] In the first of those passages the determinist affirms the following identifications: 'there is destiny' = 'there is Apportionment' = 'there is Retribution' = 'there is law' = 'there is right reason commanding what to do' = 'there are good and bad actions' = 'there are forbidden actions and enjoined ones' = 'there are virtue and vice' = 'there are what is praiseworthy and what is blameworthy' = 'there are reward and punishment'. From which derives: 'there is destiny' = 'there are reward and punishment'.

But there are many differences between the two texts: the basis of the identification in the determinist's arguments is both the 'negated conjunction' and a form of the conditional, whereas the basis of the identification in Socrates' argument is the assent of the respondent grounded on the (supposedly) endoxastic nature of the theses proposed. Besides, the determinist's argument is used to prove a controversial thesis such as 'destiny is not incompatible with reward and punishment', whereas Socrates' argument tends to establish a definition by a series of pseudo-endoxical identifications. The logic of those passages should be analysed more fully than I can do here, and the connections between the logic of the early fourth century BC on one side, and Aristotelian and Stoic logic, on the other, need to be studied in detail.[47]

To sum up. Xenophon thinks that Socrates was useful to his fellow citizens, by both words and deeds. He gave a marvelous example of virtue and self-control,

---

[44] Cf. S. Taragna Novo, *Economia ed etica nell' Economico di Senofonte* (Turin, 1968), 19 n. 11; Brancacci, *Oikeios logos*, 133.

[45] Cf. Morrison, 'Justice et legalité'.

[46] I would like to thank R. Sharples who has discussed these passages with me in connection with what Xenophon says.

[47] There is no paragraph on Xenophon in the standard histories of ancient logic, such as W. C. Kneale and M. Kneale, *The Development of Logic* (Oxford, 1971).

and with his conversation offered a good philosophical training to his friends and disciples.

Socrates' encounters with friends, according to Xenophon, were not simple discussions. To help his audience to become better citizens he followed different methods; the best known among them, the *elenchos*, despite what some commentators may think, was only one procedure among others, and perhaps not the most important.

In a first phase of his encounters, to encourage (*protrepein*) them to philosophize, Socrates used to undermine the apparent strength of other people's convictions. To do that he used both argument and refutation. In a second phase, and only if people who survived the first phase of the treatment were not too angry with the philosopher, he used more civilized methods.

His teaching, at the new level, consisted mainly in giving positive advice on different situations, advice of which we have a long series of examples in the *Memorabilia*. But he also used to train his disciples on dialectic.

Dialectic, as described in the *Memorabilia*, has two aspects: definition of *pragmata* and sorting *pragmata* in two kinds, good and bad. The first step is preliminary to the second and is more intellectual; the second is strictly connected with praxis and demands self-control as a necessary condition.

Xenophon maintains the idea of Socratic intellectualism, but he wants also to stress the strength of emotions and feelings, which need to be controlled by *enkrateia* and *karteria*. The two positions are compatible because he thinks that people unable to control themselves have no knowledge: it is impossible to be at the same time wise and *akratês*.

Xenophon dedicates an entire chapter to showing the method used by Socrates in reaching a definition of such moral realities as 'justice', 'piety', 'courage', and so on. This is the most interesting part of the *Memorabilia* from our point of view. Socrates proceeds step by step, passing from an idea to what seems to be a slightly different formulation of the same idea ('behaving properly' = 'behaving well' = 'acting well': *chrôntai hôs dei* = *kalôs chrôntai* = *kalôs prattein*), till he arrives at the definition he is looking for. Here the semantics of the terms employed is clearly at stake, and an accurate study of the procedure is still a desideratum. Anyway, we can say, at least, that Xenophon's dialectic is different from the dialectic of Plato's early dialogues and also from that of Aristotle. I think that it is an indispensable piece in the reconstruction of the puzzle constituted by the history of ancient dialectic.

2

If you Know what is Best, you Do it: Socratic Intellectualism in Xenophon and Plato

Gerhard Seel

I PRELIMINARY REMARK

In the following, I shall do something most scholars consider senseless: putting the question of Socrates again. This question is exactly the opposite of the other great question of ancient scholarship, i.e. the question of Homer. What the latter is about is best expressed in the following joke: *Someone in Oxford has discovered that it was not Homer who wrote the* Iliad; *it was somebody else who happened to have the same name.* Obviously such a story could not be told about Socrates at all. In the case of Homer, we are familiar with the work; what we do not know is the identity of the author. In the case of Socrates, it is the other way around. We know pretty well who Socrates was, but we do not know what exactly he taught.

Why is it so difficult to find this out? The first reason is the fact—one of the few facts about Socrates we know with sufficient certainty—that he did not write anything. Therefore we must rely on what other people wrote in order to learn about his teaching. But how reliable are these sources? The ideal situation would be to have several reliable sources independent of each other and confirming the very same point. None of these conditions seems to be fulfilled. Our two main sources,[1] Plato's early Socratic writings and Xenophon's *Memorabilia*, seem to be not very reliable in themselves; their independence is doubtful and on many important points they contradict each other. These are the reasons why today most scholars want to get rid of the question once and for all.[2]

I had the opportunity to finish this paper during my stay at the Institute for Advanced Study (Princeton). I thank Heinrich von Staden, John Cooper, Alexander Nehamas, Hendrik Lorenz, and Jonathan Beere for their helpful comments. Jonathan Beere also checked the English.

[1] I disregard Aristophanes, *Clouds*, though this contains important information as well.

[2] In the first chapter of Prior (1996: i) which concerns the Socratic Problem, most of the recent articles express doubt that there is a solution to it: articles by Chroust, Morrison, Beversluis, and Kahn. The latter writes (pp. 161–2): 'Our evidence is such that . . . the philosophy of Socrates himself, as distinct from his impact on his followers, does not fall within the reach of historical

Let us look at these reasons more carefully. First, the reason generally given for the non-reliability of our sources is the fact that Xenophon and Plato did not intend to write exact, reliable, and objective historical reports on Socrates' teaching (see Dorion 2000: p. civ), but wrote a new form of literature, *logoi sokratikoi*, which is a kind of fiction in which 'Socrates' appears as a literary character.³ Of course, this is accurate. Before the invention of history as a science in the nineteenth century, nobody, not even the historians, intended to write exact, reliable and objective reports. But does that mean that their texts are useless as historical sources? Even the most deceitful text can furnish valid information to a historian who understands the intention of its author and avoids taking his claims at face value.

This is true of Xenophon and Plato's texts as well. In order to determine their value as historical sources we have to look to the intentions of their authors, evaluate their potential sources of information and their inclinations and capacities to transform this information. There is no doubt about Xenophon's intentions. He says it in so many words. He wanted to defend Socrates against the accusations of the Athenians by showing that he did not do what he was accused of. This could be and has been taken as sufficient to show that Xenophon had a good reason to falsify Socrates' portrait. But things are more complicated. Could he hope to be successful in defending Socrates if evidently false statements compromised his credibility? To be sure, he was tempted to improve his credibility artificially by purporting to report from memory, as he was tempted to embellish Socrates' portrait concerning the main points of the accusation. There is evidence that he succumbed to both temptations.⁴ But why should he have falsified points that have nothing to do with the accusation, for example, certain particular features of Socrates' philosophical doctrine? Concerning the reliability of his sources of information, some scholars have been extremely skeptical, saying that his personal relation with Socrates was too short to give him the opportunity to learn much from him, that his long exile from Athens deprived him of the information available in the Socratic literature, and so on. Here, again, I refer to A.-L. Dorion who has convincingly shown that these allegations are unfounded (2000: pp. xxii–xxxii). Furthermore, in order to falsify a report successfully, one must be sufficiently clever. The many failures of dexterity that critics have found in

---

scholarship. In this sense the problem of Socrates must remain without a solution.' See also A. Dorion (2000: pp. cxiii–cxvi 'La pensée du Socrate historique est hors de notre portée').

³ See Dorion (2000: p. cv): 'Les *logoi sokratikoi* sont des œuvres littéraires où l'auteur peut laisser libre course à son imagination, en respectant plus ou moins les bornes que lui impose la vraisemblance d'une représentation crédible de l'"êthos" de Socrate. La part de fiction et d'invention inhérente au *logos sokratikos* interdit de le considérer comme un témoignage visant à l'exactitude historique.' Rossetti (2004: 88) has a more differentiated attitude towards the reliability of the *logoi sokratikoi*. He acknowledges their 'average faithfulness to the real Socrates' and thinks that the portrayal of Socrates as a living person has 'documentary value'.

⁴ Many scholars argue that he overdid the defense (see Dorion 2000: p. lxv, n.2). On the other hand, there are passages in the text which show Socrates as critical of the democratic Athenian institutions, a point that would speak in favor of the accusation.

his text make us doubt that he had this 'virtue'. But this gives even more value to his text as a source. Finally, we must say that he was not a philosopher. This makes it unlikely that he used Socrates as his mouthpiece—at least in philosophical matters. Instead, one expects him to stick to the arguments he had heard and to report them as they stood, for fear of some mistake he could inadvertently make.

In many ways, Plato is the opposite of Xenophon. But, as we shall see, that does not mean that he is less credible. Though some of Plato's texts have a clearly apologetic character (*Apology, Crito*), most of his Socratic dialogues are not apologetic. Nor did Plato intend to accurately report the teaching of Socrates. What Plato intends in the first place is to present philosophical questions and possible answers to these questions. In most cases, he sets the figure of Socrates on stage to argue for positions Plato seems to sympathize with. Does that mean that he uses Socrates as a mouthpiece to express his own philosophy? Here again things are more complicated. If we compare the many master–student relations we find in the history of philosophy, the following schema seems to be prevalent: the student adopts his master's positions and arguments in his early works[5]—at least he believes he does so—and departs from these only later, when he finds his own stance. Shouldn't this schema apply to the case of Socrates and Plato as well? If so, the question whether we find Socrates' or rather Plato's own philosophy in the early dialogues would just be pointless.[6] Of course, we must take into account that Plato might have introduced elements in the overall theory that are his own inventions and, furthermore, it seems impossible in most cases to evaluate the extent of those elements. However, this does not mean that Plato's early Socratic dialogues are worthless as a source of information about Socrates' philosophy. Plato certainly was an eyewitness to many events and discussions in which the historic Socrates was involved; he may have learnt some of them from the other disciples.[7] Finally, of Socrates' associates, he was certainly the best prepared to understand the philosophical subtleties in Socrates' arguments. The exercise of these philosophical skills, however, might have resulted in some strengthening or reshaping of what Socrates originally taught. Here, again, we cannot evaluate the extent of these transformations.

As I said at the outset, the ideal situation would be to have several independent sources confirming each other. In this regard as well we are not in a very good position. For, as everybody knows, Xenophon and Plato contradict each other on

---

[5] Kahn (1996: 161) argues against this hypothesis that it is not plausible that Plato 'could remain fixed in a single philosophical position, that of his master, for 12 years or more after his master's death'. However, if there was a significant shift in Plato's thought during this period, a comparative investigation of the early dialogues should be able to discover it.

[6] This still leaves open the question where to draw the borderline between the early dialogues and the rest. I am inclined to follow Penner's (1992: 124) arguments in counting the *Hippias Minor, Charmides, Laches, Protagoras, Euthyphro, Apology, Crito, Ion, Lysis, Euthydemus, Menexenus, Hippias Major*, and *Republic* 1 but not the *Meno* and *Gorgias* among the early dialogues. For a different view concerning the latter, see Kahn (1988: 69–102). See also Nehamas (1999: 89–90).

[7] I do not mean to argue that the settings we find in Plato's dialogues are historically true.

many, though not on all important points. However, this has also its good side. For, the contradiction of two sources has to be taken as an indication of their relative independence.[8] The bad side is, however, that we have to find out which one is right and which one is wrong. The overwhelming majority of scholars opt for Plato, but for different reasons. The first is that nobody likes Xenophon's Socrates. Plato's Socrates seems to be much more interesting, and not only as a philosopher.

As Vlastos puts it (1971b: 3), Xenophon presents a Socrates who 'would have elicited nothing but a sneer from Critias and a yawn from Alcibiades', while Plato gives us a philosopher who revolutionized moral thinking and who could have gotten under the skin of haughty aristocrats like Critias and Alcibiades. The other—more serious—reason is that Xenophon seems not to be credible, that, as Vlastos says, his 'account refutes itself' (ibid.).

I do not intend to pursue this discussion further—I have already addressed the question of the credibility of Xenophon—for it seems to be based on a false dichotomy. The traditional parties in the dispute ask us to choose between Xenophon's portrait as a whole and Plato's portrait as a whole. But this choice cannot be made on rational grounds. No wonder then that many scholars have rejected it and prefer to abandon the question of Socrates altogether. However, this amounts to throwing the baby out with the bath water. How can we avoid this radical 'solution'? I should say, first of all, that we need not simply 'take it or leave it'. The question is not whether Xenophon's or Plato's picture of Socrates is accurate, but rather what kind of source their texts constitute and how we should use them. Concerning the latter, we should accept Plato's information where it seems more plausible and Xenophon's report where it is more credible. Secondly, we should take into account that Xenophon and Plato do not contradict each other on all the important points. Given their relative independence, we should give credit to the points where they converge. By evaluating in this way each piece of information separately and on its own merits we can hope to uncover at least some of the teachings of the historical Socrates.[9] Having said this, I should nevertheless reduce our expectations to some extent. We are not in a position to reach more than probabilities and plausibility. Therefore we should not ask for certainty. But most historical studies encounter the same difficulty. Were we to ask for more, a good part of the books on history could not have been written. In the following, I will treat a most interesting example for my general observations.

---

[8] I do not speak of absolute independence, since Xenophon certainly drew on Plato when composing his Socratic writings. His clearly expressed intention to correct the portrait of Socrates made by other Socratics (*Mem.* 1. 4. 1; 4. 3. 2) shows that his knowledge of this literature did not preclude a critical distance from it.

[9] The general methodology I recommend has much in common with the line of historical investigation G. Vlastos followed in Vlastos (1991). Vlastos actually distinguishes two figures of Socrates, Socrates of the early dialogues and Socrates of the later dialogues, as holding different positions and uses the testimony of Xenophon and Aristotle to attribute to the historical Socrates claims that can be found in the early dialogues. For a critique of this procedure see Kahn (1996) and Nehamas (1999: 91–5).

It is a topic where Plato and Xenophon agree on the general point and diverge in the details, i.e. Socrates' so-called moral intellectualism.[10]

II. SOCRATES' MORAL INTELLECTUALISM

Let me start with a systematic explanation of moral intellectualism. I distinguish 'action-intellectualism' and 'intention-intellectualism', each of which has a weak and a strong form. The core of each of these forms of intellectualism consists of two logically connected positions. I add to these basic positions three corollary positions. The latter follow from the former if one admits certain definitions and additional assumptions. The weak form of action-intellectualism consists of the following two positions:

> Pos. A': Everybody who has the opportunity to do what he believes to be the best always does it.

If we define knowledge as justified true belief,[11] we can deduce the following position from Pos. A':

> Pos. B': Everybody who knows what is the best and who has the opportunity to do it always does what is the best.

Most scholars would accept the following standard definition of *akrasia*'[12] (weakness of the will). This definition underlies Aristotle's puzzles about *akrasia* and his attempts to resolve them, though—as we shall see—Aristotle uses this term also in a larger sense:

> Someone commits an action by *akrasia*' if and only if
> (*a*) he knows what is best and
> (*b*) he has the opportunity to do what is best and
> (*c*) he does not do what is best.

Given this definition of *akrasia*', we can deduce a further position from Pos. A' and Pos. B':

> Pos. C': There are no cases of *akrasia*'.

These three positions form together what I have called 'weak action-intellectualism'. To get the strong form of action-intellectualism, we add the converse of Pos. B' to our set of principles.

---

[10] I do not use the term 'moral' in the narrow sense as opposed to 'prudential', but rather in a large sense meaning 'concerning human actions and behavior'.

[11] In formalized language: x knows that p iff x believes that p and x can justify that p and it is the case that p. Cf. Plato's definition of 'epistêmê' in the *Meno* 98a–b.

[12] I write *akrasia*' in order to distinguish action-akrasia from intention-akrasia. The latter is written *akrasia*°

Pos. B'': Nobody ever does what is best unless he knows what is best and he has the opportunity to do it.

Pos. B' and Pos. B'' taken together amount to the following position:

Pos. B''': Anyone does what is the best if and only if he knows what is the best and he has the opportunity to do it.

Somebody who accepts Pos. B''', i.e. strong action-intellectualism, has reasons to accept the following positions as well unless he rejects the underlying notions of virtue and teaching. Virtue is the permanent disposition to do what is best. We may express this conception more formally in the following definitions.

Def. 1: An action is noble and good if and only if it is done through virtue.
Def. 2: A man has virtue if and only if he always does the best when he has the opportunity to do it.

From either of these definitions together with the position of strong intellectualism, we can deduce the following position.

Pos. D': A man who has virtue has also knowledge of the best and a man who has knowledge of the best has also virtue.

It is only a small step from Pos. D' to identifying virtue with knowledge of the best. However, the latter does not logically follow from the former.

Now, if one accepts this identification and if one accepts further that knowledge is a disposition to make true judgments which is transmitted by teaching and acquired by learning, one has to accept the following thesis as well:

Pos. E': Virtue can be transmitted by teaching and acquired by learning.

Though these positions do not follow, strictly speaking, from positions A', B', and C', I consider them corollaries of action-intellectualism.

In some of our texts we find positions corresponding to those given above that speak of intending an action instead of performing it. I call this theory 'intention-intellectualism'. It consists of the following positions:

Pos. A°: Everybody who has the opportunity to do what he believes to be the best always intends to do it.
Pos. B°: Everybody who knows what is the best and who has the opportunity to do it always intends to do it.
Pos. B°°°: Anyone intends to do the best if and only if he knows what the best is and he has the opportunity to do it.

We can also have a corresponding standard definition of *akrasia*°:

Someone is in the state of *akrasia*° (weakness of the will) if and only if
(*a*) he knows what is best and
(*b*) he has the opportunity to do what is best and

(c) he does not intend to do what is best.[13]

On the basis of our explanation of moral intellectualism, one can easily see how the Socratic paradox[14] arises. If virtue can be taught and one acquires virtue by learning, one needs a moral teacher to become virtuous. However, a man—like Socrates—who does not know what is the best and who, moreover, knows that he does not have this knowledge, seems not to be the right man to do this job. But as there is nobody else who could do it, virtue seems not to be within human reach (cf. *Meno* 89c–96d).

It is extremely important to see that all our sources confirm that Socrates held the theory of moral intellectualism as defined above, at least in the weak form. For Plato, we have first to look to the *Protagoras* 352a–357e. Here Socrates tries to undermine[15] the thesis held by 'the many' that there are acts of weakness of the will. This position is to be found in 352d:

(T1) They [the many] say that many people who know the best things do not intend to do those things, even if they have the opportunity to do so, but do something else.

This formulation corresponds to our definitions of *akrasia*; it has elements of both the action form and the intention form. This shows that the difference between these forms is not important in the context of the *Protagoras*. For it seems to imply that acts of *akrasia* result from not intending to do what is best and not from some other factor. In 355c, we find a variant of this position:

(T2) Having established this [that the pleasant is the same as the good and the unpleasant is the same as the evil], let us say that a man, who knows of the bad things that they are bad, does them nevertheless.

The position that Socrates opposes to the thesis of 'the many' is formulated at the end of the long discussion at 358c–d.

(T3) Nobody pursues voluntarily the bad things nor what he believes to be bad and it is not in accordance with human nature, it seems, to intend to pursue what one believes to be bad instead of the good things and whenever one is forced to choose one of two bad things, nobody will take the greater evil when he is allowed to take the lesser.

---

[13] I introduce these variants of intellectualism because we find them in our texts. However the difference between action-intellectualism and intention-intellectualism does not play a decisive role in the arguments. For it seems that it is understood in the texts that the intention to do *a* is always followed by the action *a* unless, of course, the agent is hindered by some external factor. In *Met*. IX. 5 Aristotle introduces this principle.

[14] I refer to the *Paradox of Socrates* as described by Vlastos (1971*b*).

[15] What Socrates actually does is to show that the explanation of the alleged cases of *akrasia* given by 'the many' is absurd. As Santas (1979, 197–8) has convincingly argued, this by itself does not prove that there is no *akrasia*. It would only refute the position of the many if their explanation were the only possible explanation. One should not forget, however, that Socrates takes a further step. He offers a different explanation of the alleged cases of *akrasia* that implies that these cases are not true cases of *akrasia*, but rather cases of lack of the appropriate knowledge. It seems that Socrates considered this explanation applicable to all alleged cases of *akrasia*. If this were true it would amount to a refutation of *akrasia*.

Here Plato says that Socrates held Pos. A°, but Pos. A' seems to be implied as well. As this is presented as the conclusion of a long argument meant to refute the thesis of 'the many', the author must have considered it as contradictory to this thesis. This presupposes that he held that Pos. A' implies Pos. B' or that Pos. A° implies Pos. B°.

It is interesting to see that in the *Protagoras*, Plato seems also to confirm that Socrates held Pos. C and Pos. D. As evidence, I only quote from Socrates' concluding observations at 361a–b:

(T4) It seems to me that the final outcome of our arguments, as if it became a person, accuses us and laughs at us and if it had a voice would say: You are strange people, Socrates and Protagoras, you [Socrates], who said at the outset that virtue cannot be taught, now argue zealously for the opposite of your former point trying to demonstrate that all useful things are knowledge, justice as well as temperance and courage, by which means virtue would appear most clearly as teachable. For if virtue were something else than knowledge, as Protagoras tried to argue, it would clearly not be teachable. Now, if it shall appear to be nothing but knowledge, as you, Socrates, argue, it would be astonishing if it were not teachable.

If we consider the thesis that wisdom (*sophia*) is identical with prudence (*sôphrosunê*) which Socrates defends in 332a–b we can even attribute to Socrates the stronger form of intellectualism. In 332b Socrates argues that prudent actions are always done by prudence and imprudent actions are always done by imprudence. He makes the same point in 332d. If we translate this into the terminology of 'doing good things' and 'doing bad things' which is allowed by the identity-thesis, we can attribute to Socrates the thesis that 'doing good things' presupposes knowledge of the good and 'doing bad things' presupposes the lack of such knowledge. Together with the thesis we found in the previous passages, i.e. that knowledge of the good has the inevitable consequence of doing good things, we thus get the following principle:

> Anybody will do the good things if and only if he knows what is good.

This is the position I have called 'strong intellectualism'.

I should add that important versions of Pos. A° and Pos. B° can be found in the *Meno* 77b–78b and in the *Euthydemus* 280a–b.[16]

Let us now look at Xenophon's testimony on this point. The most explicit statement of moral intellectualism is to be found at *Memorabilia* 3. 9. 4 (OCT 90. 14–22). Let me first quote this passage in my translation:

(T5) He did not separate wisdom and prudence, but, holding that a man who knows the noble and good things uses them and that a man who knows the shameful things avoids them, he judged this man to be both wise and prudent. When he was asked further whether he thought that those who know what they ought to do and yet do the opposite are wise and not self-controlled, he said, 'Not more than unwise and not self-controlled. For I think that all men who make a choice between possible actions do exactly the things

---

[16] A good interpretation of this difficult passage is given in Santas (1979: 185–9).

they consider most to their advantage. Therefore I hold that those who do not act correctly are neither wise nor prudent.'

The reading of the Greek text is unclear and there are other philological problems as well which make the interpretation of the text difficult. I shall deal with these problems in due detail later. For the moment let me just concentrate on the points relevant to the present issue: (1) according to the first sentence of the paragraph Socrates held Pos. B'; (2) according to the second last sentence (OCT 90. 19–21) Socrates held a variant of Pos. A'. The meaning of neither sentence is controversial.

The next paragraph (3. 9. 5) is no less interesting for our purposes. Right in the first sentence (23–4) Xenophon tells us that Socrates held Pos. D. He then (90. 24–91. 4) reports Socrates' argument for this. It can be reconstructed as follows:

> P.1: All forms of actions that are done through virtue are noble and good.

As formulated here, P.1 is a weak form of our definition of virtue; it is only a weak form because it does not say that only actions accomplished through virtue are noble and good.

> P.2: Nobody who knows the noble and good things will choose something other than these.

P.2 is clearly a variant of Pos. B°.

> P.3: Somebody who does not know the noble and good things is not capable of them.

P.3 is a form of our Pos. B''. As we found Pos. B' in the preceding paragraph, we can deduce from this that, according to Xenophon, Socrates held what we called 'strong intellectualism'. If we presuppose as the underlying definitions that the wise are those who know what is best and the unwise those who do not, we find in fact in the next sentence a formulation of strong intellectualism. In the last sentence of the paragraph (91. 2–4), Socrates is reported to draw the following conclusion from these premises.

> Conclusion: Every virtue is wisdom.

As we have seen at the outset this deduction is not sane. For P.1 is too weak to establish that wisdom and virtue are coextensive, let alone identical. In order to prove their coextension, we need our definition of virtue. On this basis, we might argue as follows:

> An action is good and noble if and only if it is done through virtue.
> An action is good and noble if and only if it is done through knowledge of the best.
> Wisdom is knowledge of the best.
> Conclusion: The set of actions done through virtue is identical with the set of actions done through wisdom.

This conclusion does not formally allow the identification of virtue and wisdom; it only allows holding them to be coextensive.

The most important result of our investigation is the fact that our two main sources attribute to Socrates a form of moral intellectualism. In the *Protagoras* (and in the *Memorabilia*), we found strong intellectualism. In both texts we found the first two corollaries of intellectualism, and in the *Protagoras* we found the third as well. In both texts, Socrates makes an effort to argue for the second corollary, and both arguments are inconclusive. In order to reach a conclusion that comes close to the identity thesis, one needs strong intellectualism together with a strong definition of virtue.

We should not forget Aristotle's testimony. To be sure, Aristotle's version of Socrates' intellectualism depends on Plato. Nevertheless, Aristotle's confirmation of the testimony of Plato and Xenophon is not without value. For Aristotle was critical of Plato and he had enough other sources at his disposal to check the information he found in Plato before reporting it under his own name.[17] Here is what he says (*EN* 1145b21–7):

(T6) Someone could find it puzzling how somebody who has the right judgment [about what is best] acts through *akrasia*. Some say that it is not possible that he has knowledge [of what is best]. For it would be outrageous, as Socrates believed, that, although knowledge is in someone, nevertheless something else masters it and drags it around like a slave. For Socrates fought against the very claim that there is *akrasia*, holding that there is no such a thing, since nobody who judges [what is best] acts against the best, he does the latter only through ignorance [of the best].

In 1145b25–6 we have our Pos. C'. In b23–4, Aristotle first gives a psychological explanation of Socrates' position: Socrates found it outrageous to accept that anything else (for instance pleasure) could be stronger than knowledge. In b26–7, he adds a logical justification: the only cause for somebody not doing what is best is his ignorance of what is best. This corresponds to our Pos. B'. We have already seen that Pos. C' follows indeed from Pos. B'. We find also indirect evidence for Socrates holding Pos. A' in Aristotle's text. In b31–5 he says:

(T7) There are some who concede some [of Socrates' positions] and reject the others. For they agree that nothing is stronger than knowledge but they do not agree *that nobody acts against what he believes to be better*[18] and therefore they define the incontinent person not as one who has knowledge [of the best] but is dominated by pleasure but rather as one who has belief [and is dominated by the pleasures].

The position these people do not accept is precisely our Pos. A'. There is no inconsistency in what they say, for while Pos. A' implies Pos. B' the converse does

---

[17] Vlastos (1991: 97) argues convincingly against Kahn (1981: 305 ff.) that Aristotle's testimony about Socrates has limited but independent value. For Kahn's rejoinder see 1996: 158–61.
[18] My emphasis.

not hold. Furthermore in *MM* 1182ª15–26 and *EE* 1216ᵇ2–9 Aristotle confirms that Socrates held Pos. D'.

Given the evidence of the three sources, it seems to me highly plausible that the historical Socrates held the position of moral intellectualism at least in its weak form.

III. IS MORAL INTELLECTUALISM PLAUSIBLE?

No doubt, moral intellectualism is a consistent theory. But is it also plausible? Aristotle finds it 'obviously contrary to the empirical evidence' (1145ᵇ27–8)[19] and he sets out to investigate how ignorance can be a source of affection leading to the wrong action.

To answer our question we should first take into account that Socrates obviously based his intellectualism on the following general principle:

Everybody strives for what is good and seeks to avoid what is bad.[20]

What is good is determined more precisely as 'eu prattein', i.e. having a good life (*Euthydemus* 278e). Consequently somebody who knows that a certain course of action is the best or leads to the best life will normally take this course of action or at least intend to take it. So far intellectualism is quite plausible. The question however is whether we can completely exclude some further factor that is not under the control of the will, a factor that could interfere with the intention to do the best and make the agent will or do something else, i.e. whether *akrasia* as defined above is possible or not.

To decide this we must first return to the arguments of the *Protagoras* and see how Socrates tries to explain the empirically evident cases of *akrasia* in a way that is consistent with his theory. What he has to show is that, in all the alleged cases of *akrasia*, the wrong action does not result from pleasure overcoming our right judgment but from errors we make in our judgments. How does Socrates proceed in this?

Instead of the details of the discussion in *Protagoras* 352d–357e, a general outline of the steps of the argumentation will be sufficient. Those who defend the thesis that there are real cases of *akrasia* explain them in the following way (352d):

(T8) They [the many] say that they [people who commit acts of *akrasia*] do so because they are overcome by pleasure or pain or because they are dominated by some [affection] I mentioned just now.

---

[19] In the passage of *MM* (and less explicitly in the *EE* passage) mentioned above, Aristotle explicitly criticizes Pos. D' as false, leading to a simplistic conception of the soul.

[20] See *Euthydemus* 278d–282d; *Meno* 77a–78b; *Gorgias* 468b; *Protagoras* 358 c–d.

Socrates' aim is to show that this explanation of the alleged cases of *akrasia* is not correct and to replace it with what he believes is the right one. This explanation will in turn show that these cases need not be considered as cases of *akrasia*, but must be considered as cases of errors in judgment. So we can distinguish two arguments in Plato's text: (1) the *reductio ad absurdum* of the explanation of the 'many' reached in 355d and (2) Socrates' own explanation given in 355e–357e. The two arguments depend partly on the same premises. I will focus my analysis on the second argument. According to Socrates, the right explanation is that the alleged cases of *akrasia* occur because of ignorance. Therefore Socrates must show that in each and every case where pleasure or pain (or some other affection) seems to make us choose the wrong action it is rather an error in our judgment that is the cause of it.

Socrates' first step (353c) consists of interpreting the expression 'overcome by pleasure' in his own way and substituting his own formula for the expression given in the explanation of 'the many'. Thus he gets the following explanation:

(T9) Do you not say, gentlemen, that this happens to you in circumstances like these when you are overcome by food or drink or sex because these things are pleasant and you commit those acts though you know that they are painful.

Then he makes clear that those things are painful not in themselves but because they have painful consequences.

The clue to all the following arguments is the thesis reached in 354a–e that the terms 'pleasant' and 'good' designate one and the same property and that the same is true of the terms 'unpleasant' and 'bad'. Protagoras and Socrates affirm that their adversaries need to concede this kind of hedonism.[21] This allows Socrates to substitute the term 'good' for the term 'pleasant' in the explanation given by the 'many'. Thus they are obliged to say that 'somebody does bad things knowing that they are bad, and, not having to do them, nevertheless does them, because he is overcome by the good' (355d, cf. 355a–b), which Socrates considers ridiculous.

The hedonistic premise also forms the basis for Socrates' own explanation. He first establishes a common scale of measurement for all values presupposed in the alleged acts of *akrasia*. Thus he can formulate the following explanation:

(T10) So it is clear, he will say, that by 'being overcome' you mean taking greater evils instead of lesser goods.   (355e)

---

[21] Kahn (2004: 111) finds it 'difficult to believe that the Socrates we know from the *Apology* and the *Crito* could ever have identified the good with the pleasant'. It has been argued (Santas 1979: 199) that Socrates and Plato need not accept hedonism in order to make this point; they only need their adversaries to adhere to this position. However, we should not overlook that Socrates needs the hedonistic premises not only in the reduction of the explanation of the 'many' but also in his own explanation. See also Vlastos (1969), who rejects Santas's view and McKirahan (2004: 119) who agrees with the thesis of Zeyl (1980: 250–69) that Socrates never endorses hedonism in the *Protagoras*. I do not see how one can avoid the contrary conclusion unless one interprets—as Zeyl actually does—Socrates' affirmations as 'ironical'.

In turn, this is explained by the fact that those people are deceived in their value judgments, giving too much weight to immediate goods in comparison to goods occurring later (356a–357c). So the final explanation of acts people normally call acts of *akrasia* is the following: 'People who commit those acts do so because they lack knowledge of the exact value differences between present and future goods and evils.'[22] Of course, this amounts to denying that there is *akrasia* as defined at the outset.

Is Socrates' argument convincing? I think it convinces only those who are prepared to accept that the only cause for taking (the Greek term is *lambanein*) the lesser good instead of the greater is a wrong value judgment about those goods. Of course, if 'taking' means 'choosing' and if the latter presupposes an act of judging, intellectualism of some kind is inevitable (see Santas 1979: 205). But one might take a course of action without having made a choice; thus taking a course of action might be a completely irrational act, which does not express any judgment at all.[23] In fact, as we may understand, Socrates' adversaries explained *akrasia* as the effect of non-intellectual motivations (pleasure, anger, lust, etc.) overcoming intellectual motivation. To rebut this it is not sufficient simply to deny that there are non-intellectual motivations. Therefore Socrates' argument is question-begging.

IV. SOCRATES' ARGUMENT ACCORDING TO XENOPHON

Does Xenophon's Socrates have a better argument for the denial of *akrasia*? I think he does. In order to show this, let me first introduce two different conceptions of the interference of *akrasia* in human actions. I call the first 'post-deliberation *akrasia*' and the second 'pre-deliberation *akrasia*'. It is important to note that these two conceptions are not my inventions. They are to be found in the *EN* under the terms of *astheneia* (weakness) and *propeteia* (impetuosity). Here is Aristotle's text (*EN* 7. 7, 1150b19–22):

(T11) One type of akrasia is impetuosity, the other is weakness. For some people, after deliberation, do not stick to the result of their deliberation because of the affect, the others act under the influence of affect because they have not deliberated.

Aristotle explains the case of impetuosity three lines further down saying (^{b}25–8):

(T12) Those who lack self-control according to the impetuosity type of *akrasia* are mostly quick-tempered and ardent people. For they do not wait for reason, some because of

---

[22] This is my formulation. It summarizes a long passage in the *Protagoras*, i.e. 355e–356d.
[23] Santas (1979: 209) calls this the 'Strength model'. He sees that Plato did not take this model into account, but he defends this. According to him, Plato, by emphasizing that the agent 'did not have to do what he did', presupposes freedom of choice. Therefore he argues the 'Strength model' does not apply to the cases discussed in the *Protagoras*. I do not find this argument very convincing.

quick temper, others because of ardor, because they are inclined to follow sensible imagination.

Aristotle makes it clear that, in the *astheneia* case, people have already carried out their deliberation about the right course of action; in this case, *akrasia* interferes between deliberation and action, so that the result of the deliberation is not carried out and realized in action. As we see, the *astheneia* case corresponds to the standard definition of *akrasia* given at the outset. In the case of *propeteia*, on the contrary, *akrasia* interferes before the deliberation can take place. Here, *akrasia* has the effect that people immediately follow their non-intellectual motivation, bypassing deliberation. So the *propeteia* type of *akrasia* does not fulfill the standard definition of *akrasia*, or so it seems.[24] It is important to note that *propeteia*, though resembling *akolasia*, is not identical with it. As Aristotle makes clear in 1152^{a}4–6, 'both [the *akratês* and the *akolastos*] pursue the pleasures of the body, but the latter believes that he ought to do so, while the former does not'.[25] Though Aristotle does not mention in this context the two types of *akrasia*, it is clear that what he says applies to both of them.

In the *Protagoras*, the discussion is concerned with the first type of *akrasia*. As we have seen, none of Socrates' adversaries doubts that deliberation occurs in all cases of *akrasia* and, moreover, reaches the right result; the only point of discord is whether some kind of affect can make the agent do the contrary of what was the result of his deliberation. If so, *akrasia* intervenes after the deliberation. Therefore here only the post-deliberation type of *akrasia* is at stake.

Table 1

	t1	t2	t3	t4
Astheneia	No interference of *akrasia*	Deliberation: to perform action *a* is best	Interference of *akrasia*	Performing some action other than *a*
Propeteia	Interference of *akrasia*	No deliberation	No interference of *akrasia*	Performing some action other than *a*

[24] Charles (1984: 141 n. 36) tries to avoid this consequence. He thinks that both the impetuous *acratês* and the weak *acratês* act against preferential choice. The former, however, 'acts against, not his immediate preferential choice, but a preferential choice he has previously made (or would have made, if he had deliberated)'. Irwin (1985: 354) makes a similar point. In fact, the way Aristotle describes *propeteia* suggests that it precludes deliberation in a particular situation of decision and not the acquisition of general practical knowledge. However, as we shall see, the way Xenophon conceives of *akrasia* does not allow restricting it to the first case. In this regard there may be a difference between Aristotle's conception of *propeteia* and Socrates' conception of pre-deliberation *akrasia* as reported by Xenophon. Charles's way of applying the general idea of *akrasia* to the case of impetuosity as well is very attractive.

[25] Pace Vlastos; see n. 26 below.

In the *Memorabilia*, on the contrary, both types of *akrasia* are at stake. As we shall see, Xenophon reports that Socrates denies the existence of the post-deliberation type of *akrasia*, while he admits the existence of the pre-deliberation type. How can we explain this? The effect of pre-deliberation *akrasia* is to hinder and preclude deliberation. Therefore, whenever someone suffers from this type of *akrasia*, no judgment is formed about what it is best to do. In this case, post-deliberation *akrasia* has simply no object to interfere with. Here the question whether some force is stronger than practical knowledge is beside the point. On the other hand, if someone comes to deliberate, he is not under the influence of pre-deliberation *akrasia*. It would be very strange then, if after forming a judgment, he suddenly came under the influence of post-deliberation *akrasia*. This explains why Xenophon's Socrates totally denies the existence of post-deliberation *akrasia*, while he affirms the existence of pre-deliberation *akrasia*. However, this position must be characterized as intellectualism, since it implies all the positions by which the latter is defined.[26]

Let me first give some evidence from Xenophon's text that Socrates actually argues along these lines. The first relevant passage is Socrates' long speech on self-control reported in chapter 5 of the first book. Let me quote from the end of that speech (OCT 27. 4–7):

(T13) Does not every man need first of all to establish self-control in his soul, being convinced that this is the foundation of virtue? For who, without this, would either learn any good or care for it in a worthwhile way?

Here self-control is called the foundation of virtue, not something that helps one put virtue into action. That this means that one needs self-control before even acquiring virtue is made clear in the second, explanatory sentence. Nobody is able to learn what good and evil is, i.e. to acquire practical knowledge, which is identical with virtue, without self-control. Socrates must mean—as the context shows—that somebody who spends his time looking for immediate bodily pleasures of all kinds will not ever engage in reflection on what is good and evil.

This point is most clearly expressed in a passage of 4. 5.11 (OCT 130. 25–131. 4). Here Socrates is reported to ask Euthydemus:

(T14) In which property, Euthydemus, he said, does a man lacking self-control differ from the most ignorant beast? How would one who does not consider things that matter most, and seeks in every way to do what is most pleasant, be different from the most thoughtless cattle? Rather, only the self-controlled are able to consider the things that

---

[26] Vlastos (1991: 100–1) is tempted to charge Xenophon with 'gross confusion', on the grounds that he both affirms and denies the existence of *akrasia*. See also Klosko (1986: 55, n. 5) who makes a similar criticism. To clear Xenophon of this charge, he supposes that Xenophon uses 'the word "*akrasia*" differently from Aristotle .... as a synonym of *akrateia*, to mean not "incontinence" but "intemperance".' Vlastos does not see that Aristotle himself uses the term *akrasia* in two senses, of pre-deliberation and of post-deliberation *akrasia*, and that he clearly distinguishes both types from *akolasia*. It is sufficient to point to this distinction to clear Xenophon of Vlastos's charge.

matter most, and, sorting them out according to classes by word as well as by deed, to give preference to the good things and abstain from the bad.

Let us also consider the following question put to Euthydemus (4. 5. 6; OCT 129. 10–16):

(T15) As for wisdom, the greatest good, does it not seem to you that lack of self-control drives men away from it and throws them into the contrary of it. Or does it not seem to you that lack of self-control prevents them from attending to useful things and learning them, by drawing them away toward what is pleasant and often after having stunned them in their perception of good and evil makes them choose the worse instead of the better.[27]

Here lack of self-control is described as having two negative effects: (*a*) preventing the acquisition of practical knowledge, (*b*) preventing the correct choice by disturbing the perception of good and evil. So all the passages we analyzed confirm our interpretation.[28]

The next question is whether according to Socrates as depicted by Xenophon self-control is not only a necessary condition for practical knowledge but also a sufficient one. The passages quoted above—with only one exception—suggest that Socrates did not consider it as a sufficient condition. In fact he never says that it is sufficient, but emphasizes that it is necessary.[29] The only text that seems to contain a different view is (T5). I shall deal with the problems of this text later. There is also a systematic reason for attributing the latter position to Socrates. If self-control were sufficient for acquiring wisdom, everyone who engages in deliberation would necessarily discover the truth. In this case, however, there would be no place for a teacher of morality. The fact that Xenophon presents Socrates as a moral teacher is therefore a clear indication that—according to him—Socrates could not possibly consider self-control as a sufficient condition for practical wisdom. This is also consistent with what we found in the

---

[27] Vlastos (1991: 100) translates: 'and often so stuns men that, though perceiving both the good and the bad, that it makes them do the worse instead of the better'. On the basis of this translation, which is possible, he then charges Xenophon to make Socrates teach the position he explicitly rebuts in the *Protagoras*. This translation, however, makes no sense at all. For if the object of the stunning is the men who do the perceiving, the effect of the stunning must be the hindrance or perturbation of the perceiving. Therefore I follow Marchant who has 'stuns their perception'. But even if one translates 'stuns those who perceive' the perceiving must not be taken, as Vlastos does, as an act conducing to a belief of what is good and bad. Therefore we find Xenophon's report in perfect agreement with what we have in the *Protagoras*.

[28] Dorion (2003: 645–72) follows by and large the same line of interpretation. Concerning Vlastos's claim that 4. 5 contradicts 3. 9. 4–5 (our T5) he states that 'aucun commentateur ne semble avoir remarqué que IV 5 confirme la position de III. 9. 4 sur un point essentiel, à savoir que la *sophia* et la modération sont étroitement liées et que l'*akratēs* ne possède ni l'une ni l'autre' (654). He doesn't mention that I did exactly this in the paper I gave at the *International Conference on Socrates* in Athens in 2001. This omission is the more astonishing as Dorion attended my talk. Whatever his reason for this might have been, I can only express my agreement with his rebuttal of Vlastos's critical remark.

[29] In *Mem*. 4. 5, Xenophon calls *akrasia* the greatest hindrance to caring for what is right. So the opposite of *akrasia* must be a necessary condition for caring for what is right.

Protagoras. The alleged cases of *akrasia* are, in Socrates view, clearly cases where people engage in deliberation, but come to the wrong conclusions. What they lack is practical wisdom, not self-control. Therefore self-control cannot be sufficient for acquiring practical knowledge. We have to consider a further possibility that played an important role in Aristotle's solution of the puzzle of *akrasia*, i.e. the possibility that somebody acquires general practical knowledge but fails to apply it in a particular decision because of *akrasia*. There are, however, no traces in Xenophon's text that Socrates considered this possibility.

Let me summarize the results of our investigation in a systematic way, putting the four main terms under discussion—*sophos, asophos, egkratês*, and *akratês*—in a two by two table (see figure). Now the question is which kind of action (right or wrong) results from each combination of properties of the acting subject. Let us first consider the standard theory as found in Aristotle's *Nicomachean Ethics*. According to this theory cases I and IV lead to a right action, while cases II and III imply a wrong action. That case IV implies a right action seems somewhat paradoxical; Aristotle calls it in fact the 'sophistical paradox' (*EN* 7. 1146^{a}27–33). But this is only a consequence of the fundamental idea of *akrasia* according to which weakness of the will makes people act against what they believe to be best.

What is Socrates' answer to our question according to Xenophon? A first point is quite obvious: Socrates holds that I implies a right action and IV implies a wrong action. Though the first is perfectly in line with the standard theory, the latter presents a first important difference from it. This point is important because it avoids the sophistical paradox. As for III Socrates seems to deny that it could ever occur. This denial is of course a consequence of Socrates' intellectualism and should not surprise us. The most puzzling case is II. If Socrates considers having self-control a necessary but not sufficient condition for having practical wisdom, he must admit that there are cases where the agent, though acting in a self-controlled manner, makes the wrong judgments and thus acts in the wrong way. As a consequence Socrates must admit II as a case of acting wrongly.

	Sophos	Asophos
Egkratês	I	II
Akratês	III	IV

Now, according to (T5), Socrates seems to deny this. Let us first look to the last sentence of the paragraph. If we understand the Greek term *sôphrôn* as meaning more or less the same as *egkratês*, Xenophon has Socrates saying that all cases of wrong actions are due to both lack of practical wisdom and lack of self-control. This means that case II does not occur.

We can avoid this consequence by translating *sôphrôn*, not by self-controlled, but rather by 'of sound mind', 'discreet', 'prudent', or 'moderate'. The Greek allows these translations. If we look to Xenophon's usage of this term and related terms like *sôphroneô* and *sôphrosunê*, we find that one of the latter meanings is more likely.[30] In *Mem.* 4. 5. 7 he asks to which person *sôphrosunê* belongs less than to the *akratês*. The question makes sense only if *sôphrosunê* and *egkrateia* have different meanings. For this reason I opted for the translation given in (T5) above. However, this does not entirely eliminate the problem. For it seems that the central passage of our text still allows us to attribute to Socrates the denial that there are any instances of case II.

Whether this is in fact so depends on which reading we adopt for lines 18 and 19 of the OCT edition and how we interpret the *Ouden ge mallon ê* clause in these lines. Let me first explain the problems linked to the uncertain reading of lines 18 and 19. In the OCT edition, Marchant reads *akrateis* in both lines. However, in his edition for the Loeb Classical Library, he has *egkrateis* in the first line and *akrateis* in the second, presumably by mistake, for he translates *akrateis* in both lines (see Cooper, 2000: 24 n. 42). In fact, many of the eighteenth- and early nineteenth-century editions (Dindorf, Weise, Finckh, Herbst, Schütz) read *egkrateis* in the first line. They probably took the *Ouden ge mallon ê* clause as expressing a contrast between the two formulae. Others like Delatte follow them in looking for a contrast, but interchange the two terms (Delatte 1933: 115–16). Now, there is no doubt that we should read *akrateis* in line 18 OCT, for—as Hude notes—except for the Marcianus 590, Marcianus 852, and the Vaticanus 1619, all the manuscripts have this reading. The main manuscripts, however, do not support Delatte's reading of line 19 OCT. So the reading best supported by the main manuscripts would be to have *akrateis* in both lines as the OCT does.[31] This means that the contrast between the two formulae is lost.

Carlo Natali[32] considers this contrast unnecessary, arguing that the 'answer does not maintain the opposition of the qualities'. He keeps *akrateis* and follows Marchant who translates 'Not so much that, as both unwise and vicious'. To be sure, *Ouden ge mallon ê* sometimes means 'Not so much this, but rather...' though it sounds odd in the present context.

---

[30] In *Mem.* 1. 2. 17–20 Xenophon speaks of 'sôphrosunê' as a virtue and as something that can be taught or learned. By contrast 'egkrateia' is never called a virtue. In *Mem.* 1. 2. 19 Xenophon opposes 'sôphrôn' and 'hybristês', which suggests the meaning 'moderate' for the former.
[31] The Marcianus 590 and the Vaticanus 1950 have *amatheis*, which makes perfect sense.
[32] See his contribution to this volume.

Given the main variants of the reading and the two possible meanings of the *Ouden ge mallon ê* clause we have the following four possible translations of line 19 OCT:

(1) 'Not more than "unwise and not self-controlled" '
(2) 'Not more than "unwise and self-controlled" '
(3) 'Not so much that, but rather "unwise and not self-controlled" '
(4) 'Not so much that, but rather "unwise and self-controlled" '

I think we should stick to the reading of the main manuscripts and therefore exclude (2) and (4). Concerning the remaining alternative, I give preference to (1) for the following reasons. First, *Ouden ge mallon ê* mostly means 'Not more than'. There are two other places in Xenophon where this or a similar formula occurs, i.e. *Mem.* 3. 12. 1 and *Oec.* 12. 18. 2. In both places, it has this meaning. Second, according to (3) people who know what they ought to do and do the contrary have to be called unwise and lacking self-control. That seems at least awkward. Third, by contrast with (4), interpretation (3) does not exclude the strong thesis that wrong actions always result from both lack of wisdom and lack of self-control. This thesis implies the denial of case II. I have already argued that it would create problems of consistency had Socrates adopted this position. What one would expect of Socrates is instead the denial of case III, which is implied in the question. To say that the characterization advanced in the question is not more acceptable than the characterization 'unwise and not self-controlled', which is excluded by it seems to be a rhetorically elegant way to do exactly this.

At the end of this chapter we should put one final question: which of the two versions of practical intellectualism, Plato's or Xenophon's, is more likely to be the one the historical Socrates actually held? To answer this question the following points have to be taken into account. First, Xenophon's version corresponds better to the experience of the man in the street. Second, Xenophon's version is more plausible in itself. Third, as we have seen, the justification of Plato's version partly depends on Xenophon's version. All three points speak in favor of Xenophon's version.

But there is a further argument that is even more compelling. In the *Apology* (25d–26a) Socrates asks Meletus whether, when charging him with corrupting the young people, he meant that he does this on purpose or that he does this unwillingly. Meletus answers that he meant that Socrates does it on purpose. Socrates then tries to show that this is unlikely, because this would mean that he intentionally harms himself. So only two possibilities remain: either he does not corrupt the young people at all or he does it unwillingly (26a). In the latter case, however, it would be appropriate to teach him the right course of action and not to bring him to justice. For 'it is evident that, if I am taught, I will stop to do what I did unwillingly'. This point, namely that those who do something wrong by some mistake in their judgment, and not on purpose, must be taught the right course of action, is perfectly in line with plain moral intellectualism as we found it in the *Protagoras*. However, this is not true of what immediately follows. Socrates continues, arguing that Meletus brought him to court instead of teaching him, where according to the law one must bring those who need punishment rather than teaching. Socrates seems to admit that there are cases where in fact people need punishment rather than teaching in order to become better. This is not in line with the moral intellectualism as found in the *Protagoras*. For according to this position the only way to make people better is to teach them. Who are those who need punishment? The most plausible answer is: those who lack self-control as Xenophon describes them. It seems that the only way to make sense of Socrates' argument in *Apology* 25d–26a is to attribute to him the form of intellectualism we found in Xenophon.

Now, if the *Apology* is the work of Plato's that relates with most fidelity the core of the positions of the historical Socrates, as most scholars believe, we have good reason to think that he actually held Xenophon's version of moral intellectualism and not Plato's. In this case, how can we explain the difference between the position found in the *Apology* and the position found in the *Protagoras*? The most plausible way to explain this is to consider the *Apology* as an earlier work than the *Protagoras* and as the Socratic writing that shows the least impact of Plato's own philosophical ideas. On the other hand, the theory we find in the *Protagoras* seems to be the result of a radicalization of the original position by Plato, a radicalization that perfectly serves the dramaturgical structure and the purpose of this dialogue.[33]

V. IS SOCRATES A DEONTOLOGIST?

It is important to see that—according to Xenophon's testimony—the pre-deliberation type of *akrasia* has two kinds of negative effects on knowledge: it hinders the acquisition of general practical knowledge and it makes us rush to wrong decisions in concrete situations. That means that in some way Socrates must have distinguished two levels of practical knowledge: (1) knowledge of general principles and (2) knowledge about the best choice to make in a particular situation. As is well known, Aristotle exploits the difference between the two levels of practical knowledge in his explanation of post-deliberation *akrasia*. He actually has a rather complicated theory about the relation between the two levels (see again Charles 1984: 109ff.). What is the content of the general practical knowledge and what is its relation to the particular knowledge according to Socrates? It is a characteristic feature of Xenophon's presentation of Socrates that we find two answers to this question in his text. On the one hand, there is the picture he wants to convey. Let us call it the official version of Socrates' theory of practical knowledge. On the other hand, we find many elements of a completely different version, which he

---

[33] See Kahn (2004: 114), 'This simplification makes for a very elegant theory'.

inadvertently lets slip in the text. As we shall see, both versions are also present in Plato's early dialogues, but let us first consider Xenophon's testimony.

In the *Memorabilia*, we find two levels of general practical knowledge: (1) definitions of virtues and vices and (2) classifications of types of action. Concerning the first, Xenophon confirms the well-attested picture according to which Socrates engaged in discussions about definitions of good and bad and of the virtues and vices (see *Mem*. 1. 1. 16). However, as Carlo Natali[34] rightly emphasizes, according to Xenophon he did so not so much in order to refute other people's definitions—what he mostly does in Plato's early dialogues—as in order to find the right definitions (cf. *Mem*. 1. 4. 1 and 4. 6. 1). In fact Xenophon gives examples for this procedure in books 3 and 4. What is the function of these definitions?

We find an answer to this question in the following passage:

(T16) Whenever somebody contradicted him about a point without having anything clear to say, but claimed without proof that the person he mentioned was either wiser or better in political affairs or braver or something else of this kind, he would lead the whole argument back to the basic hypothesis, much in this way. (*Mem*. 4. 6. 13; OCT 135. 1–5)

The context makes it clear that the basic hypothesis Xenophon speaks about is the definition or a part of the definition of wisdom, political ability, courage, and so on. Socrates, or so it seems, considered the general knowledge (e.g. the definition of courage) as the appropriate criterion to settle a dispute about a particular case (e.g. whether some particular person is brave).

Besides the definitions of good and bad, virtues and vices, Socrates was after a more special but still universal form of practical knowledge, which seems to have been the proper object of Socrates' dialectical method.[35] In (T14) Xenophon describes it as follows (*Mem*. 4. 5. 11; OCT 131. 1–4):

Only the self-controlled are able to consider the things that matter most, and, sorting them out according to classes by word as well as by deed, to give preference to the good things and abstain from the bad.[36]

Carlo Natali conjectures that the procedure Xenophon here describes in general terms is exemplified by the dialogue between Socrates and Euthydemus in *Mem*. 4. 2. 13 ff. If this is correct, the procedure must have consisted of sorting out types of actions and classifying them under the headings 'works of justice' and 'works of injustice' or—as we see later in the dialogue—of sorting out states of affairs and classifying them under the classes of good and bad things. One would expect that the definitions of good and bad, just and unjust, and so forth would play an important role in this task. However, there is no sign that Euthydemus

---

[34] See his contribution to this volume
[35] See Natali's contribution to this volume
[36] See *Mem*. 4. 5. 12.

uses any such definition when he subsumes a type of action under a heading. On the other hand, Socrates uses his definition of good or a part of it, as given in *Mem.* 4. 6. 8, in order to refuse Euthydemus' proposals. According to the paragraph following (T14), Socrates was convinced that, once this list was completed, one could teach it.

On the other hand, (T14) also says that this second type of general practical knowledge was meant to make us choose the good things and avoid the bad. It can easily be explained how this is accomplished. When someone has to choose between two particular courses of action, he wants to choose the good one and avoid the bad one. In order to know which is good and which is bad, he has to see, first, what type the particular courses of action are cases of and, second, under which heading the corresponding types fall. So, here again the general practical knowledge serves as a criterion for deciding which particular course of action has to be chosen in a concrete situation. In today's terminology, a moral theory that tries to determine which types of action are good or bad, obligatory or forbidden, without considering the consequences of the corresponding actions, is called 'deontologist'. Accordingly, if Xenophon's description were accurate, Socrates would figure most prominently along with Kant on the list of the deontologists.

When we consider Plato's early Socratic dialogues, we understand why someone like Xenophon could come to believe that this was a correct description of Socrates' philosophy. For not only do we find all the elements of this description in the early dialogues, but we also realize that modern scholars drew similar conclusions from these elements (see Santas 1979).

I do not need to emphasize that in several of the early dialogues definitions of virtue and of different virtues are at stake. Aristotle too confirms that Socrates was the first to look for universal definitions of the virtues (*Met.* 13. 1078^{b}18–30). As Santas has argued quite convincingly,[37] these definitions were meant to serve as criteria for deciding whether a particular thing or a particular course of action was good or bad, just or unjust, pious or impious, and so forth. This particular practical knowledge is used in turn to choose the right course of action.

We also have examples of the second level of general practical knowledge in the early dialogues. In the *Laches*, for instance, Socrates establishes a list of types of action that fall under the heading 'courageous action', in the *Euthyphro* he does the same for 'pious action'. In the *Euthydemus* (279a) Socrates asks Kleinias: What sorts of things happen to be good for us? This leads to the—later classical—threefold classification of external goods, goods of the body and goods of the soul (see *Meno* 87e–88a). Among these only the latter (knowledge) gets through Socrates' examination. However, in establishing these lists, Socrates never uses any definition of courage or piety or good. He could not because

---

[37] Santas (1979: 115–18) calls it 'the diagnostical use' of the definitions.

neither he nor his interlocutor knows such a definition.[38] Instead, in some contexts (*Republic* 1) he uses these types of actions to check whether a proposed definition is acceptable or not. Again, once the subsuming of an action-type under the heading of a kind of virtuous action is accomplished, this knowledge can be used to decide whether a particular action has to be done or, if already done, be praised or blamed. The *Euthyphro* affords the best example of this.[39]

Though the picture given in Plato's early Socratic dialogues differs in many details from Xenophon's, the general view seems to be the same: Socrates held a form of deontologism. If this were accurate, Socrates would be a proper object of the criticism one normally addresses to deontologist positions. However, I have serious doubts that the prima facie view of Socrates' theory of practical knowledge we found in Xenophon and Plato gives the whole picture.[40] Let me first explain these doubts concerning the picture given in Plato's early dialogues.

As is well known, Socrates emphasizes on several occasions that he knows that he has no knowledge. To be sure, many scholars have argued that this cannot be taken seriously, and Xenophon too must have shared this opinion, for an explicit mention of Socrates' avowal is absent from his Socratic writings. Others, like Vlastos[41] and Nehamas (1999: 70–6) try to show that Socrates' confession has to be taken seriously. But how can we take it seriously, given that Socrates also claims on many occasions to have moral knowledge?[42] The answer to this objection must be—as Beversluis[43] has argued—that the knowledge Socrates avows to lack is knowledge of definitions, i.e. knowledge of the kind presupposed in the deontological model, and the knowledge Socrates claims to have is of a completely different kind.[44] Actually, as I shall argue, it is either moral meta-

---

[38] To be sure, in his examination of the things on Kleinias' list Socrates uses as a criterion whether they benefit us or not (*Euthydemus* 280b). This can be taken as an element of a definition of 'good'.

[39] Concerning the relation between the two levels of knowledge Geach (1966) has charged Socrates with the following methodological inconsistency. On the one hand, he claims that without knowledge of what F-ness is one can never know whether something is an F. On the other hand, he tries to find out what F-ness is by abstracting the definition of the general notion from particular cases of things that are Fs. I do not believe that Socrates committed this methodological error, but I cannot address this question here.

[40] For reasons of space, I cannot argue my views in full detail. I content myself with stating my claims, and sketching some of my reasons for them.

[41] See Vlastos (1991: 32). More precisely, Vlastos attributes to Socrates what he calls a 'complex irony': Socrates denies having knowledge in the traditional sense, but claims to have knowledge in a new Socratic sense.

[42] See Beversluis (1996: 222–6) who gives a list of such claims.

[43] Ibid. 223–6. See also Lesher (1996: i. 261), who holds that Socrates' denial of knowledge concerns 'basic thesis about virtue, the good, and the noble, and is therefore compatible with claims to knowledge about the moral character of specific actions' and Woodruff (1996: i. 275), who makes a distinction between expert and non-expert knowledge.

[44] Vlastos (1991: 238) doesn't accept Lesher's and Woodruff's solution of the problem. He argues that Socrates' denial of knowledge is so global that there is no room left for a distinction of different kinds of knowledge. However, his own concept of 'complex irony' involves a distinction of kinds of knowledge as well, i.e. the usual one and the Socratic one.

knowledge[45] or knowledge of particular moral facts.[46] The latter must be the 'human' wisdom Socrates claims to have at *Ap.* 20d–e.

In most of the early dialogues of Plato, a definition of the virtue under discussion is never reached.[47] This may be explained by the fact that, in these dialogues, Socrates' primary aim is the testing of his interlocutors' claims that they have knowledge.[48] However, would we not normally expect Socrates to give the right answer after having refuted the false ones? Should we not take his silence on this point as a sign that he does not dispose of such an answer? So the first point which makes me doubt Socrates' deontologism is that the general knowledge in question is not available either to him or to anyone else.

One might object to this that the early dialogues do not always leave us with an open question. But whenever, as in the *Protagoras* (361b–c), the examination of false beliefs leads finally to a positive answer, the definition Socrates gives does not fit into the deontological model. To know that virtue is knowledge is a kind of formal metaknowledge, which is of very little practical use. To be sure, this knowledge could be of some use for somebody who wants to acquire virtue, but when it comes to choosing a particular course of action this definition does not give any applicable criterion. The same holds of Socrates' 'definition' of the good as the beneficial used in the *Euthydemus*. To apply this definition one has to know what is beneficial and what is not in a concrete situation.

Some scholars (Irwin 1996: 226: Penner 2004: 131–51) have argued—in my opinion convincingly—that Socrates has a prudentialist approach to ethics. This means that he would justify moral claims by means of hypothetical imperatives. In the paper mentioned above, T. Penner tries to show that this even holds for Socrates' arguments in the *Crito*. If he is right, Socrates appears to be a consequentialist rather than a deontologist. Against this conclusion, one might argue that the goods we choose for their own sake must have an intrinsic value and this value cannot be justified instrumentally. In fact, as Irwin (1977:85) has shown on the basis of *Lysis* 219c–220b, Socrates distinguishes two kinds of goods: those that are loved for the sake of something else and those that are loved for their own sake. Does Socrates hold a deontological view concerning the latter? The good we choose for its own sake is the good or happy life. Irwin argues that Socrates must have conceived happiness as the fulfillment of (all) our desires (see Irwin 1996: 234–41). To reach this kind of happiness, Socrates seems to have recommended

---

[45] A good example is the knowledge claim Socrates makes in the *Apology* (29b 6–7): 'But I know that to do wrong and to disobey my superior ... is bad and dishonorable.' This looks like an analytical truth. Without knowing what types of action are wrong or who the legitimate superior is and what he orders, it is obviously useless for making decisions.

[46] A good example is Socrates' confession in the *Apology* (37a): 'I am convinced, that I acted unjustly against nobody.'

[47] Aristotle already remarked the absence of positive answers in Socrates' refutations and explains this by Socrates' acknowledgement of his ignorance (*Soph. elenc.* 34. 183^{b}6–8).

[48] See on this point Benson (1996: 246–56).

the adaptation of our desires to the circumstances in which we find ourselves by giving up desires that cannot be satisfied (see Irwin 1996: 237). If this was in fact Socrates' view, he could not have held a deontologist position concerning the intrinsic good either. For the adaptation view of happiness implies that what is good depends on the situation and what has to be chosen is relative to the circumstances of the choice.

We come to the same conclusion if we analyze the type of moral knowledge Socrates recognizes and recommends in the *Protagoras*. The kind of knowledge people lack in the alleged cases of *akrasia* is the science of measuring correctly present and future pleasures and pains. Is this a universal knowledge that could be taught? I think it is not. The only thing that could be taught in connection with it are some general methodological rules, like: always take into account all the consequences of a course of action and evaluate the amounts of pleasure and pain they imply. However, nobody can teach somebody else what will win him pleasure and pain and how much. Pleasure and pain are essentially private experiences, knowable only by the person who has them. Therefore they are not teachable. If virtue is this kind of knowledge, it does not consist of definitions of virtues and vices or of classes of types of actions falling under the heading of different virtues and vices as presupposed in the deontological model.

Let me now come to Xenophon. There is no doubt that he understood Socrates' moral teaching according to the deontological model. However, he inadvertently lets elements of the prudentialist model slip into his text. These elements have to be taken the more seriously.

1. By contrast with Plato and Aristotle, Xenophon never refers to Socrates' confession of ignorance, and what is more, he explicitly says that he boasted of his knowledge of definitions.[49] However, if we look at these definitions we find that they contain a kind of metaknowledge that is not of direct practical use. For not only wisdom but also piety, justice, courage are defined as a kind of knowledge. In 4. 6. 4, for instance, the pious man is defined as the man who knows the laws about the gods; in the same chapter, paragraph 6, the just man is defined as the man who knows the laws about men. These definitions simply reformulate Socrates' intellectualism on the level of the theory of virtues, but they are useless as criteria for a concrete decision. Most important for our question are the definitions of 'good' and 'fine' given in *Mem.* 3. 8. 5 and 4. 6. 8–9. In the first passage (OCT 88. 24–7) Socrates says:

---

[49] The most convincing example is Socrates' dispute with Hippias over the definition of justice (*Mem.* 4. 4. 5–25). In this text, Hippias charges Socrates twice with refusing to give positive definitions and Socrates answers (OCT 123. 19–21): 'About the just, however, I strongly believe I have something to say, against which neither you nor anyone else could make objections.' Then he says first that he shows by his deeds what things are just in his view, and then, when pressed by Hippias again, he declares that the just is the lawful.

(T18) It is in relation to the same things that men's bodies look beautiful and good and it is in relation to the same things that all other things men use are considered beautiful and good, namely, in relation to those things for which they are of good use.

This is a confirmation of Socrates' prudentialism that has been found in some of the early dialogues as well.

2. In the second passage (OCT 133. 14–20), Socrates asks Euthydemus whether he would call anything else good but the useful. Socrates then adds that the useful is good for precisely the person it is useful to. This clearly is a relativistic conception of good which contradicts directly any form of deontologism. In the following lines, the notion of 'fine' receives the same treatment. Something is fine because it is useful and it is useful for a particular purpose only.

3. Socrates' hedonism is not missing from Xenophon's report either. The argument in 4. 5. 9–10 presupposes as a fact commonly agreed upon that pleasure is a good, though the text does not say that it is the only good.

4. Though in the official portrait Xenophon presents Socrates as a teacher of morality (*Mem.* 4. 7. 1–2), he tells us (*Mem* 1. 2. 3; OCT 26–29) that Socrates 'in no way ever professed to be a teacher of this (virtue), but by being visibly of this character, he made those who spent time with him hopeful to become of such a character by imitating him'. In fact, as Carlo Natali[50] rightly emphasizes, Socrates' *dialegesthai* is not a kind of unilateral transfer of pre-established knowledge but a way to gain practical insight step by step, in which the interlocutors have to give their free assent to each step (4. 6. 15. 1–3).

5. Among the examples of Socratic moral argument Xenophon reports, there is one in which Socrates himself seems to reduce to the absurd the deontological positions officially attributed to him. This argument is to be found in the long interrogation of Euthydemus in the second chapter of book 4—one of the rare examples of a genuine *elenchus* in Xenophon—in which Socrates tries to make Euthydemus aware of his ignorance. In paragraph 13 of this chapter, Socrates proposes to Euthydemus that they establish a list of the just and the unjust types of actions; as we have seen, Xenophon elsewhere describes Socrates' method of moral teaching just in this way. But, whenever Euthydemus proposes a type of action to be put under the heading of the just actions, Socrates shows that there are circumstances in which an action of this type has to be considered unjust.[51] In paragraph 31, Socrates does the same exercise with the headings 'good' and 'bad'. Once again, he demonstrates that for every good Euthydemus proposes under certain circumstances it has bad consequences and thus turns out to be bad in these circumstances.[52] Thus health, wealth, even wisdom are shown to be relative

---

[50] See his contribution to this volume.
[51] This reminds us the procedure in book 1 of the *Republic* 331b–c, where Socrates shows by means of a counterexample that the proposed definition of justice does not work.
[52] In the *Euthydemus* 279a ff. and the *Laches* 195c–d, Socrates argues along similar lines.

goods, their usefulness depending on the circumstances in which they are used. Obviously this kind of argument depends on the definition of good we found in *Mem.* 3. 8 and 4. 6.

6. When Euthydemus plays his last card, saying that at least happiness is a good, Socrates agrees, imposing as a condition that the ingredients of happiness are unquestionable goods. As a matter of fact, he has just shown that they are not. This argument presupposes what Irwin has called the adaptive account of happiness (1996: 237–9). Socrates wants to say that happiness cannot be defined once and for all; rather what happiness amounts to depends in each case on its ingredients and that these change according to the situations of life. We find an adaptive account of happiness also in the discussion with Antiphon reported in *Mem.* 1. 6. 4–10. Socrates here states that 'to have no needs is divine'. This could be taken as an ascetic position, but when he says in 1. 6. 5–6 (OCT 28. 14–17) that 'the one who drinks most pleasantly least desires unavailable drinks', he makes it clear that he wants to emphasize the adaptation of one's desires to the conditions under which they may be satisfied.[53] A further aspect of the adaptive account Irwin emphasizes is also present in Xenophon's report. The happy person must have confidence in the future fulfillment of his future desires. In 1. 6. 8. (OCT 28. 28–29. 1) Socrates says that the pleasures he enjoys 'provide hopes that they will benefit always'.

The conception emerging from *Mem.* 4. 2 is an extraordinary and very astonishing piece of theory. It reduces the deontological model of practical knowledge to the absurd and proposes a kind of ethical relativism based on prudentialism. To be sure, this relativism seems to be inconsistent with what we find elsewhere in the *Memorabilia* and in Plato's early dialogues. In the latter, justice and wisdom are presented as goods that benefit everybody in any situation, while here Socrates' arguments imply that they are harmful in certain circumstances. However, the appearance deceives. Socrates here presupposes the popular conception of justice and wisdom. Justice and wisdom as popularly conceived can in fact have harmful consequences under certain circumstances. However, if we presuppose the meaning Socrates attaches to these terms in accordance with his intellectualism, we see immediately that neither justice nor wisdom can ever harm.[54] Xenophon presents the interrogation of Euthydemus as an example of Socrates' way of making people acknowledge their ignorance.

---

[53] Irwin (1996: 240) recognizes that an adaptive account of happiness, though different from asceticism, will lead to some form of asceticism and seems to imply that Xenophon misunderstood Socratic self-sufficiency as pure asceticism. Even if this is so, Xenophon still inadvertently lets slip the true position of Socrates in the passages we quoted.

[54] Penner (2004: 131–51) argues concerning the *Crito* that the only way to harm somebody (to do injustice to him) is to make him less wise and that by doing this to an other person one harms oneself. For everybody depends on the wisdom of everybody else in order to examine their lives. See also *Euthydemus* 281a–282d.

Therefore he does not take Socrates' affirmations seriously. I think, however, that we have to take them seriously and consider them as a testimony of the very moral theory of the historical Socrates.

What is the conclusion we must draw from these points?

1. The official portrait Xenophon gives of Socrates' conception of practical knowledge is false. However, if we exploit Xenophon's text as a source, reading 'between the lines' as I proposed at the outset, we find the true Socrates reappearing under the layers of his false portrait.[55] Despite a number of differences in the details, we find the same overall picture in Plato's early Socratic dialogues.

2. A careful reading of the dialogues also makes us understand how Xenophon could have gotten his false picture. For the deontological model of practical knowledge is present in the early dialogues. Sometimes it even seems as if Socrates considered it the ideal form of practical knowledge. However, Socrates uses this model critically to show that the sophists and other pretenders to such knowledge do in fact not have it. He confesses, at the same time, that he does not have it either. As a consequence, there is no way to teach this form of knowledge.

3. The only knowledge Socrates has concerns meta-ethical questions. In fact, the content of this knowledge is his intellectualism, his prudentialism and—though less clearly expressed—his adaptive eudaimonism. However, this knowledge is of no immediate practical use. Therefore there would not be a lot of people who want to be taught such knowledge.

4. The only type of knowledge that really counts in one's life is particular knowledge about the course of action to choose in a concrete situation. The best example is the choice Socrates faces in the *Crito*. However, this knowledge cannot be deduced from the general meta-ethical knowledge. One can only expect to come close to it by engaging in endless conversations with other people who have the wisdom, the patience and the motivation to discuss questions of this kind. In fact, Plato and Xenophon both present Socrates as a 'hunter' of suitable interlocutors and as a tireless questioner. For, as he says in the *Apology*, 'the unexamined life is not worth living'.

---

[55] Rossetti (2004: 81–94) makes the same attempt to discover the 'real Socrates' behind what he calls the 'literary barrier', though confining his task to the living figure and excluding the teaching.

REFERENCES

Bandini, M., and Dorion, L.-A. (2000). *Xenophon Mémorables; Texte et traduction*, i (Paris).

Benson, H. H. (1996). 'The Priority of Definition and the Socratic Elenchus', in Prior (1996: 230–72); first published in *Oxford Studies in Ancient Philosophy*, 8, (1990), 19–65.

Beversluis, J. (1996). 'Does Socrates Commit the Socratic Fallacy?', in Prior (1996: iii. 211–29); first published in *American Philosophical Quarterly*, 24 (1987), 211–23.

Charles, D. (1984). *Aristotle's Philosophy of Action* (London).

Cooper, J. M. (2000). *Reason and Emotion* (Princeton).

Delatte, A. (1933). *Le Troisième Livre des souvenirs socratiques de Xénophon* (Liège and Paris).

Dorion, L.-A. (2000). 'Introduction', in Bandini and Dorion (2000: pp. vii–cclii).

—— (2003). 'Akrasia et enkrateia: dans les *Mémorables* de Xénophon', *Dialogue*, 42: 645–72.

—— (2004). 'Socrate et la basilikê teknê: Essai d'exégèse comparative', in *Socrates, 2400 Years since his Death, International Symposium Proceedings*, ed. Vassilis Karasmanis (Athens), 51–62.

Geach, P. T. (1966). 'Plato's *Euthyphro*: An Analysis and Commentary', *Monist*, 50 (1966), 369–82.

Ildefonse, F. (1997). *Platon: Protagoras: Introduction, traduction et notes* (Paris).

Irwin, T. H. (1977). *Plato's Moral Theory: The Early and Middle Dialogues* (Oxford).

—— (1985). *Aristotle*, Nicomachean Ethics (Indianapolis).

—— (1996). 'Socrates the Epicurean?', in Prior (1996: iv. 227); first published in *Illinois Classical Studies*, 11 (1986), 85.

Kahn, C. H. (1981). 'Did Plato Write Socratic Dialogues?', *CQ* 31: 3OS ff.

—— (1988). 'On the Relative Date of the *Gorgias* and the *Protagoras*', *Oxford Studies in Ancient Philosophy* 6 (1988), 69–102.

—— (1996). 'Vlastos's Socrates', in Prior (1996: i. 157–78); first published in *Phronesis*, 37 (1992), 233–58.

—— (2004). 'Socrates and Hedonism,' in *Socrates, 2,400 Years since his Death, International Symposium Proceedings*, ed. Vassilis Karasmanis (Athens), 111–15.

Klosko, G. (1986). *The Development of Plato's Political Theory* (London).

Kraut, R. ed., (1992). *The Cambridge Companion to Plato* (Cambridge).

Lesher, J. (1987). 'Socrates' Disavowal of Knowledge', *Journal of the History of Philosophy*, 15: 275–88.

McKirahan, R. (2004). 'Socrates and Hedonism. Comments on Charles Kahn's paper', in *Socrates, 2,400 Years since his Death, International Symposium Proceedings*, ed. Vassilis Karasmanis (Athens), 117–19.

Natali, C. (forthcoming). 'Socrates' Dialectic in Xenophon's Memorabilia'.

Nehamas, A. (1999). *Virtues of Authenticity: Essays on Plato and Socrates* (Princeton).

Penner, T. (1992). 'Socrates and the Early Dialogues', in Kraut (1992: 121–69).

—— (2004). 'Towards a Prudential Reading of the *Crito*', in *Socrates, 2,400 Years since his Death, International Symposium Proceedings*, ed. Vassilis Karasmanis (Athens), 131–51.

Prior, W. J., ed. (1996). *Socrates, Critical Assessments* (4 vols., London and New York).

Santas, G. X. (1979). *Socrates' Philosophy in Plato's Early Dialogues* (London).
Vlastos, G. (1969). 'Socrates on Akrasia', *Phoenix*, 23: 71–88.
—— ed., (1971*a*). *The Philosophy of Socrates: A Collection of Critical Essays* (Notre Dame).
—— (1971*b*). 'Introduction: The Paradox of Socrates', in Vlastos (1971*a*: 1–21).
—— (1991). *Socrates, Ironist and Moral Philosopher* (Ithaca, NY).
Woodruff, P. (1987). 'Expert Knowledge in the *Apology* and *Laches*: What a General Needs to Know', *Proc. of Boston Area Colloquium in Ancient Philosophy*, 3: 79–115.
Zeyl, D. J. (1980). 'Socrates and Hedonism: *Protagoras* 351b–358d', *Phronesis*, 25: 250–69

3

Socrates and Hedonism

Charles H. Kahn

The *Protagoras* is a puzzling dialogue in many respects, but none more puzzling than the apparent endorsement of hedonism by Socrates in the final refutation of Protagoras. Since Aristotle clearly takes some of the views expressed by Socrates in this dialogue to be the views of the historical Socrates (notably the denial of *akrasia*), some scholars have been tempted to see the identification of pleasure as the good as in fact a view defended by the historical character Socrates, and not just by Socrates in the dialogue. But most of us find it difficult to believe that the Socrates we know from the *Apology* and the *Crito*—the Socrates who claimed that the only consideration for a good man is whether a proposed action is or is not just—could ever have identified the good with the pleasant. And other dialogues, from the *Gorgias* to the *Philebus*, make clear that hedonism was not Plato's view. So what is Socrates doing in the *Protagoras* when he makes use of the identity between pleasure and the good as a premise in an elaborate argument designed to prove that courage is inseparable from wisdom?

Many interpreters point out that the hedonist premise is presented in the context of a dialogue with the many and that when it is accepted by Protagoras he is speaking in the name of the many. So hedonism here can be seen not as Socrates' own view but rather as a vulgar view acceptable to a mass audience, and Socrates' goal is to show that both Protagoras and the other sophists are ready to accept such a view (as they eventually do, at 358a). Gregory Vlastos, however, in his classic 1956 Introduction to the *Protagoras*, rejected this interpretation on the grounds that 'it is most unlikely that Socrates would deliberately offer a false proposition as a premise for establishing his great proposition' that knowledge is virtue.[1] Vlastos suggested, instead, that 'what Socrates most likely meant to assert' was (*a*) that pleasure is a good (not the only one) and (*b*) that whatever is best will *in fact* be the most pleasant, namely, the life of virtue (ibid., p. xli). Vlastos correctly pointed out that both (*a*) and (*b*) are maintained by Plato in other dialogues. Vlastos suggested that Socrates might not have realized the

---

[1] *Plato's Protagoras*, ed. M. Ostwald and G. Vlastos (New York: Liberal Arts Press, 1956), p. xl n. 50.

logical distinction between this position of quasi-hedonism and the strict identification of the good with pleasure.

Most of us will be less worried than Vlastos was about allowing Socrates to make deliberate use of a false premise in the argument for a good conclusion. But otherwise my motive in citing Vlastos is not to disagree with him. I want instead to call attention to a feature of the text that has not been sufficiently noted, namely, that Socrates *in propria persona* asserts precisely the proposition Vlastos designated as (*a*), namely, the claim that pleasure is *a good*, although Socrates allows his interlocutors to understand him to be making the stronger claim. That is to say, it is Protagoras who is guilty of the logical oversight that Vlastos is inclined to attribute to Socrates. When Socrates asks him 'isn't pleasure itself good?' Protagoras understands the question to be whether 'pleasant and good are the same' (351e). If we read the text carefully, we see that there is a repeated logical ambiguity between Socrates' own formulation, which asserts only (*a*), 'the pleasant is good, the painful is bad' (358a5), or 'you pursue pleasure as being good, you avoid pain as bad' (354c4), on the one hand, and the use Socrates makes of this as a premise in the argument, on the other hand, as if the interlocutors had agreed to the identity between pleasure and the good. I want to suggest that, with his usual cunning as an author, Plato has here attributed to Socrates only his own position, the position I have called quasi-hedonism, while making use of the cruder premise of hedonistic identity for the sake of the argument. The precision with which this is done shows, to my mind, that the author is fully aware of the kind of confusion that Vlastos has identified (which includes a confusion between 'All As are B' and 'A and B are the same').

But what is the argument after all, and why is it useful for Socrates to take hedonism as a premise? I want to connect this to another question: why does Socrates deny *akrasia* in this context, and what is the function of this denial in the argument? These two questions are not usually linked together, because whereas Socrates' endorsement of hedonism in our dialogue is generally regarded as problematic, his rejection of *akrasia* is thought to be historically confirmed, on the authority of Aristotle. But once we begin to suspect the historical validity of Aristotle's testimony—as we certainly should—we see that there is no *other* reason to attribute the denial of *akrasia* to the historical Socrates.[2] And we can also see that Aristotle's basis for such an attribution is precisely this dialogue, which he quotes verbatim in reporting Socrates' view (*Nicomachean Ethics* 7. 2, 1145^{b}24). So I propose to ignore Aristotle's reading of the *Protagoras* and thus leave aside all problems about the historical Socrates, and to ask instead: what is

---

[2] Unless we also follow Aristotle in attributing to Socrates the identification of virtue with knowledge, and infer that this implies a denial of *akrasia*. But here again, I believe, Aristotle is simply interpreting Plato's representation of Socrates in the dialogues. See my *Plato and the Socratic Dialogue* (Cambridge: CUP, 1996), 85 f.

Plato's philosophical motivation for introducing these two surprising premises in Socrates' final argument?

I submit that the endorsement of hedonism and the explicit denial of *akrasia* belong together, as equally isolated and equally anomalous in their appearance in the *Protagoras*. They are part of the systematic strangeness of this dialogue, together with the deliberate misinterpretation of Simonides' poem, and the almost total absence of the genuinely Socratic view of *aretê* as the healthy condition of the soul. It is important to note that there is no explicit denial of *akrasia* in other versions of what is called Socratic intellectualism, for example in the *Gorgias* and the *Meno*. Scholars have claimed that a denial of *akrasia* is implied by the inference in the *Gorgias* that anyone 'who has learned just things' (ὁ τὰ δίκαια μεμαθηκώς) will be just and will act justly (460b7), by the argument in the *Meno* which proves that no one desires bad things (78a), and more generally by the equation of virtue and knowledge. But it is one thing to defend a thesis that can be taken to entail a denial of *akrasia*, or that simply ignores this possibility, and it is something else to claim expressly that no one ever acts against their better judgment. These other dialogues (including the *Laches* and the *Charmides*) do emphasize that moral knowledge, or the knowledge of good and bad, is inseparable from *aretê* or equivalent to *aretê*; but nowhere except in the *Protagoras* (and later in the *Republic*) is the case discussed of someone who might know what is good but nevertheless act otherwise. Before the *Republic*, and except in the *Protagoras*, the possibility of *akrasia* is never mentioned, and hence never denied. Since two notorious examples of *akrasia* (namely, Medea and Phaedra) had been brilliantly portrayed in Euripidean tragedies produced about the time Plato was born, Socrates' denial here that a person's better judgment might be overwhelmed by their passion would seem just as implausible and paradoxical in Plato's day as in our own.

Why then are hedonism and the denial of *akrasia* introduced into Socrates' last argument? Let us consider the context. The argument serves to refute Protagoras' claim that courage is very different from the other virtues, and that many people who lack the other virtues are nevertheless outstandingly brave. (Note that Protagoras speaks here with the voice of common sense.) Socrates first offers a short proof designed to show that wisdom and courage are the same, but Protagoras finds fault with this argument. Socrates then begins with an apparently unrelated series of questions about the role of pleasure in the good life. In response, Protagoras agrees that they should examine the relation between pleasure and the good. Socrates begins this examination by questions about the role of knowledge and whether it can be overcome by the passions. As a consequence, they are apparently diverted into the discussion of an entirely different question, the problem of *akrasia*. The issue of hedonism returns not as a question in its own right but only as a component in the analysis of *akrasia*, as a basis for explaining 'what this is that you (the many) call being overcome by pleasures' (354e). Although the topic of hedonism was invoked first, its discussion turns out to be justified only as a necessary prerequisite for the reinterpretation of *akrasia* as a miscalculation of pleasures and pains. Why are we spending so much time analyzing relative pleasures and pains? asks Socrates, and he provides his own answer: because the whole account of *akrasia* depends upon this (354e7), namely, upon showing that the many have no other standard (*telos*) in judging pleasure bad, or in judging pain good, than the long-term balance of pleasures and pains (354d). It is just this result, the disclosure of the unspoken hedonism of the many, that makes nonsense of the ordinary notion of 'being overcome by pleasure'. Thus it is hedonism that permits Socrates to reinterpret *akrasia* as an error in the measurement of pleasures and pains (355a–357e).

We can only be dazzled by Plato's brilliance in working out a hedonistic calculus as the model for human decision-making, and thus pointing the way for Epicurus, Bentham, the utilitarians, and the modern exponents of rational choice theory. Perhaps no passage in the dialogues better illustrates Whitehead's characterization of the history of Western philosophy as a series of footnotes to Plato's work. But if we leave aside this broader historical perspective and focus on the logic of the text, we see that hedonism is required in this final argument *only* as a basis for rejecting the ordinary notion of *akrasia* and for replacing it by the metrical theory of decision-making. In the context of the dialogue, the hedonistic premise serves simply as an instrument for the radical reinterpretation of the phenomenon known as weakness of will or acting against one's better judgment.

Why is the elimination of *akrasia* so important for Socrates in this argument? At the beginning Protagoras himself asks why they should bother with the opinion of the many in such matters. Socrates' answer is that this will contribute to finding out 'how courage is related to the other parts of virtue' (353b). In strictly formal terms, Socrates' goal is to refute Protagoras' claim that courage can be separated from the other virtues. More generally, Socrates is concerned to show that Protagoras and common sense are mistaken in thinking of the virtues as functionally independent of one another, like the parts of the face. In this argument he achieves both goals by obliging Protagoras to accept the identification of courage with a kind of wisdom, namely, with the knowledge of what is and is not to be feared. This conclusion, and indeed the whole force of the argument, depends upon the purely cognitive or intellectualist definition of fear as the expectation of evil (358d). It is crucial to Socrates' line of reasoning that any emotional or non-rational aspects of fear (for example, the desire to run away) be excluded from consideration, and this exclusion is achieved not only by the cognitive definition of fear but also by the reinterpretation of *akrasia* as a mistake in calculation. If cowardice could be seen as acting against one's better judgment, as running away because one is overcome by fear, Socrates' refutation of Protagoras would collapse.

Thus far I am simply explicating the logic of the text. If we reflect now on the larger philosophical strategy, I suggest the following account of Socrates' final argument. His goal, here as always, is to show that virtue is impossible without a correct understanding of good and bad, and hence that wisdom is an essential ingredient, a necessary condition, for any kind of virtue. Here, as often, he exaggerates this point by arguing, paradoxically (in this case for courage, but by implication for the other virtues as well) that the virtues are *identical* with wisdom understood as the knowledge of good and bad. Socrates is of course fond of paradox. Like the sting of elenctic contradiction, paradox can serve as a stimulus for the interlocutor to reflect critically on his previously unquestioned assumptions. But in this case there is more at stake. For in the passage in the *Phaedo* where Plato's Socrates explicitly rejects the hedonistic calculus as a model for virtue, he nevertheless seems to maintain that wisdom is not only necessary but sufficient for virtue.

'This is not the right exchange in reference to virtue: pleasures for pleasures, pains for pains, fear for fear, the greater for the less, like coins, but the only right coin is wisdom ... Together with this there is real courage and temperance and justice and, in sum, true virtue.' The text goes on to say that, without wisdom, what appears to be virtuous behavior is merely slavish virtue (69ab). Perhaps this text means only that wisdom must be *added* to virtuous conduct in order to constitute real virtue. But we can also read this passage as asserting that wisdom *alone* is sufficient to guarantee true virtue. This reading would bring the *Phaedo* into agreement with familiar passages in the *Meno* and *Euthydemus*, as well as with the identification of courage with wisdom in the *Protagoras*.[3]

What all these texts have in common is an apparent neglect of the emotional factors in moral character and in decisions to act. This neglect is what Vlastos took to be a psychological error committed by the historical Socrates. But we are speaking here about the Socrates of Plato's dialogues. I want to suggest a two-part answer to the question why Plato was willing to have Socrates occasionally affirm not only the necessity but also the sufficiency of wisdom for moral virtue.

First, the *Gorgias* presents, and Aristotle in the *Ethics* develops, what we may call the classical theory of rational action. This theory assumes that all actions are done for the sake of the good, i.e. that there is a rational desire for the good (or for good things) present in all human beings, as a fundamental principle of their psyche.[4] By 'good' here is meant both (*a*) good for the agent, beneficial, and also (*b*) good absolutely, that is, good for any agent as the final goal of all his actions. (It is the task of moral theory to show how these two conceptions of good coincide.) The classical view is clearly expressed by Aristotle in his claim that we desire something because we judge it good; we do not judge it good because we desire it (*Met.* λ 7. 1072^{a}29).

This notion of things done 'for the sake of (something) good' amounts to an implicit definition of rational action. Thus for Plato in the *Gorgias* an action

---

[3] Compare *Meno* 89a3, *Euthydemus* 280d–281e.
[4] For the claim that all action is for the sake of the good see *Gorgias* 468b7, *Republic* 505d11; compare Aristotle on *boulēsis* as rational desire for good.

counts as rational, as an expression of *boulesthai*, only if the agent has an end in view that he perceives as good, and if he deliberately pursues that action as a means to achieving this end.[5] Thus all rational actions are done for the sake of a *perceived* good. They are done because the agent judges the action or its consequence to be good.

But of course the agent may be mistaken. That is why wisdom is necessary for virtue. But why is it sufficient? Plato's implicit answer, I take it, is because the desire for the good is universal in human beings. So anyone wise enough to know what is good will necessarily desire it, and act accordingly. This is Plato's interpretation of the Socratic paradox: anyone who acts badly, or for the sake of a bad outcome, is not doing what he really wants (since what he wants is the good). So his action in this case is involuntary.

Secondly, this classical theory of action, outlined in the *Gorgias* (in Socrates' discussion with Polus) and implied in the *Meno* and elsewhere, does not entirely ignore the emotions, but it takes account only of the rational desire for what is judged good. But what about non-rational desire such as sexual passion, fear, or anger? And what about weakness of the will, acting contrary to one's judgment of what is good, because of the force of these other motivating passions?

These are questions that the Platonic Socrates generally ignores before the *Republic*, when for the first time he attempts to develop a comprehensive theory of human motivation. The earlier dialogues are concerned with the fundamental need for moral wisdom rather than with its limitations. Only occasionally, as in the confrontation with Callicles in the *Gorgias*, is there a serious discussion of non-rational desires, and even then not in the context of a general theory of human motivation. Of all dialogues earlier than the *Republic*, only the *Protagoras* suggests such a theory, a general moral psychology, as distinct from a theory of rational action. But the theory of the *Protagoras* turns out to be not so different after all—it simply reduces all human motivation to a problem of rational choice. Before the *Republic*, only in the *Protagoras* does Socrates raise the question of the limits of rational control over human action, and here he gives the highly paradoxical answer that there are none: what is generally thought to be the distorting effect of the passions is really a mistake in calculation.

Why does the *Protagoras* take such a hard line, reducing the power of the passions to a metrical mistake, and reducing human motivation to the pursuit of pleasure and the avoidance of pain? I suggest two different answers. First of all, this simplification makes for a very elegant theory. And on the other hand, we must remember that this is a dialogue in which Socrates is prepared to behave unscrupulously. The entire meeting between Socrates and Protagoras, 'the wisest

---

[5] Of course some actions are done for their own sake, because they are intrinsically good. For Aristotle, virtuous actions are of this kind: they are done for their own sake, because they are something noble, *kalon*. For Plato in *Republic* 2, an action is better if it is desired both for its own sake and also for its consequences.

man in Greece', is staged as a contest for the crown of wisdom, a highly competitive contest in which Socrates figures as the young challenger, whose skill in dialectical manipulation will bring down the reigning champion in defeat. This is not a context chosen by Plato for presenting the first attempt in history to provide a realistic theory of human psychology, of the kind that he will offer in the *Republic*. Just as Socrates outdoes Protagoras in creative misinterpretation of Simonides' poem, so he trumps Protagoras' very sensible account of moral education in the Great Speech by a brilliantly perverse account of *akrasia* and cowardice as miscalculation. The *Protagoras* is not the place to look for Plato's own theory of moral psychology—just as it is not the place to find Socrates' conception of virtue as the health of the soul.

Still, we are left with the two questions we began with. Why hedonism? And why the interest in *akrasia*?

I take *akrasia* first. As we have seen, it is necessary for Socrates to eliminate *akrasia* in order to win his argument against Protagoras. At a more general level, *akrasia* poses a problem for the Socratic paradox that no one is voluntarily bad or unjust. The classical theory of action was originally designed to support this paradox: since everyone desires the good and acts for the sake of the good, bad action must be due to ignorance of the good and be in this respect involuntary. But suppose one knows what is good but nevertheless does what is bad because of moral weakness, because one's better judgment is overcome by fear or by lust? In the end, Plato (unlike Aristotle) will count akratic actions as involuntary, just like actions due to ignorance, since they do not aim at the good. In the *Protagoras* he has taken the more direct course of simply identifying acratic actions with acts done *in ignorance of the good* (i.e. by a mistake as to what is better).

Somewhat to our surprise, Plato shows no theoretical interest in the Aristotelian distinction between *akrasia* and vice.[6] But he is insightful enough to realize that acratic acts are going to be a stumbling block for his fundamental claim that all actions are done for the sake of the good. In the *Gorgias* and other 'early' dialogues he systematically avoids this problem by never confronting Socrates with the apparent objections to his paradox that could be based on acratic behavior. In the *Republic* he will develop a broader motivational theory that takes non-rational desires into account. In the *Protagoras*, on the other hand, he salvages the Socratic paradox and the conception of virtue as wisdom by simply denying the reality of moral weakness and reinterpreting the appearance of weakness in intellectualist terms. Hence in this dialogue Plato is able to present rational choice theory as a general theory of human action.

We are left with the issue of Plato's quasi-hedonism. The *Protagoras* is the only dialogue in which Socrates seems to endorse hedonism, but it is not the only text in which pleasure is presented as a popular candidate for the good. In the *Gorgias* Callicles defends an identity between pleasure and the good, and this is named

---

[6] See *Plato and the Socratic Dialogue*, 253–7.

again as the view of most people in *Republic* 6. 505b. The entire *Philebus* is constructed as a contest between pleasure and knowledge as competitors for the nature of the good, and the interlocutors agree that a life without pleasure cannot be 'choiceworthy'. In the *Laws* Plato goes even further and claims that 'no one would voluntarily consent to perform an act unless more pleasure follows than pain' (*Laws* 2. 663b).

Clearly there is more at stake here than a popular preference for hedonism. There is a concern on Plato's part to take account of the profound psychological appeal of hedonism, in the natural connection between pleasure and motivation. This connection is mirrored in the normal connotations of non-technical language (as in the exchange between Callicles and Socrates in the *Gorgias*), where there is an almost tautological link between pleasure and desire: desire suggests the pursuit of pleasure, and pleasure implies the satisfaction of desire. This strong conceptual connection poses a problem for any theory of action that wishes to avoid hedonism. Aristotle deals with this problem by a distinction between *epithumia* as desire for pleasure and *boulêsis* as rational desire for good. But Plato is not a philosopher to be satisfied by terminological distinctions, and the attempt to do justice to the deep psychological appeal of hedonism is a major theme of his life's work. It is in the context of this larger project that we can best understand the hedonism of the *Protagoras*. Meeting the many halfway, this dialogue offers hedonism as a general theory of human action, a popular and persuasive simplification which the more complex theory of motivation in the *Republic* is designed to replace.

4

Socrates and Euthyphro: The Argument and its Revival

Terence Irwin

I

In the *Euthyphro* (10a–11b) Socrates argues against Euthyphro's suggestion that piety is what all the gods love. His argument, sometimes known simply as 'the Euthyphro Argument', is the source of a long sequence of philosophical reflexions on definition, and on related issues in meta-ethics. The continuing prominence of these issues in contemporary philosophy demonstrates the depth and breadth of the questions raised by the Euthyphro Argument.[1]

I want to comment on the significance of the Euthyphro Argument in three contexts: (1) Socrates' views on religion and morality; (2) Plato's views about the nature of Forms and of adequate accounts of them; (3) attempts to identify morality with the content of divine commands.

I will try to show how some developments of the Euthyphro Argument raise worthwhile questions both about the interpretation of Plato and about the relevant meta-ethical issues. In particular, I will refer to the revival of the Euthyphro Argument in the late seventeenth and early eighteenth centuries by Ralph Cudworth and Samuel Clarke. These philosophers exploit the Euthyphro Argument to introduce questions about realism, anti-realism, and response-dependence. Without trying to explore these questions, I simply want to indicate their connexion with historical applications of the Euthyphro Argument.[2]

---

[1] See e.g. Crispin Wright, *Truth and Objectivity* (Cambridge, Mass.: Harvard UP, 1992), 109–39 (section entitled 'The Euthyphro Contrast').

[2] I discuss these later uses of the Euthyphro Argument more fully in 'Morality and Immutability: A Platonic Contribution to Meta-Ethics', in R. W. Sharples (ed.), *Perspectives on Greek Philosophy* (Aldershot: Ashgate, 2003). Ss. 1–3 of that paper overlap with this chapter.

II

Socrates concedes to Euthyphro that the two predicates 'pious' and 'god-beloved' are coextensive, but he still argues against Euthyphro's definition. His argument is this:

(1) The god-beloved is god-beloved because the gods love it, and it is not the case that the gods love the god-beloved because it is god-beloved (10d9–10, e5–7).
(2) The gods love the pious because it is pious, and it is not the case that the pious is pious because the gods love it (10d1–7, e2–3).
(3) Hence the pious and the god-beloved are not identical.
(4) Hence the pious is not correctly defined as what the gods love.

Though the conclusion is significant, some crucial premisses are not fully defended, and they need to be examined more closely.[3]

Socrates does most to support the first step of the argument. He appeals to simple logical, perhaps even grammatical, considerations (10a1–d12). To support (1) he appeals to a simpler case:

(1a) x is being-carried (*pheromenon*) because x is carried (*pheretai*), and it is not the case that x is carried because x is being-carried.

Socrates expresses his point by claiming that the participial form ('being-carried' or 'a being-carried thing') is to be understood through the passive form ('is carried'), and that the converse is not true. His point is easier to grasp in English if we use the passive and active forms:

(1b) x is carried because S carries x and it is not the case that S carries x because x is carried.

In (1) Socrates applies the pattern illustrated in (1b) to the case of 'god-beloved' (*theophiles*).

The general claim illustrated in (1) and (1b) is easy to accept. It is plausible to claim that carried or seen things, as such, have no nature in common beyond the fact that someone carries or sees them; what makes them carried or seen is simply the fact that someone carries or sees them. Similarly, then, loved things, as such, have nothing in common beyond the fact that someone loves them.

It is more difficult to say why we ought to accept Socrates' second premiss. Since Euthyphro accepts it without question, Socrates neither explains nor

---

[3] I will not discuss the argument in detail. Two helpful treatments are: S. M. Cohen, 'Socrates on the Definition of Piety', in G. Vlastos (ed.), *The Philosophy of Socrates* (Garden City, NY: Doubleday, 1971), ch. 8, from *Journal of the History of Philosophy*, 9 (1971), 1–13; R. Sharvy, '*Euthyphro* 9d–11b: Analysis and Definition in Plato and Others', *Nous*, 6 (1972), 119–37.

defends it at length. He expects us to recognize that pious things, as such, differ from god-beloved things, as such, because pious things, as such, have something in common beyond the fact that the gods love them. Because they differ in this way, the pious and the god-beloved are entirely different (*pantapasin heteron*, 11a4), as Socrates claims in (3).

To show that the pious and the god-beloved differ in the way expressed in (2), Socrates appeals to an explanatory asymmetry: 'For the one [sc. the god-beloved], because it is loved, is of a sort to be loved (*hoion phileisthai*), but the other [sc. the pious], because it is of a sort to be loved, is loved because of that' (11a4–6). The pious has some property, distinct from being god-beloved, because of which it is loved, whereas the god-beloved, as such, has no such property. Socrates alludes to this property by saying that the pious is 'of a sort to be loved' or 'of a character to be loved'; by having this character it is suitable to be loved antecedently to being actually loved.

These claims about the pious and the god-beloved lead to the conclusion in (3) that they are not identical. The conclusion cannot be understood extensionally, so as to claim that the set of god-beloved things is not identical to the set of pious things; for Socrates and Euthyphro agree (for the purposes of the argument) that these are the same set. Nor does Socrates suggest that the two sets are only contingently identical. For his purposes we may take the two predicates 'pious' and 'god-beloved' to be necessarily coextensive. The two non-identical things that Socrates calls 'the pious' and 'the god-beloved' must be non-extensional. If his argument is sound, their non-identity can be discovered by recognition of the explanatory asymmetry that Socrates asserts.

How, then, do we recognize the relevant explanatory asymmetry, and what does it show about whether the pious and the god-beloved are non-identical? We might try two possible answers.

(a) An appeal to meaning

A correct definition of the pious would say what 'pious' means. But we can see that 'pious' does not mean the same as 'god-beloved'; for it is not self-contradictory (even though it is false) to say that x is pious but the gods do not love x, whereas it is self-contradictory to say that x is god-beloved but the gods do not love x. The proposed definition of the pious as the god-beloved is therefore (we may say) 'logically inadequate'; the denial of the proposed definition is not self-contradictory.

(b) An appeal to moral judgment

It would be unacceptable to suppose that the gods could make everything that is pious pious simply by loving it; it must already be pious if it is to be an appropriate object of their love. Hence the proposed definition of piety is 'morally inadequate'; to know that an action has the property mentioned in the proposed definition is not thereby to have given sufficient reason for concluding that it is pious.

These two ways of grasping the asymmetry imply two different ways of distinguishing the pious and the god-beloved. According to the logical argument, the god-beloved and the pious are different concepts, because the meanings of the terms are different. This difference in meaning is established by appeal to what is and is not self-contradictory. According to the moral argument, we do not establish difference of properties by meanings and by appeals to analyticity, but by appeal to the different explanatory roles identified by moral judgments. A definition that is morally adequate might apparently be logically inadequate, since the denial of such a definition might not be self-contradictory. A morally adequate definition of the pious would not analyse the concept 'pious'; it would give an account of the property of piety. Even if the concepts of the pious and the god-beloved were different, it would not follow that they pick out different properties.[4]

Though some of the concepts used in drawing this distinction between logical and moral argument arouse familiar philosophical controversies, the distinction itself is difficult to avoid. A familiar modern meta-ethical illustration concerns the status of an account of rightness as what maximizes utility. We might attack the truth of this account either (*a*) by arguing that is not self-contradictory to claim that an action is right but does not maximize utility, or (*b*) by arguing that some actual or possible actions are right whether or not they maximize utility. These different objections are relevant to different sorts of accounts. The first is relevant to a question about the concept 'right', whereas the second is relevant to a question about the property of rightness.

From the Euthyphro Argument, taken by itself, it is difficult to decide whether Socrates is concerned with concepts or with properties. The appeal to explanatory asymmetry does not help us to decide. In 'x is carried because S carries x' one might claim that Socrates has a conceptual (or semantic) connexion in mind; but even here it is not clear whether the explanatory priority of S's carrying x is conceptual or metaphysical. And even if the 'because' in this example were conceptual, it would not follow that the 'because' in the example of the pious and the god-beloved is also conceptual.

III

We may be able to clarify this issue if we step back from this particular passage and consider its relation to the dialogue. Many readers are legitimately surprised

---

[4] For present purposes, I assume that concepts are, or necessarily correspond to, meanings, and that this is not true of properties. This is not the only way of speaking of meanings, concepts, and properties.

to find that Euthyphro does not consider denying step (2) of Socrates' argument, about the explanatory priority of being pious to being loved by the gods. The argument for (1b) does not make it obvious that we must accept (2).

If neither Socrates nor Euthyphro thinks of denying (2), ought we to infer that they treat (2) as analytic, something that could not be denied without self-contradiction? This inference is questionable in the light of their earlier discussion. The dialogue begins with a reminder of Socrates' prosecution for impiety on the charge that he does not recognize the gods recognized by the city (*Ap.* 24b8–c1; cf. *Eu.* 3b1–5). On this point Socrates and Euthyphro have something in common; for Euthyphro remarks that, despite his superior knowledge of religious matters, he is ridiculed when he speaks about them in public (3b–c). The prosecution he is undertaking at the moment exemplifies his disdain for popular religious views. He is prosecuting his father for causing the death of a slave; he thereby violates a traditional bond of filial loyalty, but he argues that if an injustice has been committed, the gods demand punishment for it (*Eu.* 4b7–c3, 5d8–6a5, 7b7–9).[5]

Euthyphro's convictions do not add up to a systematic theory, as Socrates soon makes clear. But it is not unfair of Socrates to expect him to agree that gods are guided by considerations of justice in forming their loves and hates. If he holds this moralized conception of the gods, he might fairly be expected to agree that pious actions have some property that makes them antecedently worthy of the gods' love.

If this is how Plato presents Euthyphro, he implicitly warns us against assuming that principles acceptable to Euthyphro must therefore be acceptable to common sense. In accepting step (2) of Socrates' argument, Socrates and Euthyphro accept a moral judgment about piety that separates them from many of their contemporaries.

Probably, therefore, we should understand Socrates to be claiming not only that 'pious' and 'god-beloved' are different concepts, but that the pious and the god-beloved are different properties, and that being pious explains being god-beloved. The explanatory relation is metaphysical, not conceptual, and Socrates argues for it by relying on moral judgments, not simply on appeals to what is or is not self-contradictory.

IV

Though this is a reasonable conclusion about the Euthyphro Argument, it is not certain; the distinctions I have used to explain Socrates' point are not drawn

---

[5] I have discussed Euthyphro further in 'Common Sense and Socratic Method', in J. Gentzler (ed.), *Method in Ancient Philosophy* (Oxford: Clarendon Press, 1998), ch. 2, at pp. 41–3, 52–3.

explicitly in the dialogue. The conclusion will be confirmed if it fits Plato's implicit or explicit practice in other dialogues.

The Euthyphro Argument makes it clear that we have not found an adequate Socratic definition if the definiens and the definiendum are coextensive; to find an adequate definition we must also find the property that explains the other properties of the definiendum. How far does Plato rely on this condition for an adequate definition?

In the Socratic dialogues, many of the objections to proposed definitions seem to rest on counter-examples. Sometimes these are actual examples. Socrates reminds Laches of how the Scythians, the Homeric Aeneas, and the Spartans at Plataea actually fight or fought (*La.* 191a8–b6). The examples he offers Charmides are not specific historical examples, but they are examples (writing quickly, learning promptly, appropriate and inappropriate shame) that we can easily see to be actual (*Ch.* 159b7–161b2). But the actual occurrence of the actions described does not seem to be necessary for Socrates' objections to be effective. Their point is to show that the proposed definition of, say bravery, either excludes actions which, if they were to occur, would clearly be brave, or includes actions, which if they were to occur, would clearly not be brave. The proposed definition, therefore, has the wrong extension.

The same objections seem to underlie Plato's arguments for non-sensible Forms. As Aristotle sees (in *Metaphysics* 1.6), Plato believes that Forms must be distinguished from sensibles because sensibles are in flux and change. The flux Plato has in mind is not primarily change in particular sensible objects, but the fact that (for instance) a certain type of action changes from being just in some circumstances to being unjust in others.[6] This fact reveals mutability in some sensible properties. Repaying what was borrowed is sometimes just and sometimes unjust, so that it (the action type) changes from being just to being unjust. Hence the property of being a repayment of what was borrowed changes from making an action just to failing to make an action just. Since the property of being just always makes an action just, justice cannot undergo the sort of change that is undergone by repaying what was borrowed. The properties that are wrongly identified with justice have the wrong extension. These are 'the many justs' that the sight-lovers of *Republic* 5 identify with justice.

Should we infer, then, that Plato's appeal to the flux of sensibles and the immutability of Forms rests on an appeal to the different extensions of sensible properties and of the non-sensible properties that are Forms? The Euthyphro Argument should make us hesitate to infer this. For it insists that piety is identical only with the property that makes things pious, and is therefore not identical to the property of being loved by all the gods, even though this property is coextensive with piety.

---

[6] This interpretation probably goes back to Alexander, in *Met.* 83–9. See G. Fine, *On Ideas* (Oxford: Clarendon Press, 1993), 152 f.

When Plato discusses conditions for an adequate definition, he recognizes the explanatory component as distinct from the demand for a coextensive property. The *Euthyphro* requires an adequate definition to identify a form that we can attend to (*apoblepein pros*) and use as a pattern (*paradeigma*) in saying whether something is or is not pious (6d–e). This demand might be understood as epistemological ('Tell me a characteristic of the pious that I can recognize and use in making judgments about which things are pious') or as metaphysical ('Tell me a characteristic that I must grasp in order to understand why things are pious'). My discussion of the Euthyphro Argument supports a metaphysical interpretation. This interpretation is confirmed by the *Meno*. Socrates wants an account of the form of F because of which F things are F (*Meno* 72c6–d1). When he tells Meno he would be 'content' (*agapan*) if Meno could find an account providing a coextensive property (75b11–c1), he distinguishes such an account from one that would meet Socrates' explanatory condition.[7]

Concern with this explanatory condition reappears in the *Phaedo*. Plato argues that a correct account of the Forms must provide a satisfactory explanation of why things have the relevant properties. Being beautiful cannot be the same as being bright coloured, because being bright coloured is not the property that makes things beautiful (*Phd.* 101c9–e3).

The *Phaedo* also insists that the Form of F must be free of flux, not liable to variation between being F and being not-F (78d–e). He does not discuss the relation of the explanatory demand to the demand for freedom from flux. If the latter demand is simply a demand for properties with the right extension, it is weaker than the explanatory demand.

Plato, therefore, has a choice between different lines of argument. An appeal to actual counter-examples excludes the identification of justice with returning what has been borrowed, but it does not exclude the identification of piety with what all the gods love. Other arguments rule out properties that provide inadequate explanations; such properties are relevant to (say) justice because they embody justice in different cases, but actions (etc.) that have these properties are just only because these properties embody some further property that really makes the actions just.

A modified appeal to flux might expose the non-explanatory character of these embodying properties. Even if we believe that necessarily the gods love only what is pious, we might argue as follows:

(1) If the gods were to love unjust action, unjust action would be pious.
(2) But it is impossible for unjust action to be pious.
(3) Therefore the god-beloved changes from being pious to being impious.
(4) Therefore the god-beloved is not the pious.

---

[7] In his contribution to this volume, David Charles argues that the account with which Socrates says he would be content is a different kind of definition (saying what the name 'F' signifies) rather than (as I interpret Socrates) an inadequate answer to Socrates' single demand for a single kind of definition (providing an explanatory account of the F).

The 'change' mentioned in (3) is counterfactual rather than actual flux; it is change that would result from the truth of the antecedent of (1), which is allowed to be impossible.

If proposed accounts of Forms may be refuted by appeal to counterfactual flux, it is understandable that Plato does not point out that his explanatory demand is more exacting than his demand for freedom from flux. The latter demand might be understood so as to include the former. None the less, they are two distinct demands; for the point of appealing to counterfactual flux is clear only if we accept the explanatory demand.

Plato ought to rely, therefore, primarily on explanatory inadequacy rather than on actual examples of flux. Actual flux is relevant, since it exposes some cases of explanatory inadequacy, but it cannot expose all the cases of explanatory inadequacy that Plato wants to expose.

How, then, does Plato understand the relevant explanatory relation? We saw that the *Euthyphro* might understand 'x is F because of the F' as a conceptual or a metaphysical connexion; we found some reasons for taking it to introduce a metaphysical connexion. Some of the same questions return in the *Phaedo*. Socrates rejects explanations according to which things are beautiful by being bright coloured or symmetrical in shape in favour of the explanation that says things are beautiful by the beautiful. This conception of a 'safe' explanation (100d8–e3) might be taken to rest on an appeal to a conceptual connexion. Perhaps Plato means that 'x is F by the G' is refuted if it is not clearly self-contradictory to claim that x is F but not G.

We might even find a more extreme claim in the *Phaedo*. When Plato favours the explanation 'x is F by the F', perhaps he means that no substitution of any other predicate for 'F' in 'by the F' yields an acceptable explanation. Perhaps he assumes that nothing of the form 'x is F by the G' can avoid logically conceivable counter-examples. In that case he takes the demand for a safe explanation to imply that the Form is indefinable; any attempt to substitute another predicate for 'F' in 'by the F' yields an unsafe explanation.

V

We need not attribute these views to Plato, however. As I mentioned earlier, we might take him to reject Euthyphro's definition on the basis of moral judgments, not because of appeals to what is or is not self-contradictory. In that case, he is concerned with properties rather than with concepts.

To see what he means, we should notice that he relies on moral judgments, not simply on intuitions about what is or is not self-contradictory, to refute definitions. To show that justice is not returning what was borrowed, we have to agree that in some circumstances it would be unjust to return what was borrowed. To show that the good is not pleasure, we have to agree that there are bad pleasures (*R*. 505c6–d1).

We will have a firmer basis for deciding Plato's views, if we consider not only proposed definitions that he rejects, but also definitions of moral properties that he accepts. Such definitions appear in *Republic* 4, when he offers accounts of the different virtues.[8] Even if these are imperfect definitions, they offer a more informative explanation than we find in 'x is just by the presence of the just'; Plato tells us that the just person is just by the harmony between the three parts of the soul in which each of the parts does its own work (443b1–6); and he offers similar explanatory accounts for each of the other three cardinal virtues (442b11–d3).

These definitions do not capture the concepts of bravery, temperance, wisdom, and justice. This is especially clear in the case of justice. One might express the familiar objection that there is a 'fallacy' in Plato's argument about justice by pointing out that it is not self-contradictory to deny that a just person has the psychic harmony that Plato identifies with justice. Plato, however, believes he has given an account of the relevant property; we can see by moral judgment and moral argument that the appropriate sort of psychic harmony explains the justness of just actions and people. The interpretation of the *Euthyphro* that fits Plato's own attitude to definitions is the one that takes him to be concerned with moral properties, discovered by the exercise of moral judgment, rather than with moral concepts.

VI

According to this interpretation of the Euthyphro Argument, Socrates and Euthyphro agree in accepting a controversial claim about the explanatory priority of piety over being loved by the gods; they agree that the gods love the pious because it is pious, and they reject the converse claim. At this stage in the argument they assume that 'because it is pious' gives the right sort of explanation. But this assumption is only tentative. For they agree that what is pious is also just, and they find some difficulty in distinguishing piety from the rest of justice. They have not yet settled whether piety is a different property from justice. This question leads to further questions about the unity of the virtues. If Socrates accepts the unity thesis, it is possible that 'because it is virtuous' is the right explanation of why the gods love the pious.[9]

To examine this possibility, we would need to explore some familiar disputes about the unity of the virtues and its implications for definition and explanation. But it is at any rate plausible to take Socrates to claim that choice and will do not

---

[8] It would also be relevant to discuss the treatment of the 'clever cause' in the *Phaedo*, and its relevance to moral properties.

[9] An argument against this possibility is offered by C. C. W. Taylor, 'The End of the *Euthyphro*', *Phronesis*, 27 (1982), 109–18.

constitute moral rightness, and that morally correct choice and will presuppose antecedent moral rightness.

In affirming this position Socrates rejects a position that we may call 'voluntarist', claiming that choice and will constitute moral rightness. A voluntarist about piety holds that actions are pious because the gods love them. More generally, a voluntarist holds that actions are right because they are chosen by some agent. In the *Euthyphro* Plato does not discuss this general voluntarist position, but he probably rejects it. If the gods do not make actions pious by loving them, it is difficult to see how human beings could make actions just by choosing or preferring them.

Another version of a voluntarist position about rightness is the conventionalist position of Protagoras (as Plato represents him in the *Theaetetus*), who holds that what is just is just because of the law or convention (*nomos*) of a particular city (*Tht.* 167c). If the position rejected in the *Euthyphro* is theological voluntarism, the position of Protagoras is social voluntarism, or (more specifically) legislative voluntarism. Plato does not draw our attention to this connexion between the issues discussed in the *Euthyphro* and those discussed in the *Theaetetus*; but the connexion helps to explain why he takes the anti-voluntarist position on both issues.

VII

With this generalization beyond the specific case of piety we come to the version of the Euthyphro Argument that is prominent in the later history of ethics, in accounts of moral properties that identify them with the contents of divine commands. In the *Euthyphro* itself Euthyphro does not take seriously either a voluntarist thesis about piety or a more general voluntarist position. But we have seen that traditional Greek views about piety give some support to a voluntarist position, and that Protagoras maintains legislative voluntarism. The voluntarist position finds serious defenders when philosophers consider more closely how divine law or divine will could be a source of moral requirements.

Some Christian moralists make some apparent concessions to voluntarism, by allowing God to make an action wrong simply by prohibiting it. This is Augustine's view of the wrongness of eating from the tree of the knowledge of good and evil: 'But they [sc. Adam and Eve] were also taking other kinds of food, apart from one tree, which had been forbidden not because it itself was an evil, but in order to commend the good of pure and simple obedience.'[10] Adam and Eve could not have been expected to work out for themselves that it would be wrong to eat from this tree, and indeed they would have had no reason to refrain from eating if they had not been prohibited.

[10] Augustine, *De Civitate Dei* 13. 20.

In order to allow God to make actions wrong simply by prohibiting them, Christian moralists introduce a division between actions that are bad because prohibited (*mala quia prohibita*) and those that are prohibited because bad (*prohibita quia mala*): 'But Adam sinned by doing what was bad only because it was prohibited. Many, however, sin by doing what is bad in both ways, both in its own right and because it is prohibited.'[11] The division between these types of bad actions may appear to endorse both Socrates' position, for the second class of actions, and the voluntarist position, for the first class.

This appearance, however, is not accurate. To say that God's legislation can make some actions wrong that would not otherwise be wrong is not to say that rightness and wrongness consist in being prescribed or prohibited by divine legislation. For one might argue that it is right to obey divine commands because disobedience to God is wrong. The possibility of God's legislation making specific actions right or wrong presupposes the antecedent wrongness of disobedience.

To maintain the stronger position, that rightness and wrongness consist in being commanded and prohibited by God, one needs to go beyond recognizing some actions that are bad because they are prohibited. One also needs to claim that divine prohibition is the whole explanation of the wrongness of wrong actions.

According to Duns Scotus, this explanation is required by a correct account of divine freedom. In Aquinas's 'Socratic' (i.e., non-voluntarist) conception of the principles of natural law, the requirements of justice are grasped by the divine intellect, because they are best all things considered; that is why God prescribes them. But, according to Scotus's conception of freedom, God's will, being free, is free to reject what is best all things considered, so that Aquinas's explanation of God's acceptance of the requirements of justice must be rejected.

If, therefore, we combine a correct account (as Scotus believes) of divine freedom with a Socratic account of justice and the divine will, we might endorse all these claims:

(1) The requirements of justice are best all things considered, not because of God's will.
(2) Since God is free, God is free to violate the requirements of justice.
(3) Since it is possible for God to do what God is free to do, it is possible for God to violate the precepts of justice.
(4) It is necessarily true that only what God wills is just, and that what God does not will is not just.

Since (3) and (4) conflict, something must be rejected. The simplest resolution of the conflict might appear to be the rejection of (4). But since Scotus refuses to make God capable of willing anything unjust, he resolves the conflict by retain-

---

[11] Aquinas, *2 Sent* d21 q2 a2 sc1.

ing (4) and rejecting (1). Since he rejects (1), he can reject (2) and (3), and hence maintain (4) without any conflict. He takes the requirements of justice to result from God's choice, undetermined by any knowledge of what is best all things considered.

The divine will is not inclined determinately through anything within itself towards any secondary object in such a way that it would be inconsistent for it to incline to the opposite object to that one, because just as the divine will can will the opposite without contradiction, so it can will it justly; otherwise it could without qualification will something and not will it justly, which is inappropriate.[12]

God cannot, therefore, act unjustly and cannot instruct us to violate justice. Scotus's belief in divine freedom gives him a clear reason for accepting voluntarism, reversing Socrates' views about the explanatory priority of rightness in itself to divine commands.

The medieval philosophers who discuss these questions discuss them without any reference to the Euthyphro Argument. Though the division that relies on asymmetry of explanation corresponds to the Euthyphro Argument, we have no reason to trace it, either directly or indirectly, to this Platonic source.

VIII

None the less, it is relevant to mention these Scholastic discussions of morality and divine legislation, in order to trace the historical influence of the Euthyphro Argument. These discussions form the background for the use of the Euthyphro Argument in modern moral philosophy, especially by Cudworth.

In *Eternal and Immutable Morality* Cudworth seeks to show that some influential views of the nature of moral principles and moral obligations overlook the fact that morality is eternal and immutable. He rejects the positivist view that identifies morality with the requirements of some positive law:

As the vulgar generally look no higher for the original of moral good and evil, just and unjust, than the codes and pandects, the tables and laws of their country and religion; so there have not wanted pretended philosophers in all ages who have asserted nothing to be good and evil, just and unjust, naturally and immutably; but that all these things were positive, arbitrary and factitious only.[13]

Cudworth finds the ancient sources of this view of morality in the various philosophers who assert that moral properties hold by convention and not by nature. He finds this opinion asserted by Protagoras in Plato's *Theaetetus*. Among modern moralists he find the opinion in Hobbes.

---

[12] *4 Sent* d46 q1 #8. See A. B. Wolter, *Scotus on the Will and Morality* (Washington, DC: CVA Press, 1986), 246.
[13] *Eternal and Immutable Morality*, ed. S. Hutton (Cambridge: Cambridge University Press, 1996), 9.

He connects this 'positive' view with the theological voluntarism that places morality in the commands of God.

> ... certain it is, that divers modern theologians do not only seriously, but zealously contend in like manner, 'that there is nothing absolutely, intrinsically and naturally good and evil, just and unjust, antecedently to any positive command or prohibition of God; but that the arbitrary will and pleasure of God (that is, an omnipotent being devoid of all essential and natural justice) by its commands and prohibitions, is the first and only rule and measure thereof'. (p. 9)

In Cudworth's view, the Protagorean position opposed by Plato makes the same basic errors as those he finds in theological voluntarism. Hence he takes Plato to provide the basis for refuting both positivism and theological voluntarism.

In connecting the Protagorean position with theological voluntarism, Cudworth makes explicit a connexion that is at most implicit in Plato. We saw earlier that both the position rejected in the *Euthyphro* and the position defended by Protagoras might be understood as versions of voluntarism. Plato himself does not say that they should be understood in this way. Cudworth, by contrast, suggests that they are different manifestations of the same basic voluntarist error.

Though Cudworth notices the connexion between Protagoras and theological voluntarism, he does not trace it to the *Euthyphro*.[14] The relevance of the *Euthyphro* is noticed by Samuel Clarke, in recapitulating Cudworth's argument against Hobbes. Clarke quotes the relevant passage of the *Euthyphro* to show what is wrong with Hobbes's claim that the laws of nature are laws because they are commanded by God.

> As this law of nature is infinitely superior to all authority of men, and independent of it, so its obligation, primarily and originally, is antecedent also even to this consideration, of its being the positive will or command of God himself... As in matters of sense, the reason why a thing is visible is not because it is seen, but it is therefore seen because it is visible, so in matters of natural reason and morality, that which is holy and good... is not therefore holy and good because it is commanded to be done, but is therefore commanded of God because it is holy and good.[15]

In Clarke's view, the obligation of the law of nature is antecedent to any command or will of God, for the reason made clear by the *Euthyphro*.

Cudworth and Clarke place the Euthyphro Argument in a historical context, and adapt it for wider use. These arguments show that Scholastic controversies about morality and divine legislation raise the issues about explanatory asymmetry that Plato raises in the Euthyphro Argument. They also suggest that some contemporary views that do not take a theological voluntarist view of morality

---

[14] Cudworth cites and paraphrases the Euthyphro Argument elsewhere. See C. A. Patrides (ed.), *The Cambridge Platonists* (Cambridge, Mass.: Harvard UP, 1970), 102. (I owe the reference to Terry Penner.)

[15] Clarke, *Discourse upon Natural Religion*, in L. A. Selby-Bigge (ed.), *British Moralists* (Oxford: Clarendon Press, 1897), ii, §507. In a footnote Clarke cites *Euthyphro* 10–11.

are none the less open to objections derived from the Euthyphro Argument; hence they apply the Platonic argument to Hobbes.

This revival of the Euthyphro Argument is not the end of a story, but the beginning. The rationalist successors of Cudworth and Clarke adapt the argument for use against moral sense theories, and so they introduce it into the discussion of fundamental questions in meta-ethics. An examination of this later adaptation of the argument would demonstrate the importance of the issues raised by Socrates' discussion with Euthyphro.

5

Did Socrates Agree to Obey the Laws of Athens?

Lesley Brown

Plato's *Crito* contains a justly famous discussion of what has come to be known as the problem of political obligation, of what obligations a citizen has to the government, and what are the grounds of those obligations. To many, the most surprising aspect of the work is that it appears to argue, on many grounds, that a citizen owes absolute obedience to the laws; a position scarcely to be credited to Socrates of all people. But one argument in particular caught the attention of David Hume. His essay 'Of the Original Contract' is an attack on political theories such as Locke's which held, in Hume's words, that men 'owe allegiance to no prince or government unless bound by the obligation and sanction of a promise' (1985: 469). Hume thought this an absurd theory, and concludes his attack on it by remarking that it was a view not found in ancient writers, with the one exception of the *Crito* where Socrates 'refuses to escape from prison because he had tacitly promised to obey the laws'. 'New discoveries are not to be expected in these matters. If scarce any man, till very lately, ever imagined that government was founded on compact, it is certain, that it cannot, in general, have any such foundation.'

In this paper I explore the *Crito*'s argument from agreement, paying particular attention to the arguments *for* agreement, that is, to the arguments which purport to show that Socrates has made an agreement of the appropriate kind. I am convinced that the arguments on this point in the *Crito* are unsuccessful.[1] But they have a tremendous appeal. I find that most of those with whom I discuss these issues believe that they themselves have (in one way or another) agreed to obey the laws, and that this agreement is the (or one) ground of their obligation to obey. I shall suggest that the (erroneous) claim that Socrates, or a present-day citizen, has agreed to obey the law is made plausible in part due to a conflation of different notions of agreement, a conflation to which Plato was especially prone

---

[1] Below I consider the views of those who claim that Socrates (in the *Crito*) does not endorse the arguments put in the mouth of the personified Laws.

thanks to his interest in another kind of agreement, that involved in Socrates' examination of the beliefs of another, the *elenchus*. These different kinds of agreement are set out in section I and explored further in what follows. First, some scene-setting.

I

It is simplest to read the development of the arguments in the *Crito* as follows.[2] To counter Crito's insistence that, for the sake of his friends, his children, and himself, Socrates ought to escape from prison and avoid his sentence, Socrates proceeds by first securing Crito's agreement that living well is the aim, and that to live well one should never act unjustly (*adikein*). Next he gets Crito to agree to the following: one shouldn't do harm of any kind, including returning harm for harm, or retaliating (*antikakourgein, antadikein*), and one shouldn't break just agreements. What follows is put into the mouth of the personified Laws of Athens, with a few interjections and replies from Socrates. The Laws set out to show that Socrates' conduct in escaping would contravene both these principles, for in breaking the law which enjoins that verdicts be carried out he would be attempting to destroy the city (i.e. to harm it), and he would be breaking an agreement he had entered into with the laws. And they add a new argument, comparing Socrates' obligation to the laws with that of offspring to father. Arguing from the benefits they have provided and from their superior status, they insist that a citizen, and hence Socrates, must obey them in whatever they command, and that not to do so would again be to *adikein*.

There is a well-known problem that the Laws' arguments seem to aim for a conclusion that is both far stronger than is needed and unacceptable. All that needs to be established (to counter Crito) is that it would be wrong for Socrates to escape, i.e. to disobey the law which holds that verdicts be carried out. But the arguments used by the Laws, and in particular the last mentioned, seem to argue that it would be wrong for Socrates to disobey any law at all. As well as being undesirably authoritarian, this would seem to conflict with the guiding principle of the dialogue, that one should never *adikein*. For might a law not command one to *adikein*, and how could Socrates possibly regard himself bound, in that case, to obey it?

Though my aim is not to offer a solution to this problem, I mention here two recent, independent, attempts to solve it by finding indications from Plato to the reader that Socrates does not endorse the arguments used by the Laws, and so does not endorse their apparently authoritarian stance. They are those of Roslyn Weiss (1998) and Verity Harte (1999). Though they argue the case in very

---

[2] See the analysis and discussion of Bostock (1990) who defends the 'three arguments' interpretation.

different ways, both read the Laws as using arguments which are directed principally at Crito, and each discerns Socrates' views only in what he says *propria voce*.[3] I am not persuaded by either of these subtle and careful treatments, but, though important for our overall understanding of the *Crito*, the issue is to some extent irrelevant to my purpose here. First, the arguments deserve scrutiny, whether or not Socrates is presented as endorsing them, and whether or not we suppose Plato endorsed them. Second, my interest in the stretches of argument concerning agreement focuses mainly on the claim that Socrates *did make an agreement* with the Laws to obey them. And Socrates does twice *in propria persona* interrupt the flow of the Laws' speech to concede that he has made an agreement with them (52a6–9 and 52d3–6).[4]

The next preliminary is to look closely at kinds of agreement. There are two distinctions that must be drawn, the first between different kinds of agreement, agreeing to do something, and agreeing that something is so. Borrowing the labels from Raz (1986: 80–1), let us call agreement to do something a *performative agreement*, and agreement that something is the case *cognitive agreement*. The second distinction concerns the public and the private, and I illustrate it first in connection with cognitive agreement. 'She agreed that p' can describe either public assent or private belief. One who publicly *asserts* that p (agrees that p) may or may not *believe* that p (may or may not agree—inwardly—that p), though in asserting that p you present yourself as believing that p, and the assertion (agreement) is insincere if you don't believe it. So cognitive agreement can be either public or private, and, if public, either sincere or insincere.

But agreement to do something must be public, as the label 'performative agreement' signals. As such it must be sharply distinguished from an intention to do the thing in question, and from approval or other pro-attitudes. One who agrees with someone to do something undertakes an obligation to that person, and in making the agreement performs an action which, in Raz's formulation, 'changes the normative situation of another'. In other words, it gives the person with whom the agreement was made rights they did not have before, namely, the right to require that I do the thing I promised, unless they release me from my agreement. For me to agree with you to do something, it is irrelevant whether I actually intend to do it, or whether I have one or another pro-attitude towards it. I may have these without agreeing (performative) to do the thing in question, and conversely I may agree without having the pro-attitudes. In the former case I have not bound myself, and in the latter I have. So performative agreement is always public, and as such can be sincere or insincere. And, as the dialogue reminds us, it

---

[3] Weiss (1998) holds that Socrates gives a full account of his reasons for not escaping before the speech of the Laws begins. One surprising feature of her case is to understand Socrates' appeal to the principle of keeping just agreements at 49e5–7 in such a way that it has no connection with the Laws' subsequent claim (endorsed by Socrates) that Socrates has agreed to obey them. See n. 7.

[4] I do not find a satisfactory account, in either Harte or Weiss, of Socrates' repeated assertions, in his own voice, that he did make an agreement.

can be made verbally or non-verbally. The Laws claim that it is by what he did, not by what he said, that Socrates agreed to obey them.

Both kinds of agreement figure prominently in the *Crito*, and we shall shortly trace them.[5] The focus of this chapter is the argument from agreement to obey: you agreed to obey, and you ought to keep your agreements, so you must obey. This is of course a performative agreement, an agreement to do something. Before moving on, a word about the relation between performative agreement, consent, and promising. All of these are public acts, which generate obligations. Both consent and agreement may be to the actions of others—such as permitting or authorizing. But one can promise only one's own actions. Since the kind of agreements we are interested in (from the *Crito*) are agreements to do something, they are more akin to promises than to authorizations. Locke's tacit consent—which, in a manner highly reminiscent of the *Crito*, he held to be given by anyone who resides in the country or uses the highway—is at once a promise to obey and an authorization which legitimates the government's authority. Significantly, only the former aspect is prominent in the *Crito*'s argument, a topic to which I return in the conclusion. Remembering that we must be clear in all cases which kind of agreement is in question, we can safely continue to use the word agreement, which, fortunately, has just the same range of uses as Greek *homologia* and the cognate verbs *homologein* and compounds.

II

Before any mention of agreements to act, we find, as in so many dialogues, much play with the language of cognitive agreement. Socrates reminds Crito of what they had agreed before Crito's urgent plea that Socrates should let him arrange an escape (48b11, 49a7–8: the second passage refers to 'all those former agreements of ours'). In an important exchange at 49d, Socrates urges Crito that in agreeing these things he should be sure not to agree them contrary to his belief; for no common counsel, no *koinê boulê*, can obtain between those who do and those who don't accept these principles. The political metaphor 'no common counsel' is striking. Socrates emphasizes that Crito's beliefs are what matter to Socrates, not (or not merely) his assent. This is an important theme to which I return (section IV). Pressed on whether he abides by these principles, Crito replies that he does, and that he shares Socrates' beliefs (49e2–4).

---

[5] A distinction between what she labels 'agreement in argument' and 'agreement in act' forms the heart of Lane's paper (1998). But the contrast as she draws it is misconceived. The crucial point about the agreement which Socrates is said to have made 'by what he did' is not that it was made by an action (remaining in Athens) but that it was an agreement to do something. Such an agreement could as well have been made by words as by an action. There is no suggestion that it is less binding because it has been made by an action, not by a verbal promise.

At this point Socrates introduces a new principle, this time that one should do what one has agreed with someone to do, provided they (the agreements) are just.

(T1) Should one do whatever one has agreed upon with someone, providing that it is just, or should one play false?

πότερον ἃ ἄν τις ὁμολογήσῃ τῳ δίκαια ὄντα ποιητέον ἢ ἐξαπατητέον; (49e4–6)

Pace some commentators[6] it is clear that a new kind of agreement is under discussion: an agreement made *with someone* to *do* something. This ethical principle, that one should do what one has agreed with someone (promised someone) to do, and not play false, is a commonplace which Crito naturally accepts, especially with the qualification, 'provided it is just', which evidently is equivalent to 'provided it (the action promised) is not unjust'. We may think of the familiar exchange in *Republic* 1. Returning a sword, something you have promised to do when borrowing it, should be done—the agreement should be kept—unless (say) the owner has become a lunatic, for to return his sword would then be unjust. Unlike the earlier principle forbidding *antadikein*, which Socrates acknowledges as controversial, this new one, the principle that just agreements should be kept, is one on which they swiftly agree.[7]

Armed with this principle, together with the earlier ones to which Crito has assented, Socrates begins a line of argument which will only be completed during the speech of the personified Laws. He asks Crito whether by escaping

(T2) ... we are [*a*] treating badly those whom we should least treat badly and [*b*] abiding by those things we have agreed, they being just, or not?

πότερον κακῶς τινας ποιοῦμεν, καὶ ταῦτα οὓς ἥκιστα δεῖ, ἢ οὔ; καὶ ἐμμένομεν οἷς ὡμολογήσαμεν δικαίοις οὖσιν ἢ οὔ; (49e–50a)

Crito is at a loss how to reply: he doesn't understand. What the reader can already guess, and what the Laws will spell out with relish in their speech, is that the minor premiss is about to be established. In escaping from prison Socrates would be acting in a way which contravenes both principles: he will be treating badly those he least should, and he will not be abiding by, but breaking, agreements which were just. In other words, Socrates is here continuing the theme he has just introduced, that of agreements to do something (again with the proviso *dikaia*

---

[6] Surprisingly, and surely incorrectly, Adam takes this to involve an agreement 'that such-and-such'. He glosses the sentence 'it is our duty to carry out in practice that which we have in theory admitted to be right' (1891: 56) and he glosses ἐξαπατητέον thus: 'to believe a theory and not to carry it into practice is a living lie' (p. 60). Lane (1998: 321) seems to share Adam's view, as she glosses the question 'Should we do the things we've agreed definitionally to be just?'

[7] Weiss (1998: 73) accepts that here Socrates is discussing agreeing with someone to do something. But she disputes the standard interpretation which takes this to be the enunciation of a general principle whose application to the case in hand will be explained in the lines that follow: in Socrates' question at 50a2–3, and in the Laws' speech, when it is argued that in escaping Socrates would be breaking an agreement he had made. Instead she holds that this must rely on 'old ideas and events with which Crito is familiar', that here Socrates is referring to 'an actual agreement Crito has witnessed', which she locates in *Apology* 39b6 'I will abide by my penalty'.

onta), to prepare for the demonstration that he *did make* such an agreement, so that in escaping he would be breaking an agreement—contravening this newly enunciated principle. Note the language used: would we (if we escaped) be abiding by (*emmenein*) our agreements? Here to abide by an agreement is to keep a promise, whereas in the earlier passage it was to stick to—to continue to believe—the things one agreed and so assented to.[8] Crito, not surprisingly, cannot yet see how Socrates' conduct counts as (*a*) and (*b*) above. And that is where the Laws come in.

Their arguments will be scrutinized in section III. But first let us jump to the end of their speech, and note how they end by echoing Socrates' question (T2). After their lengthy rhetorical arguments, they have a final minatory flourish: not only we but our brothers in Hades will be angry with you,

(T3) ... if you depart having so shamefully retaliated and returned ill for ill, having broken your agreements and treaties that you made with us, and having treated badly those you should least so treat: yourself, friends, country and us.

| ... ἐὰν δὲ ἐξέλθῃς οὕτως αἰσχρῶς ἀνταδικήσας τε καὶ
ἀντικακουργήσας, τὰς σαυτοῦ ὁμολογίας τε καὶ συνθήκας τὰς πρὸς
ἡμᾶς παραβὰς καὶ κακὰ ἐργασάμενος τούτους οὓς ἥκιστα ἔδει,
σαυτόν τε καὶ φίλους καὶ πατρίδα καὶ ἡμᾶς,   (54c2–5)

These closing lines, with their close echo of Socrates' words which puzzled Crito (T2), confirm two points. First, that T2 'are we abiding by what we agreed?' continues the theme of T1 'doing what one agreed with someone to do' of 49e6–7; this is indicated by the echo of T2 in T3 where the words are 'agreements and treaties you made with us'. In all three passages, agreeing is agreeing to act. Second, in making the Laws in T3 deliberately echo Socrates' phraseology in T2 just before their speech began, Plato indicates to the reader that the Laws are indeed to be seen as making Socrates' case for him, though no doubt in a more vulgarly rhetorical manner than had Socrates stuck to his own voice.[9]

---

[8] Weiss (1998: 79) attempts a different interpretation of this sentence. Impressed by the verbal echo of 48b11–c1, where Socrates spoke of abiding by agreements that such and such, she says, 'what can he be asking but whether he and Crito remain true to the principles they have just agreed?' I cannot accept this. The logic of 49e–50a is clear: first Socrates gets Crito to accept a new principle, that agreements (to do something) should be kept, then at 50a he asks whether his conduct satisfies this principle about keeping (now called abiding by) agreements. Weiss's attempt to read 'agreeing' differently at 49e6 (agreeing to do) and at 50a1–2 (agreeing that certain principles hold) cannot succeed, as it destroys the logic of the passage.

[9] This article does not attempt to defend at length the traditional view according to which Socrates should be read as endorsing the arguments he puts in the mouth of the Laws. The standard view involves discerning a division of labour between what Socrates does *in propria persona* (enunciate principles, and ask whether his conduct falls foul of them) and what the Laws do (demonstrate that Socrates' conduct does indeed fall foul of them). Weiss denies that reading, but at the cost of strained interpretations of T1–T3 cited above. Harte points out, correctly, that the principle accepted by Socrates about agreements contains the proviso 'provided the actions are just', while that enunciated by the Laws does not contain that vital qualification. But her view cannot explain satisfactorily the division of labour between Socrates, who argues for the major premiss, and the Laws who argue for the minor premiss. That being so, dissociating their arguments becomes problematic.

Speaking in part through the medium of the personified Laws, and in part in his own voice, Socrates now embarks on the lengthy discourse designed to establish that, if he accepted Crito's proposal and escaped, he would be breaching the principles they previously affirmed. The charge of agreement-breaking is delayed while other issues are pursued, in the voice of the Laws. They claim that to escape would be to try to destroy the city and the laws, laws which fathered, bred, and educated him and provided the legal setting for his parents to marry and rear him. They then move to the most menacing but also most puzzling part of their argument, where, comparing Socrates to their offspring or slave, they remind him that he does not meet them on equal terms, but must submit to them in whatever they (or, at one point, the *polis* and *patris*) command. Or rather, as they several times reiterate, Socrates must either persuade them or obey them.[10]

Commentators have regretted the stringency of this requirement 'you must do whatever we command', and have puzzled over the significance of the let-out clause 'or persuade us'. Since this oft-repeated phrase appears to offer some alternative to absolute obedience, and to do so where questions arise of what is just (51c1) or well done (51e7), these remarks have been scrutinized by recent writers in the hope of finding an interpretation which is consonant with Socrates' stance in the *Apology*, and with the overarching principle of the *Crito* that one must never do injustice. While the principle of keeping agreements stated by Socrates at 49e (T1) contains the proviso 'provided they are just', the thesis enunciated by the Laws 'whatever your *polis* and your *patris* commands, you must obey us' seems to leave no such scope for principled disobedience. Hence an attempt to find some leeway in the alternatives of 'persuade or obey'.

How should we understand these alternatives? Without entering deeply into the controversy, I make a few points, and first agree with Kraut (1984: ch. 3) that it is wrong to see, as many commentators from Grote onwards have done, an allusion to the citizen's opportunities to participate in lawmaking in the *ekklêsia*. The forum of persuasion envisaged is, as Kraut says, the law courts. But I disagree with the way Kraut pursues this insight. He has a highly nuanced interpretation, which reads the Laws—through their repeated alternative: persuade or obey—as envisaging various different scenarios in which disobedience would be justified. I am not persuaded that (in what the Laws say) justified disobedience is countenanced. It is far simpler to suppose that the alternative 'persuade it (the city) as to what is just' alludes to the obvious fact that a verdict and sentence (which must be *obeyed*) follow a trial, a forum where the accused has a chance to *persuade* the jury to acquit him or to impose a lighter sentence. Two other passages confirm this interpretation. Socrates' remark that, if he escaped, he would do so 'not having persuaded the city' (49e9), and the Laws' claim (51e7) that, were he to

---

[10] 51b3–4, 51c1 (do what the *polis* commands or persuade it as to what it is just); the motif reappears in the section on agreement 51e7 and 52a2–3.

escape, he would be 'neither obeying us nor persuading us if we're doing something not well (*kalôs*)', surely allude to Socrates' failure to secure an acquittal or a lighter sentence. The point is pressed home when the Laws remind him that, had he requested exile as his penalty, he would have secured legitimately an outcome which he would now be seizing illegitimately should he escape prison and the death sentence.

If I am right that references to persuading as an alternative to obeying are simply reminders that there is a trial before a sentence, then no room for principled disobedience is given by this alternative, nor does it remind the citizen of his democratic right to have a say in lawmaking. But as my aim is not to offer a solution to the problem of the apparently authoritarian line taken by the Laws, I pass on.

III

How do the Laws argue that Socrates did make an agreement with them? I discern two versions of (or stages in) their argument. In what I label the black-and-white version (51d–e) it is simply Socrates' remaining in Athens after the *dokimasia* (see below) which constitutes his agreeing to obey the Laws. What I call the full-colour version follows at 52a–e, where facts are adduced about Socrates' lifestyle and his alleged satisfaction with Athens and its laws. This complicates matters, and it will be of especial interest to my theme.

The black-and-white version starts with the Laws reminding Socrates how well they have treated him: 'we begat you, reared you, educated you, and gave you and all your fellow citizens a share of all the good things we could'. They say that they permit anyone who so wishes, once they have undergone the *dokimasia* and seen the workings of the city and the laws, to go to a colony or elsewhere, taking their property with them.

But whichever of you remains, seeing how we judge lawsuits and manage things generally in the city: he, we say, has thereby agreed with us, by what he does, to do whatever we command.

ὃς δ' ἂν ὑμῶν παραμείνῃ, ὁρῶν ὃν τρόπον ἡμεῖς τάς τε δίκας δικάζομεν καὶ τἆλλα τὴν πόλιν διοικοῦμεν, ἤδη φαμὲν τοῦτον ὡμολογηκέναι ἔργῳ ἡμῖν ἃ ἂν ἡμεῖς κελεύωμεν ποιήσειν ταῦτα ... (51e1–4)

This is the ἤδη of so-called logical proximity, and the passage is strikingly reminiscent of Locke's famous claim that 'every man that hath any possession or enjoyment of any part of the dominions of any government doth hereby give his tacit consent' (1988: ch. 8).

I said above that an agreement, to ground an obligation, must be a public act, either verbal or non-verbal. The Laws claim that the act of remaining in Athens after the *dokimasia* constitutes the making of an agreement by non-verbal means: ἔργῳ. The *dokimasia* was the procedure by which an Athenian male of 17 or 18 years was presented by his father or other male relative for membership of his deme, and thereby (if his claim was deemed legitimate, after scrutiny by the deme, and ratified by the *boulê*) became enrolled in the citizen body (*Ath. Pol.* 42).[11] Though some scholars hold that the imposition of an oath of obedience on young men on this occasion, attested to in the fourth century, must date back to the fifth century,[12] it is plain that the Laws make no claim that Socrates took such an oath of allegiance, quite the reverse. The agreeing is done by deed, not words, and the deed cited is the remaining in Athens after the *dokimasia*, and after the chance to see how the city is ordered.

Could the Laws have made the more plausible claim that in applying for enrolment in the deme a young man thereby agreed to undertake the obligations of a citizen? Kraut thinks not, on the ground that the agreement is not alleged to be made until the newly enrolled citizen has had time to see how the city works. This may be right, but a further reason against citing the application to be enrolled as the act which constitutes agreeing may be that it was the father or male relative, rather than the youth himself, who took the initiative to get the enrolment made.

What is required for an action (or a remaining) to count as an agreement? The useful discussion by Simmons (1979: 80) of tacit consent can be adapted for this purpose. He requires the following conditions:

1. The situation must be such that it is clear that consent is appropriate and that the individual is aware of it.
2. There must be a definite period when objections or expressions of dissent are appropriate.
3. It must be clear to the potential consentor when this period is ended.
4. The means acceptable for indicating dissent must be reasonable and reasonably easily performed.
5. The consequences of dissent must not be extremely detrimental to the potential consentor.

Hume and others who criticize theories (such as Locke's) which ground political obligation in the supposed tacit consent given by remaining in the country tend to focus on its inability to meet conditions (4) and (5). So it is of great interest that the Laws try, as it were, to meet these points by showing that a citizen is free to leave (reasonable means of dissent), taking his property (consequences not too serious).

But these considerations are in vain if the first condition is not met. Simmons's version of condition (1) is that it must be clear that consent is appropriate and the individual is aware of this. To put it more plainly: if my conduct is to count as

---

[11] Rhodes's commentary (1981) ad loc. opts for 18 as the crucial age.
[12] Rhodes (1981: 495): 'We should accept that the *dokimasia* of young citizens and the imposition of an oath on them were ancient institutions.'

agreeing, I and those with whom I make the agreement must know this. Kraut disagrees. He writes 'one can discover that one's previous actions constituted an agreement, even though one did not at the time think of them in that light. Socrates is claiming <in the Laws' speech> to have discovered that his previous actions constituted an agreement, and it is irrelevant that neither he nor his fellow-citizens realised it at the time' (1984: 158). But this cannot be right. To repeat: for my conduct to count as an agreement given to X to do A, then I must be aware that this is so.

It may be objected that in some circumstances I can incur an obligation by what I do without knowing it. One who orders goods or a meal is committed to paying for them even if that individual is unaware of the conventions, provided they are generally known and understood. This is sometimes called an implied agreement. And it might be suggested that the Laws' use of the perfect tense, ὡμολογηκέναι suggests that this is what should be said of Socrates. It is not that he has done anything which counts as agreeing; rather he is 'in a state of having agreed', so has incurred an obligation of the kind one incurs by agreeing, but without an act of agreeing.[13] But even if the Laws could be interpreted as making the weaker claim, that Socrates has unintentionally incurred this kind of commitment, this could not succeed either, since this can exist only against a background of general knowledge that such conduct creates obligations. There is nothing to suggest either that all citizens or that most apart from Socrates knew that to remain in Athens counted as agreeing to obey the laws, any more than there is general knowledge today that conduct such as voting in an election constitutes—as some contend—undertaking an obligation of political obedience. One reason why this is so, of course, is that most people believe they owe obedience independently of the act in question.

To sum up on the 'black-and-white' version of the argument for agreement. The Laws argue that public conduct, remaining in Athens after certain conditions were fulfilled, constituted an agreement made by Socrates with them. The right sort of agreement—a public act—is argued for, and the Laws make important and relevant points about adequate time, fair terms, and available alternatives. But their argument falls at the first hurdle, I suggest, since they fail to show that a newly enrolled citizen knows that remaining in Athens constitutes agreeing to obey its laws.

I now turn to what I labelled the full-colour version. I shall argue that the sort of considerations adduced cannot help make the case for an agreement, because they appeal to the wrong sort of thing, Socrates' attitudes. But none the less such appeals have an air of plausibility, for reasons I shall explore.

---

[13] This would be similar to the *Meno*'s use of the perfect to suggest that the soul is 'in a state of having learned' (e.g. 86a10) without there having actually been an episode of learning. But although the perfect is used (51e3, 52a9, 52d4), the aorist participle is also used, implying that there *was* an act of agreeing. And this is what the Laws are most plausibly taken as claiming, *passim*.

From 52a–53a the Laws adduce arguments why Socrates in particular has made such an agreement, citing great proofs that 'we and the city pleased you'. He remained in Athens, bar his military service and one visit to the Isthmian festival; he had no desire for other cities or other laws. Indeed, he had children here; he refused to suggest exile at his trial, priding himself on his preferring death to exile. His agreement was neither forced nor hasty; he had seventy years to leave if the laws didn't please him and 'the agreements didn't seem just'. Despite his frequent praise for the government of Sparta and Crete, he chose neither them nor anywhere but Athens, spending more time in his native city than even the lame and poor. And so on.

This fascinating passage raises obvious problems. To account for the prima-facie conflict on when the agreement was made by Socrates (version one: at or soon after enrolment; version two: 'you had seventy years'), a number of solutions have been proposed. One is to say that the first version is definitive on when the agreement was made, while the second (mentioning Socrates' satisfaction with Athens, demonstrated by his fathering children and so on) gives reasons for honouring the agreement. But that doesn't fit the text, which adduces them as showing that he agreed, not as showing why he should stick to an earlier agreement.

A second solution, due to Woozley (1979: 78–9), can also be rejected. He proposed that the subsequent period is presented as a sort of 'cooling-off period' of the kind which allows gullible purchasers the right to revoke a hastily made agreement. But neither the text nor common sense allow this reading. An agreement with an indefinite 'cooling-off period' would be no agreement at all.

We must read the text as doing what it purports to do: offering further reasons for the claim that Socrates (in particular) did make the agreement in question. Though I believe these reasons are insufficient, I think the appeal to them is highly significant. The reasons adduced are Socrates' alleged satisfaction, with Athens and its laws, as evidenced by various things he did and did not do. An obvious difficulty is that, as I stressed above (section I), a person's attitudes are strictly irrelevant to whether or not they made a public agreement. Recognizing this, Kraut insists that the appeal is not to Socrates' inner state, his attitudes, but to his public demonstration of these attitudes.[14] The appeal to these must show, he claims, that remaining in Athens was not put forward as establishing that an agreement was made. Rather, it is a citizen's continued residence plus his manifestations of satisfaction which constitute the agreement. But this is too strained an interpretation, in my view, and the suggestion that to complete an agreement one must demonstrate satisfaction is a very strange one.

---

[14] 'Any reasonable thinker ought to realise that what counts in the making of agreements is observable behaviour rather than a person's inner satisfaction' (Kraut 1984: 172). 'No-one can seriously believe that agreements are ratified by feelings of satisfaction rather than by behaviour' (ibid. 176).

A simpler reading seems correct: the new argument is simply gilding the lily, adding extra reasons for the claim that Socrates did agree. The argument from an accused's lifestyle—*ex anteacta vita*—is, after all, a familiar way of gilding the lily in forensic oratory, and this passage is an inversion of the usual appeals to the accused's lifestyle to show that he couldn't have done the act of which he stands accused.[15]

So, in adducing 'great proofs that we and the city pleased you', 'the Laws are—they suppose—adding to the case for saying that Socrates in particular did make an agreement with them to obey them, or, as they now put it, 'to live as a citizen (*politeuesthai*) according to us' (52c2). And they do so by conflating the attitudes they argue for with the agreement they are trying to pin on him. The conflation is clearest where the Laws sum up their proofs of Socrates' satisfaction as follows: 'So strongly did you choose us and agree to act as a citizen in obedience to us, that you begat children in the city: proving it really did satisfy you' (52c1–3).

Emboldened by their further 'proofs', the Laws proceed to describe the alleged agreement in thoroughly formal and political terms as 'compacts and agreements you compacted with us' (52d2–3, repeated at 52d8–9 and 54c3–4), alleging that to escape prison would be acting contrary to them (52d2), contravening them (52e1, 54c4), not abiding by them (53a5). These further proofs—appeals to Socrates' attitudes—should not be, but are naturally seen as, salient to their case that he agreed. I explain in the next section why the mistake may have been an especially tempting one for Plato, given his interest in the other kind of agreement, cognitive agreement.

IV

Let us look in more detail at Plato's focus on agreement 'that such-and-such', the stuff of the Socratic method. I have already considered the important passage where Socrates both stresses to Crito the importance of sincerity, and characterizes the agreement between them (both of them accepting the ethical principles) in political terms: *koinê boulê* is possible only between those who accept these principles. Agreement—that is, public assent—without belief is what we find Thrasymachus manifesting at the end of *Republic* 1. Several times he concedes reluctantly and with bad grace theses whose opposites he had earlier maintained. To reinforce the readers' perception that no genuine change of heart has occurred in Thrasymachus, Plato makes Glaucon reopen the issue of whether justice is a good for the agent with the question: do you want to *seem* to have persuaded us, or really to have done so? (357a5–b1). Here, as elsewhere, Plato stresses that for agreement 'that such-and-such', belief, not outward assent, is what matters. A host of passages (collected by Vlastos 1983) emphasize this salient feature of Socratic method. We may think of Socrates' rebuke to Protagoras: I'm not

---

[15] I owe this point to Lucinda Coventry.

examining *if you like* or *if you think so*, but you and me (*Prot.* 331c), or of the repeated injunction not to agree to something 'contrary to your beliefs' (*Rep.* 346a, *Crito* 49d, *Gorgias* 500b, among others).[16]

That Plato saw many affinities between the two kinds of agreement is evident from the common vocabulary. The language of sticking to what has been agreed is used for agreements 'that such-and-such' as well as agreements to act. We saw this already at *Crito* 49e2. The term used in Socrates' question and in Crito's answer—*emmenein*—is that used in oaths to abide by treaties (e.g. Thucydides 5. 18. 9), giving Crito's reply the air of an oath, though he is not talking about a promise, but about continuing to accept certain principles. *Republic* 345b combines an injunction to Thrasymachus to 'stick to what you've agreed' (where what are agreed are certain theses) with the request that, if he changes his opinions, he do so openly and not act deceitfully. The very same verb (*exapatein*) is used of making a false agreement/promise at *Crito* 49e7. In other words, the same vocabulary of agreement, sticking to agreements, contrary to agreements, and acting deceitfully is used interchangeably where both types of agreement are involved.

My thesis is that the importance, for the Socratic *elenchus*, of people's souls, of what they really believed and not just what they were willing to assert, spills over, as it were, into the field of that other sort of agreement, the one which generates obligations to act or obey or permit. As a result, an appeal to the individual's attitudes may seem relevant to the claim that they agreed to do something, when strictly it is not. And indeed I have found many who believe that—given their willingness to obey the laws, their recognition of good reasons to do so, and their feeling of obligation to obey—they have agreed to obey, and that from this agreement stems their obligation.[17] In the next section I trace in Cicero signs of a tendency—similar to that found in the Laws' arguments—to mislocate the role of the 'inner' in agreements, oaths, and promises.

V

I have suggested that, though it is an error to conflate inner states such as attitudes or intentions with promises, or to cite them as evidence that promises

---

[16] At *Prot.* 333c6–9 Protagoras defends, at Socrates' request, a thesis he has already disavowed (the thesis that one who acts unjustly may be sensible in so acting). Taylor (1976) suggests ad loc: 'The rule of the game was presumably that anyone defending a thesis of his own must give only what he believed to be true answers, while anyone answering on behalf of someone else could give whatever answers he took to express the beliefs of the person whose views he was defending.' The passage is also noted by Vlastos (1983: 37–8) as an exception to what he calls the 'say what you believe' rule.

[17] Raz (1986: 98–9) allows that very few citizens have actually consented to obey the laws, and that therefore obligation is only rarely grounded in consent. But, with the aim of establishing that political obligation is voluntarily assumed, he makes the puzzling suggestion that *attitudes of respect for the state* can ground obligation, in those who have them, in a manner analogous to consent.

were made, it is a fully understandable one. It was a hard-won insight that, where promising or contracting is involved, an actual intention (on the part of the promisor) to do the thing promised is neither necessary nor sufficient, and even less so are pro-attitudes such as approval.

Cicero's famous discussions in *De Officiis* of when promises do and don't obligate include the case of a promise given to a pirate (3. 107). Understandably Cicero wants to argue that one is not obligated to keep such a promise, but one of the grounds he cites is surely incorrect.

For if an oath is sworn in such a way that the mind grasps that this ought to be done, it should be kept; but if not, then there is no perjury if the thing is not done.

Quod enim ita iuratum est, ut mens conciperet fieri oportere, id servandum est; quod aliter, id si non fecerit, nullum est periurium.

This suggests that the salient question, determining whether you have a duty to keep the promise, is: when making it, 'did your mind grasp that it ought to be done?' If grasping that p is possible when p is false, this would be a shocking claim. Even if Cicero's language implies that one's beliefs on the matter are correct,[18] he still misstates the salient consideration. The explanation which follows is surely his considered argument why such a promise does not bind: a pirate, the common foe of all, is not someone with whom faith must be kept. None the less, he appears to endorse the earlier faulty formulation by adding that the oaths which bind are those which are sworn 'in accordance with your mind's opinion' (*ex animi tui sententia*), suggesting that it is the state of mind of the one who promises which determines whether the promise must be kept. And the impression that this is so is reinforced when he proceeds to quote Euripides' notorious line about keeping one's mind unsworn. Where the *Crito*'s line seemed to be you approved, so you agreed, Cicero's suggests if you didn't approve, you didn't agree (i.e. promise).

A similar misformulation of the salient feature in promising is found at *Off.* 1. 40. Here Cicero is reproaching the behaviour of the Roman general whom Hannibal released after he had sworn to return to the enemy camp. 'For after leaving the camp with Hannibal's permission he returned a little later saying he had forgotten something or other. He then considered that he had released himself from his oath on leaving the camp, but he had done so only in word but not in fact.' So far so good, but Cicero goes on: 'For on the question of keeping faith, you must always think of what you meant, not of what you said' (*semper autem in fide quid senseris, non quid dixeris, cogitandum*). Once again Cicero incautiously suggests that what really counts is what you had in mind, not

---

[18] Griffin's note ad loc. exculpates Cicero from holding that one can break promises one did not really mean at the time. 'It would be perjury to break a solemn promise freely made to an appropriate person, such as a legitimate enemy; then the mind would "grasp that this ought to be done" ' (Griffin and Atkins 1991: 142). But Cicero can hardly assume that, when and only when promises ought to be kept, the promisor will grasp this.

what you said. But this is not the salient feature. What matters is what you are publicly committing yourself to in promising; what you can expect others to understand by your words. The general did wrong not in saying one thing while meaning another; rather, he tried to maintain that a certain action (returning briefly before leaving again) counted as keeping the promise, when the normal understanding of the words of his promise committed him to something different. Of course, Cicero is not here claiming that what you have in mind to do when you promise is what you are committed to. Nonetheless, in putting the point by saying that 'quid senseris' rather than 'quid dixeris' is crucial, he unhelpfully suggests that what binds is a matter of the promisor's inner state, rather than his public commitment.

That concludes my discussion of the proper role of the public and the private in performative agreements. But a further reference to Cicero will help spotlight some concluding points about the *Crito*'s arguments. In an article on Cicero's *De Republica*, Malcolm Schofield (1995: 66) argued that Cicero raises 'firmly and explicitly a question about legitimacy that is never broached in Greek political philosophy, not even the *Crito*'. Schofield focuses on Cicero's concept of the *res publica* as the *res populi*, and on his notion that a free people has *entrusted itself* to its leaders. I believe that Schofield is right in playing down, in the *Crito*, an interest in political legitimacy. Its focus is on the citizen's obligations to the *polis* and its laws rather than on the legitimacy of the latter. In particular, the *Crito*'s argument from agreement cites the alleged agreement as grounding obligations to obey, but not as simultaneously grounding the legitimacy of the laws' authority over the citizen.

There are good reasons why this is so, which can be seen if we contrast the *Crito*'s arguments with those of Locke, for instance. For Locke, not only did the supposed consent ground both the citizen's obligation and the government's legitimacy, but it was a *necessary* condition of both. Without voluntary consent, no obligation, and no legitimacy. The *Crito*, by contrast, combines, in a rather unstable way, arguments for voluntary and for non-voluntary sources of obligation to obey the laws.[19] As well as the argument from an alleged agreement there are the other arguments which ground the citizen's obligations quite differently, and in considerations of a kind far more familiar in Greek political philosophy. The parent–city (or parent–laws) analogy is used to argue that citizens have obligations independently of any they have voluntarily incurred, ones which rest

---

[19] Kraut (1984: 112) writes that neither the arguments from benefits received nor the argument from the parent–city analogy is strong enough to lead to the conclusion that the obedience owed by the citizen extends to requiring them to suffer any injustice the city might impose. Only voluntary agreements commit people to suffering injustice; hence the importance of the argument from agreement, he believes. But this relies on Kraut's reading of the parent–city analogy as figuring the citizen as owing what an *adult* offspring owes his parents, rather than what a *child* owes his parents. The latter analogy is less palatable, but is arguably what the language implies, especially as Bostock (1990: 15) notes, the requirement to yield to the *polis* as to a parent.

simply on the laws' status as authority figures and as bringers of benefits. And when the Laws contend that Socrates' whole being and formation is owed to them, through the framework for marriage, rearing, and education they provide, they reinforce a picture which leaves scant room for a freely chosen obligation to obey them. Since the arguments for an agreement, a freely chosen obligation, are faulty, it is as well to have recourse to others, which argue the case from the relevant considerations of the favourable conditions a *polis* provides for its citizens. These, and not any supposed voluntary act such as an agreement, are the best hope for grounding political obligation.[20]

REFERENCES

Adam, J. (1891). *Platonis* Crito (Cambridge).
Bostock, D. (1990). 'The Interpretation of Plato's *Crito*', *Phronesis*, 35/1: 1–20.
Griffin, M. T., and Atkins, E. M. (1991). *Cicero on Duties* (Cambridge).
Harte, V (1999). 'Conflicting Values in Plato's *Crito*', *Archiv für Geschichte der Philosophie*, 81/2: 117–47.
Hume, David (1985). *Essays Moral, Political and Literary*, ed. E. Miller (Indianapolis).
Kraut, R. (1984). *Socrates and the State* (Princeton).
Lane, M. S. (1998). 'Argument and Agreement in Plato's *Crito*', *History of Political Thought*, 19/3: 313–30.
Locke, John (1988). *Two Treatises of Government*, ed Peter Laslett (Cambridge).
Powell, J. G. F. (1995). *Cicero the Philosopher* (Oxford).
Raz, J. (1986). *The Morality of Freedom* (Oxford).
Rhodes, P. J. (1981). *A Commentary on the Athenaion Politeia* (Oxford).
Schofield, M. (1995). 'Cicero's Definition of the *Res Publica*', in Powell (1995: 63–83).
Simmons, A. J. (1979). *Moral Principles and Political Obligations* (Princeton)
Taylor, C. C. W. (1976). *Plato Protagoras* (Oxford).
Vlastos, G. (1983). 'The Socratic Elenchus', *Oxford Studies in Ancient Philosophy*, 1: 27–58.
Weiss, R. (1998). *Socrates Dissatisfied: An Analysis of Plato's* Crito (Oxford).
Woozley, A. D. (1979). *Law and Obedience: The Argument of Plato's* Crito (London).

---

[20] This paper, which I gave at the Athens–Delphi Socrates conference in July 2001, was prepared for a volume to honour my colleague Dr Miriam Griffin, and was originally published in that volume, E. G. Clark and T. Rajak (eds.), *Philosophy and Power in the Graeco-Roman World* (Oxford University Press, 2002). It has also appeared in the volume of that conference, V. Karasmanis (ed.), *Socrates 2,400 Years since his Death* (Athens, 2004).

6

Aporia and Searching in the Early Plato

Vasilis Politis

INTRODUCTION

It is typical of Socrates in a number of dialogues traditionally considered early—*Laches, Euthyphro, Charmides, Protagoras* as well as *Meno*—to lead the interlocutor towards a state of *aporia*, a mental state of perplexity and being at a loss, about some ethical subject—courage, piety, temperance, virtue. The aim of this activity, as we know especially from the *Apology*, is to divest the interlocutor of the pretence of knowledge in a particular area and to bring him to a recognition of his ignorance. Following Plato's retrospective account in the *Sophist* (230a–231b), we may call this kind of *aporia* 'purgative' or 'cathartic', because the interlocutor is supposed to be purged of his hubristic pretence of knowledge and to come to recognize his ignorance. But the success of such a purgation depends just as much on his character, that is his humility and honesty as well as the extent and quality of his desire for knowledge, as it does on Socrates' activity and intentions. Cathartic *aporia* is, of course, closely associated with the Socratic *elenchus* and is typically the direct outcome of the refutation of the interlocutor; for it is his realization that he is open to refutation that is intended to make the interlocutor question whether he really knows what he thinks he knows.

On what we might call 'the traditional view', moreover, this purgation is the exclusive aim of the Socratic *aporia*. Thus Myles Burnyeat argues that the 'earlier dialogues had valued perplexity merely as a necessary step towards disencumbering someone of the conceit of knowledge'; only later, as in the *Theaetetus* with its introduction of the compelling image of Socrates as intellectual midwife, is *aporia* treated 'as a productive state, the first stirring of creative thought'.[1] On

---

[1] 'Socratic Midwifery, Platonic Inspiration', *Bulletin of the Institute of Classical Studies*, 24 (1977), 7–16, 11; reprinted in Hugh H. Benson (ed.), *Essays on the Philosophy of Socrates* (Oxford: OUP, 1992), 53–65, 58. See also Charles Kahn, *Plato and the Socratic Dialogue* (Cambridge: CUP, 1996); Gareth B. Matthews, *Socratic Perplexity and the Nature of Philosophy* (Oxford: OUP, 1999); esp. 29–30; John Beversluis, *Cross-Examining Socrates* (Cambridge: CUP, 2000).

this view, the only aim of *aporia* in these dialogues is to purge the interlocutor of the pretence of knowledge.[2] But this, I will argue, is only half the truth.

The view of Socratic *aporia* as exclusively cathartic has one very important consequence: *aporia* in these dialogues is not part of the positive search for knowledge, but at most a preparation for it. Purging someone of the pretence of knowledge about, say, piety may incline him to take up the search for the knowledge of piety, but it is not part of that search. Thus Charles Kahn argues that 'Plato recognizes the negative elenchus as a necessary preliminary, preparing but not constituting the constructive search for knowledge.'[3] This means that *aporia* is cathartic but not zetetic; it may stimulate one to take up the search for knowledge, but it is not part of any particular search. But this again, I argue, is only half the truth.

The traditional view assumes that *aporia* in the early dialogues has only one aim and that Plato uses the term ἀπορία and its cognates in only one way for just one kind of *aporia*. On this assumption it is natural that only the cathartic aim of *aporia* should stand out since it is indeed prominent and conspicuous. But this assumption is I think mistaken, and we will see that Plato, through the different characters in these dialogues, characterizes *aporia* in different ways. There are two very different characterizations, and rightly understood this means that Plato distinguishes two kinds of *aporia*: in addition to the cathartic *aporia*, there is a kind of *aporia* that is properly a part of searching (*zêtêsis*)—zetetic *aporia*. It follows that solving particular *aporiai* is a part of the search for knowledge—though certainly we must not conclude that it is all that searching for knowledge consists in or that it is sufficient for finding knowledge. *Aporia* in these dialogues is not only a stimulus towards taking up the search for knowledge; it is part of particular searches.

We are familiar, especially from Aristotle, with the view that solving particular *aporiai* is an important part of the search for certain kinds of knowledge. Indeed he goes as far as suggesting that our engagement with *aporiai* is what enables us to undertake certain searches:

Those who search (τοὺς ζητοῦντας) without first engaging with *aporiai* (διαπορῆσαι) are like people who don't know where they need to be going; moreover, they do not even know whether or not they have found what they are searching for. For the end [of a

---

[2] Beversluis takes this view to the extreme when he argues that Socratic *aporia* even fails to stimulate anyone to take up the search for knowledge. 'Does the *aporia* to which they [the arguments in the *Laches*] lead infuse anyone with self-knowledge? If so, it has eluded me. The *Laches* reveals that although the Socratic *elenchus* can expose ignorance, defined in Socratic terms, it can neither provide knowledge nor motivate the ignorant, again defined in Socratic terms, to search for it. In the end, everyone remains exactly as they were.... *Aporia* there is [in the *Charmides*], but its effects are the very opposite of those envisaged in the *Apology*. No one is seized by his ignorance and impelled to take up the philosophical quest' (*Cross-Examining Socrates*, 133–4 and 158).

[3] *Plato and the Socratic Dialogue*, 99.

search] is not clear to such a person, but it is clear to the person who has first considered the *aporiai*.⁴

Here the term ἀπορία denotes not simply a mental state of perplexity and being at a loss, but particular puzzles and problems to be solved. In the *Topics* (6. 145ᵇ16–20) Aristotle provides perhaps the best and clearest characterization of this conception of *aporia*:

Likewise it would seem that the equality of opposite reasonings is the cause of *aporia*; for it is when we reason on both [sides of a question] and it appears to us that everything can come about either way, that we are in a state of *aporia* about which of the two ways to take up.

The cause of our being in state of *aporia* is characterized as a question articulated so as to have two opposed sides with apparently equally good reasons on both sides—a puzzle or problem in the particular sense of an apparent contradiction. And though he argues that the term ἀπορία applies in the first instance to our being in that mental state, he is in general just as ready to apply it to the puzzle or problem that causes the state. But what is important for our purposes is that an *aporia* is characterized as a particular puzzle or problem conceived in this particular way. For I will argue that broadly the same conception of *aporia* is present in these dialogues of Plato; and this conception is associated with the zetetic as opposed to the cathartic function of *aporia*.

On the traditional view, the use of the term ἀπορία to denote a particular puzzle and problem is absent from Plato's early dialogues. Thus Gareth Matthews argues that 'Aristotle uses the Greek word, *aporia* . . . for identifiable conundrums, or puzzles. . . . Instead, Plato in this [the *Laches*] and other early dialogues tends to use *aporia* and its cognates for a state of mental confusion, bewilderment, or helplessness.'⁵ It follows from the traditional view that the extension of the term ἀπορία, from denoting simply mental perplexity and being at a loss to its denoting also particular puzzles and problems, was Aristotle's or, if it was Plato's, it occurred only in later dialogues. In the *Philebus*, for example, Socrates makes a

---

⁴ *Met.* B1. 995ᵃ34–b1. Apparently Aristotle intends this strong claim to be true only of the search that is metaphysics (cf. 'the science we are searching for', *tēn epizētoumenēn epistēmēn*, B1, 995ᵃ24). See my 'Aristotle on *Aporia* and Searching in Metaphysics', *Boston Area Colloquium in Ancient Philosophy*, 18 (2002), 145–82.

⁵ *Socratic Perplexity*, 29–30. This view is succinctly summed up in the review of Matthews by Iakovos Vasiliou, who thinks it is beyond dispute 'to any professional ancient philosopher or classicist': 'Aristotle uses the cognate *aporēma*, and the plural *aporiai*, not to indicate a state of cognitive helplessness, where one cannot put into words what one has in mind (e.g. *Eu* 11b, *La* 194a–b), but to refer to the set of puzzles or problems regarding some topic that needs to be solved on the way to discovering how things really are. [first para.] . . . So far, then [i.e. in Plato's early dialogues], perplexity is described as a subjective state, a feeling or experience. [para. 5] . . . The overall thesis about the change in the role of *aporia* throughout the dialogues, and the evolution of its meaning will not be news to any professional ancient philosopher or classicist. [para. 6]' (*Bryn Mawr Classical Review*, 2000. 08. 12).

striking point about *aporia* as a mode of searching: 'By finding what we are currently searching for, we shall lose the *aporia* about these very things' (εὑρόντες ὃ νῦν ζητοῦμεν, ἀπολοῦμεν τὴν περὶ αὐτὰ ταῦτα ἀπορίαν, 34d6–7). Here we have not only an immediate connection between *aporia* and searching, but arguably also the use of the term ἀπορία to indicate a particular problem.[6] Incidentally, we may note that Aristotle, in the same passage from the *Topics*, has other people, unfortunately unnamed, in mind as 'those who say that an *aporia* is an equality of opposite reasonings' (cf. 145^{a}37–^{b}2); perhaps they are supposed to include Plato.

But my overall thesis is that this innovation, from the term ἀπορία denoting simply mental perplexity and being at a loss to its denoting also particular puzzles and problems, is present already in those dialogues of Plato that traditionally are considered early. The most striking passage in support of this interpretation, and one that I will carefully examine later, is *Protagoras* 324d2–e2, where Protagoras says that some particular point is required in order to 'solve' a particular *aporia*, namely, whether virtue can be taught: 'For on this point, and this alone, depends the solution of the particular *aporia* that you puzzle over' (ἐν τούτῳ γὰρ αὕτη λύεται ἡ ἀπορία ἣν σὺ ἀπορεῖς ἢ ἄλλοθι οὐδαμοῦ, 324e1–2). Here the term ἀπορία is used to refer to a particular problem, not simply the mental state of perplexity and being at a loss.[7] Moreover, the problem is said to be capable of 'solution' (cf. *luesthai*, 324e1) if one accepts a particular assumption, the assumption here being that there is 'a single quality which every citizen must have, if there is to be a city at all' (324d7–e1).

The general issue of the aim of the aporetic dialogues and their *aporiai* is complex and controversial in the extreme, and the literature vast.[8] But the aim of the present paper is a limited one: to examine Plato's use of the term ἀπορία in these dialogues, and to argue that two very different uses must be distinguished. In §1 I consider some passages in which the term ἀπορία is used to denote simply the mental state of perplexity and being at a loss, and in which the aim is to purge the interlocutor of the pretence of knowledge. This is largely familiar territory, but it is necessary in order to prepare for the contrast to a different use of the term

---

[6] The problem in the *Philebus* is whether pleasure is one or many, with Protarchus and Socrates on either side of the argument; and here Socrates is distinguishing different kinds of pleasures, e.g. bodily versus psychical (cf. 34c6–7). In 14c7–9 Socrates said that 'the claim that many things are one and one thing many' is 'by its very nature a source of wonder' (φύσει πως πεφυκότα θαυμαστόν). Also important are Socrates' words in 36e1–2: 'Tell me, then; for I am completely and endlessly in a state of wonder (*thauma*) about the same problems (*aporêmata*) that we have just raised. What do you say? Are there not false pleasures, and other true ones?'

[7] Thus Christopher Taylor translates 'problem' (*Plato:* Protagoras (Oxford: Clarendon Press, 1991), 17). In fact Liddell-Scott-Jones mentions this passage, *Protagoras* 324d–e, as an example of ἀπορία 'in Dialectic, [meaning] *question for discussion, difficulty, puzzle*'.

[8] See Michael Erler, *Der Sinn der Aporien in den Dialogen Platons* (Berlin and New York: de Gruyter, 1987), 1–18; also Ian Kidd, 'Socratic Questions', in Barry S. Gower and Michael C. Stokes (eds.), *Socratic Questions* (London: Routledge, 1992), 82–92.

ἀπορία in the early Plato, denoting particular puzzles and problems that are part of particular searches for knowledge (§2).

1. THE USE OF THE TERM ἀπορία TO DENOTE SIMPLY A MENTAL STATE OF PERPLEXITY AND BEING AT A LOSS, AND THE CATHARTIC FUNCTION OF *APORIA*

Let us first consider some central passages in which the term ἀπορία is used to denote simply a mental state of perplexity and being at a loss, and in which, apparently, the aim of leading someone to a state of *aporia* is to purge him of the pretence of knowledge.

Laches 194a–c and 196a–b

Laches honestly admits to his inexperience in Socratic dialogue and argument (ἀήθης γ' εἰμὶ τῶν τοιούτων λόγων, 194a7); at the same time he says that he is keen to take up the argument about the nature of courage in a spirit of good-humoured competition (cf. ἀλλά τίς με καὶ φιλονικία εἴληφεν πρὸς τὰ εἰρημένα, a7–8), the kind of contest that belongs within friendly company as opposed to the adversarial law courts (cf. 196b4–6). His good humour contrasts markedly with the extreme ill feeling that Meno displays against Socrates when he warns him that in other cities his practice of inducing *aporia* in people would land him in trouble (*Meno* 806b4–7). It is this kind of feeling that Socrates refers to in the *Gorgias* when he says that people will accuse him of 'corrupting the young by inducing *aporia* in them' (νεωτέρους διαφθείρειν ἀπορεῖν ποιοῦντα, 522b7; see also *Apology* 23d and 27e). This points to a psychological and ethical dimension of *aporia*: how the interlocutor reacts to Socrates' *aporia*-inducing activity depends very much on what he is like and his character. The same aspect is visible when Laches goes on to describe Nicias' reaction to his *aporia* as dishonest and intent on concealment (ἐμοὶ μὲν οὖν φαίνεται Νικίας οὐκ ἐθέλειν γενναίως ὁμολογεῖν ὅτι οὐδὲν λέγει, ἀλλὰ στρέφεται ἄνω καὶ κάτω ἐπικρυπτόμενος τὴν αὑτοῦ ἀπορίαν, 196a7–b2), and as vain (ἐν συνουσίᾳ τοιᾷδε μάτην κενοῖς λόγοις αὐτὸς αὑτὸν κοσμοῖ, 196b6–7)—though of course Nicias is far from being like Meno.[9] However, in spite of their very different reactions, Laches and Meno describe their *aporia* in strikingly similar ways, and it is this similar state of *aporia*, rather than the psychology and ethics behind their reactions, that is our main concern.

Laches, like Meno, associates the state of *aporia* with speechlessness and inarticulateness, and he expresses irritation at his inability to put his thoughts about courage into words:

---

[9] See also *Charmides* 169d1, ἔλεγέν τε οὐδὲν σαφές, ἐπικαλύπτων τὴν ἀπορίαν.

I am thoroughly distressed (ἀγανακτῶ) at being in this way unable to put into words what I think (ἃ νοῶ). For while it seems to me that I have in mind (νοεῖν) what courage is, this has just now escaped me, I don't know quite how, so that I am unable to grasp it in words and say what it is. (194a8–b4)

Socrates likens this condition to the distressing state of being 'tempest-tossed by argument and reduced to perplexity' (cf. χειμαζομένοις ἐν λόγῳ καὶ ἀποροῦσιν, c2–3); he virtually uses the term ἀπορία for this state of speechlessness and inarticulateness and calls upon Nicias to release them from their *aporia* by formulating in words what he has in mind:

Tell us then what you believe courage to be; release us from the *aporia* (ἡμᾶς τε τῆς ἀπορίας ἔκλυσαι) and make firm in words what you yourself have in mind (καὶ αὐτὸς ἃ νοεῖς τῷ λόγῳ βεβαίωσαι). (194c4–6)

So the state of *aporia* is experienced by the interlocutor as something distressing, which befalls one as a helpless victim and renders one speechless and inarticulate.[10]

But Laches also accuses Nicias of self-contradiction (ἐναντία λέγειν ἑαυτῷ, cf. 196b4), and one might think that here he identifies the source of *aporia* as self-contradiction. In fact, however, what he objects to in Nicias' definition of courage is that on the one hand it claims that courage is a certain kind of wisdom, on the other hand it denies that it is the wisdom of any one of the familiar and recognized experts, such as doctors, farmers, or soothsayers (196a4–7, cf. 195a). This is not strictly a contradiction, and in the context the meaning need only be that Nicias behaves like the adversaries in law courts do when they contradict each other in the sense of 'speak against each other'. To identify the source of an *aporia* as something that appears to be a particular contradiction is already to be on the way to using the term ἀπορία to denote a particular puzzle or problem, namely, the problem of how to solve that contradiction. But there is little indication that Laches has reached such a degree of dialectical self-consciousness.

What is the source of Laches' *aporia*, if it is not the awareness of a particular apparent contradiction, and what does he think is the source? He does not say, but evidently the source is Socrates and the Socratic demand for definitions. What leaves him speechless is Socrates' request that he should provide a single, unitary, and completely general definition of courage, coherent with his beliefs about courage and courageous things, and explanatory of why anything courageous is so. He may not be clearly aware of the nature of Socrates' demand, but he knows that something is demanded of him and that he lacks the ingenuity and intellectual resourcefulness to deliver. He has just tried in various ways to define courage, but his attempts were refuted by Socrates on the grounds of being either

---

[10] See also *Charmides* 169c3–6, where *aporia* is described as something contagious that one succumbs to—like a yawn.

too narrow ('Courage is standing fast in the face of danger', cf. 190e4–6) or too wide ('Courage is some kind of mental endurance', cf. 192b9–c1). We may say, summarily, that he is in a state of *aporia* in the same way as the brothers Prometheus and Epimetheus are said to be in a state of *aporia* about how to provide the human race with a vital practical benefit which was demanded of them (*Protagoras* 321c): *aporos* in the sense of needful and lacking in resourcefulness and ingenuity, here the resourcefulness to advance a task of seeming importance demanded of one.

Euthyphro 11b–d

The term ἀπορία is not used here, but what is described is very much the same mental state as in the *Laches*. Like Laches' attempt to define courage, so Euthyphro's attempt to define piety as what is loved by the gods (9e1–3) is refuted by Socrates, this time not on the grounds of the definiens failing to be co-extensive with the definiendum, but on the grounds of the definition failing to be properly explanatory and even of reversing the explanatory priority. For Socrates argues that pious things are loved by the gods because they are pious; they are not pious because they are loved by the gods (10a–11b). But asked to try again, Euthyphro responds that he has been rendered speechless: 'But Socrates, I simply don't know how to tell you what I think' (οὐκ ἔχω ἔγωγε ὅπως σοι εἴπω ὃ νοῶ, 11b6–7). Again *aporia* in the face of the Socratic demand for definitions is associated with speechlessness and inarticulateness.

Euthyphro is in no doubt that Socrates is responsible for his state of mind: 'It is not I who made our statements move around like this and not stay in the same place, rather you seem to me to be the Daedalus; for as far as I am concerned they would have stayed where they are' (11c8–d2). As he sees it, the source of his confusion is Socrates' demand for definitions and the requirements that he sets on this demand. But the image of the unruly statues of Daedalus (11b9–10) indicates a kind of confusion that is associated with instability and lack of firmness in one's statements and beliefs. Thus, under the influence of Socrates, Euthyphro has been forced to give up his initial belief (cf. 10d12–13) and even replace it with its contrary (cf. 11a3–4, νῦν δὲ ὁρᾷς ὅτι ἐναντίως ἔχετον). Socrates sums up the refutation by saying that 'neither is that which is loved by the gods pious, nor is the pious loved by the gods' (οὐκ ἄρα τὸ θεοφιλὲς ὅσιόν ἐστιν, ὦ Εὐθύφρων, οὐδὲ τὸ ὅσιον θεοφιλές, 10d12–13), a formulation that is quite unwarranted and must seem utterly confusing to Euthyphro. Socrates duly corrects it when he grants that being loved by the gods may be an attribute (*pathos*) of piety, but it does not constitute its essence (*ousia*, 11a6–b1). But nothing is made of the crucial distinction between attribute and essence, and in the context this can only increase the confusion.

The image of the unruly statues of Daedalus is meant to capture the sense of confusion associated with unstable belief, but perhaps it has a further purpose. In the *Meno* (97d) the same image, described in very similar terms, is used to prepare for the idea that knowledge requires stability of belief and some means of ensuring this stability—some way of 'tying down' the statues; and this means is identified as the 'rational grasp of an explanation' (cf. αἰτίας λογισμῷ, 98a3–4). But while the *Euthyphro* contains no indication as to how such instability of belief is to be overcome, there is already the suggestion that an unstable belief is indicative of ignorance, the ignorance of which the state *aporia* in general is indicative.

Meno 80a–b and 72a

The *Meno* (80 and 84) provides virtually a summary characterization of *aporia* in these dialogues, and its remarks on *aporia* 'may', as Charles Kahn argues, 'be read as Plato's comment on the aporetic dialogues generally'.[11] The same can be said of the first part of the dialogue, which is about the nature and teachability of virtue but whose aim is just as much to articulate in an almost systematic way the requirements of Socratic definition. Let us first consider Meno's description of *aporia* (80a–b); later we will consider Socrates' response, which in fact contains a very different description (80c–d, 84a–c).

Meno describes his state of *aporia* as the effect of witchcraft and enchantment (80a2–4) and warns Socrates to stop practising the inducement of *aporia* in people lest he be 'arrested as a wizard' (b4–7). This takes to the extreme the experience of *aporia* as something entirely passive that befalls one as a helpless victim. The source of this state of mind is clearly felt to be Socrates:

I used to hear, Socrates, even before meeting you, that you do nothing else but induce perplexity in others just as you are yourself perplexed (ὅτι σὺ οὐδὲν ἄλλο ἢ αὐτός τε ἀπορεῖς καὶ τοὺς ἄλλους ποιεῖς ἀπορεῖν). (79e7–80a2)

But Meno's state of *aporia* was the result of his frustrated attempt to satisfy Socrates' demand for a definition of virtue, so again the source of *aporia* is the Socratic demand for definitions.

What stands out most strikingly in Meno's characterization, however, is the paralyzing nature of *aporia*, memorably captured through the comparison of Socrates' *aporia*-inducing activity with the paralyzing effects of the stingray (ἡ νάρκη ἡ θαλάττια, 80a5, 'the paralysis of the sea'). I will later concentrate on this image, for Socrates' response makes it complex and ambiguous in a way that is generally overlooked. The image perfectly captures the speechlessness characteristic of the *aporia* that we meet in the *Laches* and *Euthyphro*, and it is in terms of this speechlessness and inarticulateness that it is spelled out by Meno:

My mind and my lips are truly paralyzed and I have nothing to reply to you (ἀληθῶς γὰρ ἔγωγε καὶ τὴν ψυχὴν καὶ τὸ στόμα ναρκῶ, καὶ οὐκ ἔχω ὅτι ἀποκρίνωμαί σοι).

[11] *Plato and the Socratic Dialogue*, 99.

And yet I have on hundreds of occasions given countless speeches about virtue to large audiences, and with great success as it then seemed to me. But now I cannot even say in the least what it is. (80a8–b4)

This stands in direct contrast to his initial claim that the sheer plurality of virtues ensures that one is never at a loss to say what virtue is (cf. καὶ ἄλλαι πάμπολλαι ἀρεταί εἰσιν, ὥστε οὐκ ἀπορία εἰπεῖν ἀρετῆς πέρι ὅτι ἐστίν, 72a1–2). But the use of the term ἀπορία is the same in both cases, meaning a peculiar lack of intellectual and verbal resourcefulness. This speechlessness and inarticulateness in the face of the Socratic demand for definitions is not merely an accompaniment of the mental state of *aporia*, it is virtually what this state consists in.

What characterizes this kind of *aporia*?

Let us sum up this use of the term ἀπορία, which in this context it is natural to translate as 'perplexity' or 'being at a loss'. In fact 'being at a loss' is the most adequate translation since it captures what appears to be the meaning of the term in this usage: 'lack of resourcefulness'. 'Lack of resourcefulness' is itself a familiar metaphorical extension of the root meaning of the term ἀπορία: 'lack of passage' or 'lack of a means of advance'—hence our 'impasse'. For the interlocutors' *aporia* consists in their being at a loss about how to define an ethical term with which they are otherwise familiar; and to be in this state of mind is painfully to experience one's lack of intellectual resourcefulness in the face of the Socratic demand for definitions. But the cause of this state of mind is the Socratic demand for definitions. This certainly is how it appears to the interlocutors; so much so, in fact, that they tend to experience their *aporia* as an entirely passive state that befalls them as helpless victims of Socrates, a condition they naturally find distressing. But most distressing is the experience of being speechless in the face of Socrates' demand for definitions, speechless in so far as one lacks the resourcefulness to respond to that demand. Thus speechlessness is perhaps the most central feature of this kind of *aporia*.

Socrates' aim in inducing such *aporia* is stated in the *Apology* (21b ff.): it is to test whether people really know what they think they know and to lead them to the recognition that they do not, thus cleansing them of the belief in their own knowledge. Among the above dialogues this aim is exhibited unmistakably only in the *Meno*, in Socrates' geometry-lesson with the slave boy (see below); but this exchange, we may feel, is rather artificially set up precisely to demonstrate the feasibility and efficacy of that aim. Otherwise we can perhaps detect the cathartic aim of *aporia* only with difficulty, and this lends plausibility to Beversluis's extreme view about the effects of *aporia* in the early dialogues: '*Aporia* there is, but its effects are the very opposite of those envisaged in the *Apology*. No one is seized by his ignorance and impelled to take up the philosophical quest.'[12]

---

[12] *Cross-Examining Socrates*, 158.

But this interpretation is extreme. Daedalus' unruly statues in the *Euthyphro*, especially if read together with *Meno* 87–8, go some way towards establishing a plausible connection between *aporia* and ignorance, since the instability of belief credibly associated with *aporia* does naturally appear to be a symptom of ignorance or certainly of serious intellectual limitations. To the extent that the interlocutor is, if only implicitly, sensitive to this connection, he may acknowledge his ignorance and decide to take up the search for knowledge; though whether he will in fact do so depends on his character, his humility, and honesty, as well as the extent and quality of his desire for knowledge. If he is Meno, there is perhaps little hope; but if he is Laches, the prospects may look better. For Laches, we saw, possesses the right spirit of honest and good-humoured competition (*philonikia*, 194a8); and his annoyance (*aganaktêsis*, a8–b1) at his own speechlessness in the face of Socrates' demand for definitions may be interpreted as irritation, the kind of irritation that may stimulate one to take up the search for knowledge—that is, in fact, the intended effect of Socrates the gadfly (cf. *Apology* 30e1–31a1).[13]

However, my aim so far has been not so much to examine this kind of *aporia* for its own sake, but rather to prepare for the contrast with what is arguably a very different kind of *aporia* in the early Plato: *aporia* as a puzzle or problem and the awareness of a puzzle or problem; a puzzle or problem in the sense of a specific question articulated so as to have two opposed sides with apparently good reasons on both sides. I will first consider some passages in these dialogues in which the term ἀπορία is used in this sense; then ask whether and to what extent there is a real contrast between these two kinds of *aporia*.

2. PLATO'S USE OF THE TERM ἀπορία TO DENOTE PARTICULAR PUZZLES AND PROBLEMS, AND THE ZETETIC FUNCTION OF *APORIA*

Apology 21b

For a good while I puzzled over what the god can mean, then I turned with great effort to searching for this in the following way. (21b7–9)
(καὶ πολὺν μὲν χρόνον ἠπόρουν τί ποτε λέγει· ἔπειτα μόγις πάνυ ἐπὶ ζήτησιν αὐτοῦ τοιαύτην τινὰ ἐτραπόμην)[14]

This is Socrates' response to the oracle's pronouncing him the most wise, and perhaps it is Plato's first use of the term ἀπορεῖν for Socratic *aporia*. But Socrates'

---

[13] I am grateful to David Roochnik for this observation about Laches.
[14] Though perhaps nothing hangs on this, I prefer 'with great effort' to the usual choice of 'with great reluctance' for μόγις πάνυ in b8. Why should Socrates be reluctant to take up the search? Out of fear of offending the god? But riddles invite being interpreted and solved, and the god is surely challenging Socrates to do so. It seems the meaning is rather 'with great effort' or 'exertion', also since this properly characterizes his subsequent search.

description of his *aporia* contrasts strikingly with the interlocutors' description of theirs; and his *aporia* can hardly have a cathartic function, for he has just professed himself free of the pretence of knowledge: 'For I am only too conscious that I have no pretence of wisdom, great or small' (b4–5). Perhaps he cured himself of the pretence of knowledge by demanding definitions of himself and coming up against his own perplexity; but even so, the source of his present *aporia* is not the demand for definitions. Rather, he identifies the source as an apparent contradiction:

> What can the god possibly mean and why does he speak in riddles? For I am only too conscious that I have no pretence of wisdom, great or small. So what can he mean when he says that I am the most wise? For surely he does not utter falsehoods; that would not be proper for him. (b3–7)

Socrates' *aporia* consists not in being at a loss in the face of the Socratic demand for definitions, but in recognizing a particular puzzle and problem and setting out to solve it.

The source of Socrates' *aporia* is his recognition of what appears to be a strict contradiction: (1) 'I know that I am not wise in any way'; and (2) 'The god, who does not lie, pronounces me the most wise'. His immediate response is to ask what this apparent contradiction can possibly mean, that is how both its sides can be true. In fact this is how the *aporia* itself is described: 'I puzzled over what the god can mean' (ἠπόρουν τί ποτε λέγει [ὁ θεός]). So the *aporia* consists in asking how both sides of a particular apparent contradiction can be true. This is virtually a model of an *aporia* in the sense of a particular puzzle or problem whose source is an apparent contradiction both sides of which appear true.

The way in which Socrates sets out to solve the apparent contradiction is also a model of at least one way of solving an *aporia* in the sense of a particular puzzle or problem: by drawing a distinction. Thus he sets out (21b9 ff) to show that both sides of the apparent contradiction are true if we distinguish two kinds of knowledge: knowledge of something as opposed to knowledge that one knows or does not know something. He concludes that he lacks the former, first-order knowledge, and in that sense he is not wise (so (1) is true); but that perhaps he is the only one who possesses the latter, self-knowledge or reflexive knowledge, since he alone knows that he lacks first-order knowledge, and in that sense he is wise (so (2) is likewise true). This is a model solution of an apparent contradiction by drawing a distinction. But we should note that the distinction does not rely on a commonly accepted ambiguity between two senses of 'to know', rather it is an apparently original distinction between two kinds of knowledge. Later, in the *Charmides*, the viability of a strict distinction between first-order knowledge and reflexive knowledge will come under close scrutiny, and this suggests that the attempt to solve an *aporia* is likely to be an extended task that may throw up new and unexpected *aporiai*.

Finally, the *aporia* is directly associated with searching (*zêtêsis*, 21b8); for Socrates says that his *aporia* directly led him 'to search for this in a particular way' (cf. ἐπὶ ζήτησιν αὐτοῦ τοιαύτην τινὰ ἐτραπόμην), that is, search for what the god can possibly have meant. His *aporia*, in the sense of his awareness of this particular puzzle and problem, namely, how statements (1) and (2) can both be true, generates a particular search, the aim of which is to solve the *aporia*. The *aporia* is not simply a stimulus to searching, it is part of a particular search which it helps to define and direct.

Charmides 167b–c

In one passage (169c3–d1) Socrates describes Critias' *aporia* in familiar terms: it is a state that befalls the interlocutor like an affliction, reduces him to inarticulateness and confusion, and makes him want to hide his perplexity in embarrassment. But in an earlier passage Socrates refers to his own *aporia* as something to be carefully articulated: 'I am puzzled. Do you want me to spell out to you how I am puzzled?' (ἐγὼ μὲν γὰρ ἀπορῶ. ᾗ δὲ ἀπορῶ, φράσω σοι;, 167b7–8). The problem or puzzle that he goes on to develop is whether there can be a kind of knowledge whose object is whether or not one knows something, that is, the problem whether self-knowledge or reflexive knowledge is possible:

Let us begin again, and ask, first, whether it is or it is not possible that there should be such a thing, namely, the knowledge that one knows and does not know what one knows and does not know. (167b1–3)
εἰ δυνατόν ἐστιν τοῦτ᾽ εἶναι ἢ οὔ — τὸ ἅ οἶδεν καὶ ἅ μὴ οἶδεν εἰδέναι ὅτι οἶδε καὶ ὅτι οὐκ οἶδεν.

What Socrates formulates, when he formulates his *aporia*, is not his mental state or what it is like to be in such a state, as he later formulates when describing Critias' *aporia*. What he formulates is rather his being faced with a particular puzzle or problem. The puzzle is arguably generated by his own distinction between first-order knowledge and reflexive knowledge in the *Apology* 21b ff.

Moreover, the *aporia* generates and directs a particular search (167b10 ff.): how can reflexive knowledge be possible since the states of the soul that we are familiar with are not reflexive or purely reflexive? Socrates goes through a number of states of the soul, almost systematically (167c–168a); he considers sight and hearing and in general perceptual states; desirative states such as *epithumia*, *boulêsis*, and *erôs*; feelings like fear; finally opinion or judgment, *doxa*. These states have an object, but in none of them is the object ever a first-order mental state. What the upshot is supposed to be is a vexed issue of interpretation, but certainly the *aporia* is part of a particular search which it helps to define and direct.

Protagoras 324d–e and 348c

If there is one passage in these dialogues in which it is clear that Plato uses the term ἀπορία to denote a particular puzzle and problem, it is *Protagoras* 324d2–e2:

That still leaves us with the *aporia* that you puzzle over (ἀπορία ... ἣν ἀπορεῖς) with regard to good men, why it is that they teach their sons and make them knowledgeable in those subjects where there are teachers, but as far as concerns that excellence which they themselves possess, they don't make their sons any better than anyone else. On this point, Socrates, I shan't tell any more stories, but rather give a literal exposition. Look at it this way; is there or is there not one quality which every citizen must have, if there is to be a city at all? For on this point, and this alone, depends the solution of the particular *aporia* that you puzzle over (ἐν τούτῳ γὰρ αὕτη λύεται ἡ ἀπορία ἣν σὺ ἀπορεῖς ἢ ἄλλοθι οὐδαμοῦ).[15]

Plato's carefully deliberate use of the term ἀπορία, his reference to an attempt to 'solve' it (λύειν) by exhibiting its dependence on a particular question, and his extended development of the solution, suggests that he is not only using the term ἀπορία, but reflecting on what an *aporia* is and what kind of response it calls for. The expression ἡ ἀπορία ἣν σὺ ἀπορεῖς ('the puzzle that you puzzle over', 324e1–2, also d2), used twice within a few lines, may simply mean 'the perplexity that you are in', but in this context it points rather to a distinction between the mental state of being puzzled about something and what it is that one is puzzled about; and the internal accusative indicates the object of the mental state, the puzzle that one puzzles over. When Protagoras describes what Socrates is puzzled about, he describes a particular puzzle and problem: *why* is virtue, the greatest acquired good of the soul, apparently not taught, while other acquired goods of the soul are taught (cf. d3–6)? And when he speaks of what is required to solve the *aporia*, he means what is required to solve a particular puzzle and problem.[16]

But it is striking that Protagoras' attempted solution of the *aporia* appears to employ a general method for solving such *aporiai* that anticipates the method of hypothesis in the *Meno*.[17] Thus he states that the solution of the present *aporia*, namely, that whether or not virtue can be taught, depends on precisely one thing, namely, 'whether there is or there is not one quality which every citizen must have, if there is to be a city at all' (πότερον ἔστιν τι ἓν ἢ οὐκ ἔστιν οὗ ἀναγκαῖον πάντας τοὺς πολίτας μετέχειν, εἴπερ μέλλει πόλις εἶναι, 324d7–e1). In other words, we gather from the context, 'Virtue can be taught if, and only if, there is a single quality of character that every citizen must have in order for there to be a viable city-state'. This step by Protagoras is remarkably similar to the introduction of a hypothesis in the *Meno*. There the *aporia* is equally whether

---

[15] Tr. C. Taylor, with a modification: 'the *aporia* that you puzzle over', rather than merely 'your *aporia*', for ἀπορία ἣν ἀπορεῖς. I have (on the suggestion of Amanda Piesse) rendered the active verb ἀπορεῖν with the active 'to puzzle over' rather than the passive 'to be puzzled about'; for the general lesson is after all that this mental state of *aporia* is active—virtually a mental act—rather than passive.

[16] Contrast ἡμᾶς τῆς ἀπορίας ἔκλυσαι, 'release us from the *aporia*', in *Laches* 194c5, which seems to be simply the request to be rid of the mental state of being at a loss.

[17] For the connection between *aporia* and the method of hypothesis, see Michael Erler, 'Hypothese und Aporie: *Charmides*', in T. Kobusch and B. Mojsisch (eds.), *Platon. Seine Dialoge in der Sicht neuer Forschungen* (Darmstadt: Wissenschaftliche Buchgesellschaft, 1996), 25–46.

virtue can be taught, and the hypothesis is that 'Virtue can be taught if, and only if, virtue is a kind of knowledge' (cf. *Meno* 87b). The immediately following question, therefore, is whether there is a single quality of character that every citizen must have in order for there to be a city. Protagoras goes on to defend the proposition that there is. But this again is directly comparable to the argument in the *Meno* for the claim that virtue is a kind of knowledge: 'Then, it seems, we must consider what comes next, namely, whether virtue is knowledge or different from knowledge' (87c11–12). The connection between the claim that 'There is a single quality that every citizen must have in order for there to be a city' and the claim that 'Virtue can be taught' is complex and not immediately obvious. It requires that this quality of character should not be innate and that man should not by nature be a political animal, views that Protagoras defended earlier (321d–322b, 323c–d). It also involves a particular conception of teaching as habituation and training, which seems very different from Socrates' conception. But the general structure of Protagoras' solution of the *aporia* is clear and appears to employ a method of hypothesis for solving *aporiai* in general.

Moreover, the solution is particularly sensitive to the source of Socrates' *aporia*. Socrates argues that, first, virtue is not a specialized skill (*technê*), but it is specialized skills that are most clearly capable of being taught (cf. 319b–e); second, virtuous people are not reliably successful in passing on their virtue even to those closest to them (319e–320b). But Protagoras argues that this *aporia* relies on mistaken assumptions: virtue is indeed not a specialized skill, for it is precisely the one quality of character that must be common to all humans if there are to be citizens and if civic life is to be possible (cf. 322d–323a, 324e–325a); and while the success in teaching and learning virtue may be imperfect, the very existence of citizens and civic life, as opposed to savages and the state of nature, is sufficient confirmation of the presence of such success (cf. 327c–d).

In an exemplary way this passage characterizes *aporia* as a puzzle and problem and demonstrates the place of such *aporia* in searching. It is in this light that we should read Socrates' general comment, later in the dialogue, on the role of *aporia* in dialogue and searching:

> You should not think, Protagoras, that I engage in conversation with you with any other desire than to inquire about (διασκέψασθαι) those very things that I am myself in each case puzzling over (ἃ αὐτὸς ἀπορῶ ἑκάστοτε). (*Protagoras* 348c5–7)

This does not simply mean that Socrates, like other interlocutors, is at a loss about definitions but that, unlike them, he is determined to take up searching. It means rather that he is puzzled about particular puzzles and problems that he seeks to identify and articulate and that are part of particular searches—searches which they help to define and direct. But it is worth noting that Plato put this characterization of *aporia*, as a puzzle and problem, in the mouth of Protagoras, who is the closest we come in these dialogues to an interlocutor who is Socrates' equal in dialectical ability. The suggestion appears to be that it takes considerable dialectical ability to recognize that particular puzzles and problems are the real source of perplexity and being at a loss.

Meno 80c–d and 84a–c

The *Meno* contains some of Plato's most important remarks on the role of *aporia* in searching, which can be read as comments on *aporia* in the early dialogues generally. We saw that Meno characterizes his *aporia* as a state of speechlessness and mental paralysis in the face of the Socratic demand for definitions, and he compares the effect that Socrates has on him to the paralyzing effect of the stingray on its victim (80a–b). This is a good image of the *aporia* that Socrates induces in many of his interlocutors, but is it also a good image of his own *aporia*? He says that he, too, is in *aporia* and that *aporia* is a symptom of lack of knowledge, especially knowledge of definitions and answers to Socratic questions (80c8–d3). But does this mean that he, too, is simply at a loss, paralyzed in mind and tongue? Surely nothing could be further from Socrates' active, vigorous, and supremely articulate engagement with Socratic questions. His state of *aporia* is in this respect crucially unlike and even the opposite of Meno's, though both are associated with lack of knowledge. Moreover, we will see that in the immediately following interaction with the slave boy, in which *aporia* plays a central role that is expressly commented on, Socrates' active and activating role stands out conspicuously.

In response to Meno's comparison of him to the stingray, Socrates says the following:

[1]   As for me, if the stingray is itself paralyzed and it is in this way that it causes others to be paralyzed, then I am like it; but otherwise not.   (80c6–8)
[2]   For it is not that, while it is plain sailing for myself (εὐπορῶν αὐτός), I cause others to puzzle (ποιῶ ἀπορεῖν); rather, I am most of all puzzled myself (αὐτὸς ἀπορῶν) and it is in this way that I cause others to puzzle (ποιῶ ἀπορεῖν).   (c8–d1)

These lines are often understood as saying that Socrates is himself paralyzed in so far as he is in *aporia*.[18] No doubt this is how Meno understands Socrates' response, for he can only think of *aporia* in terms of paralysis. But do these lines assert or imply this? A close reading reveals that they do not; if anything, they imply the opposite. In a looser sense of 'paralyzed', it is true, we may say that Socrates is equally paralyzed: he does not know and cannot state the definition of virtue.[19] But in the sense in which Meno says of himself that Socrates has reduced him to paralysis, Socrates' response neither asserts nor implies that he, too, is paralyzed. My main point is that when Socrates says that he is just as much in a

---

[18] John Beversluis comments: 'The image of Socrates as a stingray appears for the first time in the *Meno*, but it is an apt description of his effect on his interlocutors in many of the early dialogues. Although Socrates' preferred image of himself is that of a gadfly which awakens and arouses (*Ap.* 30e1–31a1), he accepts Meno's characterization with the proviso that his philosophical discussions leave him even more numbed than his interlocutors (*M.* 80c6–d1).' *Cross-Examining Socrates*, 9 n. 11.

[19] I am grateful to Damien Storey for this clarification.

state of *aporia* as Meno, he does not mean simply that, like Meno, he is at a loss in the face of the Socratic demand for definitions.

The statement 'As for me, if the stingray... otherwise not' ([1] 80c6–8) is a biconditional. It does not assert that Socrates is like the stingray in a certain respect, or that he is not like it in a certain respect; it asserts that he is like the stingray if, and only if, the stingray is paralyzed and causes paralysis in others through its own paralysis. By itself, therefore, this statement does not imply that Socrates is unlike the stingray and is like some curious animal that is paralyzed and causes paralysis by being itself paralyzed. If Plato had wanted to make this categorical claim, he would hardly have put it in this plainly hypothetical form. In the next statement ([2] 80c8–d1) Socrates does assert categorically that he is himself in *aporia* and that he causes *aporia* in others by himself being in *aporia*. But by itself this does not say that he is paralyzed in so far as he is in *aporia*; for it is Meno, not Socrates, that characterizes *aporia* in terms of paralysis.

But what if we put the first, hypothetical statement ([1] 80c6–8) together with the second, categorical statement ([2] 80c8–d1) and even suppose that in the second statement Socrates accepts Meno's characterization of *aporia* in terms of paralysis? What follows is that Socrates is like some curious animal that is paralyzed and causes paralysis by being itself paralyzed. But is it not obvious that such an animal is fictitious and not fit to live? So if Socrates here ([2] 80c8–d1) accepts Meno's characterization of *aporia* in terms of paralysis, perhaps he does so in order to bring out (in [1] 80c6–8) the absurdity of thinking that paralytic *aporia*, that is *aporia* as simply the mental state of being at a loss in the face of the Socratic demand for definitions, can describe not only the patient in so far as he is in *aporia*—which it clearly can—but also the agent in so far as he is in *aporia* and causes *aporia* in the patient.

The impression may still persist that Socrates' response in 80c6–d1 plainly implies that he is himself paralyzed in so far as he is in *aporia*. For obviously the actual stingray is not paralyzed and does not cause paralysis by being itself paralyzed; so when Socrates says that he is like the stingray if, and only if, the stingray is paralyzed and in this way causes paralysis, he implies that he is unlike it in some important respect. So it may seem that he implies that he is unlike the stingray in precisely this respect, namely, that while the stingray causes paralysis but is not itself paralyzed, he causes paralysis and is himself paralyzed. There is, however, no such implication; for there is a third possibility. The first possibility was that the agent is not paralyzed, but causes paralysis in the patient—this is the stingray. The second possibility was that the agent is paralyzed and in being so causes paralysis in the patient—this is the fictitious and wholly unrealistic creature. But the third possibility is that the agent is not paralyzed and does not, or not as his ultimate aim, cause paralysis in the patient.[20] This is the relation between

---

[20] Granting, as we did, that there is a sense in which Socrates too is paralyzed, there is also another version of the third possibility: the agent is paralyzed$_1$ (striving to solve a dilemma-like

Socrates and the slave boy, and it is the relationship that he aims at. The proper image is not the stingray, or the fictitious creature, but the gadfly; for the gadfly does not paralyze, but rather arouses and activates what it stings.

The image of Socrates as intellectual midwife, first introduced in the *Theaetetus* (148e ff.), is likewise an image of an active and activating power. But now we have seen that in these dialogues Socrates' own *aporia*, as opposed to the *aporia* of many of the interlocutors, is active and potentially activating; whether it actually activates depends on the condition of the interlocutor. This removes an important reason—the view that *aporia* in these dialogues is not 'a productive state'[21]—for denying that the compelling image of Socrates as midwife is supposed to refer to these dialogues.[22] Furthermore, the image of Socrates as intellectual midwife fits well the relationship between him and the slave boy; and the comments on *aporia* that Socrates makes in the course of the lesson with the boy (cf. 84a–c) can be understood independently of the intervening theory of recollection, which is arguably a departure from these dialogues, and may likewise be read as a comment on them.

Socrates has brought the boy to recognize that he does not know the answer to the question he was asked, namely, how to determine the side of a square whose area is twice the area of a given square (cf. 84a2–3). At this point Socrates comments on the role of *aporia* in the boy's search for an answer; he says that it is the boy's recognition of his state of *aporia* that made him recognize and admit his ignorance (84a5–b2). This change is beneficial since the recognition of one's ignorance will motivate one to search for the particular answer that one is ignorant of, whereas unrecognized ignorance will prevent one from searching (84b–c). He concludes that, with the help of some questioning but not instruction, the boy will even succeed in finding the answer to the search 'from out of this *aporia*' (cf. ἐκ ταύτης τῆς ἀπορίας ... καὶ ἀνευρήσει ζητῶν μετ' ἐμοῦ, 84c10–11).

The *aporia* here is not the perplexity and being at a loss in the face of the Socratic demand for definitions; it is a particular puzzle and problem, the problem of how to determine a certain line. What is more, when Socrates says that the boy will even succeed in finding the answer to the search 'from out of this *aporia*', he does not mean simply that the boy's perplexity will stimulate him to take up geometry, but rather that a particular geometrical discovery emerges from a particular geometrical puzzle and problem. In fact the discovery, which consists in constructing the desired square by using as its side the diagonal of the original square, does emerge from the recognition of a particular problem in the boy's previous, unsuccessful attempt to determine the side of the square. Socrates

problem but not yet able to do so) and via this paralysis$_1$ causes in an interlocutor paralysis$_2$ (a state of being rendered speechless by the probing questions of someone in paralysis$_1$). I am grateful to William Lyons for this clarification.

[21] Burnyeat, 'Socratic Midwifery', 11.
[22] Just as the comparison in the *Sophist* (230–1) of *aporia* to a purgative against the pretence of knowledge is supposed to refer to these dialogues.

indicates what this problem consists in when he invites the boy to look for an answer, no longer by trying to calculate the desired side of the square as he was doing so far, but by trying to point it out in the drawn diagram (cf. καὶ εἰ μὴ βούλει ἀριθμεῖν, ἀλλὰ δεῖξον ἀπὸ ποίας, 84a1–2). The problem is that if one keeps looking for the answer by trying to calculate the desired side, that is, by trying to determine the numerical relation between the desired and the original side of the square, one will find it difficult to succeed; in fact impossible since, as we know, the relation between the side and the diagonal of a square cannot be expressed as an arithmetical proportion. But there is a different kind of solution, one that is purely geometrical, and it is this solution that the boy discovers, with the assistance of Socrates' questioning (84d–85b), 'from out of' his previous *aporia*.

What this shows is that the *aporia* that Socrates argues is beneficial because it stimulates one to search is not so much the perplexity and being at a loss in the face of the Socratic demand for definitions, but puzzlement about particular puzzles and problems. Such *aporia* not only gives one a general desire to be rid of one's ignorance, rather it is part of a particular search which it helps to define and direct. By reflecting on the particular puzzle that one is puzzled about, one becomes clearer about what is required for its solution. It is in this sense that we should understand the highly suggestive statement that the solution to a search originates in a particular *aporia* (cf. ἐκ ταύτης τῆς ἀπορίας ... καὶ ἀνευρήσει ζητῶν μετ' ἐμοῦ, 84c10–11). So if we go back to the difference between Meno's and Socrates' *aporia*, we may conclude that, while Meno is simply perplexed and at a loss in the face of the Socratic demand for definitions, Socrates is above all puzzled about particular puzzles and problems.

What characterizes this second kind of *aporia*?

Let me now sum up this use of the term ἀπορία, which it is natural to translate as 'puzzlement', 'puzzle', or 'problem'. Here I note that 'puzzlement' refers to the mental state whereas 'puzzle' or 'problem' can refer either to the mental state or to what one is puzzled about. This already points to the fact that, on this usage, the term ἀπορία can refer just as much to what one is puzzled about as to the puzzlement itself; and this distinction is indicated in the expression ἡ ἀπορία ἦν σὺ ἀπορεῖς ('the puzzle that you puzzle over', *Protagoras* 324e1–2, also d2). On the previous usage, by contrast, it appears that the term ἀπορία can only refer to the mental state of perplexity and being at a loss, and not to the content or object of that state, for example, *courage, piety, temperance*, or *virtue*. Thus one can be in a state of *aporia* about virtue, but virtue as it figures within one's *aporia* cannot be characterized as an *aporia*; only a particular question about virtue, as, for instance, whether virtue can be taught, can be described as an *aporia*, and then it is not any kind of question, but a puzzle or problem. This is perhaps the most central contrast between the two uses of the term ἀπορία.

The following features are characteristic of this use of the term ἀπορία in these dialogues: *aporia* as puzzlement about particular puzzles and problems.

First, the object of one's *aporia*, i.e. what one is puzzled about, is a particular question articulated so as to have two sides. In the *Apology* the question was 'Do I possess knowledge, or not?', as asked by Socrates; in the *Charmides*, 'Is reflexive knowledge possible, or not?'; the *Protagoras*, 'Can virtue be taught, or not?'; the *Meno*, 'Is the relation between the sides of two squares, if the one square is double the other in area, an arithmetical proportion, or not?' But not all questions are articulated so as to have two sides, and in particular so-called Socratic questions, questions of the form 'What is courage? Piety? Temperance? Virtue?', are not so articulated.

Secondly, there are apparently good reasons on both sides of such a question. In the *Apology*, Socrates believes he lacks knowledge in so far as he cannot answer Socratic questions; but he also believes that he possesses the ability to test people with regard to the possession of knowledge and that perhaps this itself provides a kind of knowledge, purely reflexive knowledge. In the *Charmides* this Socratic motivation behind the belief in purely reflexive knowledge is set against the observation that no other kind of knowledge is purely reflexive. In the *Protagoras* Socrates argues, on certain assumptions which he defends, that virtue cannot be taught; but Protagoras argues against these assumptions and for the claim that virtue can be taught. With regard to the geometrical question in the *Meno*, we who know the solution may find it difficult to appreciate why anybody should think that the relation between the sides of the two squares must be an arithmetical proportion. But from the perspective of someone still searching for the solution, as is the slave boy, there is a natural and perfectly intelligible tendency to think this (this is nicely exhibited in *Meno* 82e14–83e10).

Thirdly, the apparent contradiction between the two sides of the question helps to define and direct a particular search, namely, the search for a solution to the *aporia*. The search may take two directions, at least. One may develop hypotheses in support of either side, and even develop further support for these hypotheses (cf. *Protagoras* and *Meno*). Or one may develop an argument for thinking that the two sides can be reconciled, perhaps by drawing some appropriate distinction (cf. the *Apology* and *Charmides*, and the distinction between first-order knowledge *versus* reflexive knowledge).

We may conclude that when Aristotle speaks of 'those who say that an *aporia* is an equality of opposite reasonings' (ὅσοι λέγουσιν ὅτι... ἡ ἀπορία ἰσότης ἐναντίων λογισμῶν, *Topics* 6. 145^{a}37–^{b}2), he is referring to a characterization of *aporia* that fits well a number of Plato's dialogues traditionally considered early. There are, then, two kinds of *aporia* in the early Plato: *aporia* as the mental state of perplexity and being at a loss in the face of the Socratic demand for definitions; and *aporia* as the puzzlement about particular puzzles and problems.

How different are the two kinds of *aporia*?

But how different are these two kinds of *aporia* and how important is the difference?

First, the two kinds of *aporia* differ in respect of their object: what one is puzzled about. The object of the former kind of *aporia* is a concept, or what a concept signifies: *courage, piety, temperance, virtue*. But the object of the latter kind of *aporia* is a question, articulated so as to have two sides. But is this a real difference? For we can perhaps speak of 'the question of courage, piety, etc.', and certainly we can speak of 'the question "What is courage, piety, etc.?" ' So it may seem that both kinds of *aporia* can be about questions. Still, these will be syntactically different questions: questions not articulated so as to have two sides, such as Socratic questions, versus questions articulated so as to have two sides.

But I think the difference goes deeper and that there is an important sense in which only the latter kind of *aporia* is about questions. For we need to distinguish questions in the sense of interrogative sentences from questions in the sense of issues, puzzles, and problems that can be expressed in interrogative sentences—real questions as it were. My point is that while the former kind of *aporia* can be about questions in the former sense, it is primarily the latter kind of *aporia* that is about real questions. Thus take any concept one pleases, for example, *virtue*. It requires only elementary grammatical skill to turn this into a question of the form 'What is virtue?'; and this grammatical device does not imply that there is an issue, puzzle or problem about virtue or what virtue is. Moreover, compared to the activity of identifying a real question about virtue, this device is mechanical, automatic, and mindless—hence the sinking feeling one sometimes has when one hears talk of 'the problem of knowledge', 'the problem of morality', or whatever. It is primarily the latter kind of *aporia* that is about real questions, that is, issues, puzzles, and problems; and the former kind of *aporia* is about real questions only if it is associated with the latter kind. That is, Socratic questions, questions of the form 'What is X?', are about real as opposed to merely grammatical questions only if associated with particular puzzles and problems.

Second, the two kinds of *aporia* differ in respect of their aim. The aim of the former kind is cathartic: to purge the interlocutor of the pretence of knowledge in the hope that he may take up the search for knowledge. But the aim of the latter kind of *aporia* is zetetic: to generate particular searches, defined and directed by the puzzle and problem at hand. This is perhaps the most important difference between the two kinds of *aporia*.

Third, the two kinds of *aporia* differ in respect of their cause. The former kind, we saw, is caused by the Socratic demand for definitions: the interlocutor lacked the resourcefulness to provide definitions that satisfied the Socratic requirements for definition—unity, generality, coherence, explanatoriness—and this resulted in the experience of perplexity and being at a loss. But the latter kind of *aporia* is not caused by the demand for definitions, but by particular puzzles and problems. It is in fact remarkable that there does not appear to be an immediate connection between the search for Socratic definitions and the engagement with puzzles and problems. Thus searching for solutions to particular puzzles and problems does not directly imply searching for definitions; and, conversely, one may think that it is possible to search for definitions without searching for solutions to particular puzzles and problems—that it is possible to search for definitions non-dialectically.

Plato, we must suppose, thinks there is some important connection between these two searches, the search for definitions and the search for solutions to particular puzzles and problems; but how he conceives this connection is a large and difficult issue, which we can barely touch on here. Perhaps we may confidently say this much. Our overall conclusion is that this kind of *aporia* has a zetetic function and aim: particular puzzles and problems are part of particular searches that they help to define and direct. But if the ultimate aim of the search for knowledge in these dialogues is to find definitions, we may conclude that engaging with and trying to solve particular *aporiai* is part of the searches for particular definitions. Thus while the other kind of *aporia* was the result of failing to find definitions and being at a loss about how to search for them, this kind of *aporia* is an integral part in the search for definitions.

Fourth, with regard to the latter kind of *aporia*, the term ἀπορία may denote either the mental state of puzzlement or the puzzle that one is puzzled about—as in the expression ἡ ἀπορία ἥν σὺ ἀπορεῖς ('the puzzle that you puzzle over', *Protagoras* 324e1–2, d2). This is because the object as well as the cause of the *aporia* is a real question, indeed a puzzle and problem. But with regard to the former kind of *aporia*, the term ἀπορία can only denote the mental state of perplexity and being at a loss, presumably because neither its object or cause is a puzzle and problem. Aristotle argues that the term ἀπορία, even when it means 'puzzle' as it does when he uses it, denotes in the first instance the mental state of puzzlement and only by extension does it denote the puzzle that one is puzzled about and that is the cause of one's puzzlement (*Topics* 6. 145^{a}37–^{b}20). And this does seem plausible. But this innovative extension and transfer of the term ἀπορία goes back to the early Plato, if not further.[23]

How important is the difference between the two kinds of *aporia* in the early Plato? No doubt the two kinds of *aporia* are not sharply separate states of mind; rather, there may be a continuous path from the one to the other. Thus a person may at first experience the encounter with Socratic dialectic as confusing,

---

[23] The transfer of the term ἀπορία, from denoting perplexity and being at a loss to denoting a particular puzzle of this sort, is facilitated by the grammatical fact that a number of abstract nouns in -ία can also be used to denote instances of themselves, taking the role of a neuter in -μα. Thus εὐπορία can also mean a particular *euporia* (as in the famous passage of Aristotle, *Met.* B1. 995^{a}29); ἀδικία can denote a particular wrongful act (alongside ἀδίκημα); εὐβουλία can mean 'individual instance of good counsel'.

bewildering, and simply a cause of perplexity and being at a loss; but gradually he may come to think that the cause of his perplexity is particular puzzles and problems that he may try to articulate and solve. Meno and Euthyphro remain largely at the one end, but Laches is already moving in the direction of other, and Socrates is already there. So in fact is Protagoras, the closest that Socrates has to an equal in these dialogues.

But it is still important to distinguish sharply between the two kinds of *aporia*. For one thing, there is nothing obvious or inevitable about the transition of the term ἀπορία from the one use to the other; rather this is a real innovation. For there is nothing obvious about the view that the cause of the perplexity and being at a loss in the face of the Socratic demand for definitions is particular puzzles and problems. We can imagine perplexity and being at a loss in the face of the Socratic demand for definitions, but without the emergence of a dialectical response, a response involving engagement with particular puzzles and problems. Meno, for one, thinks that the state of perplexity and being at a loss in the face of the Socratic demand for definitions is a disease of the mind caused by poisoning of a sort (cf. *Meno* 80a3); so his response would be to look for an antidote. But equally conceivable are responses that are perhaps intellectual, but not specifically dialectical. Thus, as we know, a non-dialectical search for definitions may take the form of thinking that definitions can as it were be inspected in the language we use.[24]

To conclude, the most important difference between the two kinds of *aporia* in the early Plato lies in their function and aim. For while the aim of the former kind of *aporia* is to purge us of the pretence of knowledge and stimulate us to take up the search for knowledge, the latter kind of *aporia* is part of particular searches which it helps to generate, define, and direct. Plato from the start thought that the search for knowledge involves the endeavour to solve particular puzzles and problems—it is a dialectical search.[25]

---

[24] Thus Matthews: 'Consider Meno and Socrates again. They are trying to figure out what virtue is. Yet, in a way, they both already know perfectly well what virtue is. They are, after all, both competent speakers of Greek. The Greek word for virtue, *aretê*, is not a technical term, but rather a term in quite ordinary usage.... So what's the trouble?... Aristotle's [that is, Matthews's Aristotle] idea of how to break the logjam is as follows. Instead of trying to aim our inquiry even more clearly at virtue, the very thing we are unclear about, and so cannot focus our sights on, we should instead focus on the perplexity or perplexities that stand in the way of our being able to call on our pre-analytic understanding of what virtue is.' (*Socratic Perplexity*, 111.)

[25] For helpful comments, I am grateful to Bert van den Berg, Justin Broackes, David Charles, John Cleary, John Connolly, John Dillon, Christopher Dustin, Vassilis Karasmanis, James Levine, William Lyons, Arthur Madigan, Brendan O'Byrne, Amanda Piesse, David Roochnik, and Damien Storey.

7

Types of Definition in the *Meno*

David Charles

1. INTRODUCTION

It has become a commonplace to say that Socrates in the *Meno* and elsewhere did not have one clear idea of the type of answer he was seeking as an answer to his famous definitional question: 'what is F?'[1] Recent critics have distinguished three different types of account which (in their view) Socrates offers in answer to this question. They have separated

(a) *real definitions*: propositions which give the essence of the thing to be defined (possible example: colour is the efflux of shapes, commensurate with and perceptible to sight),

(b) *conceptual definitions*: true propositions about the thing to be defined, known a priori by anyone who understands the concept (possible example: shape is the limit of solid), and

(c) *true factual claims which identify the phenomenon* (for example, shape is the only thing which always accompanies colour).

In their view, Socrates failed to determine which of these three types of definition of F is to be preferred. Some have found it difficult to see how he could have taken type (c) accounts as definitions at all, since these are merely true identificatory claims about the object in question. Others have suggested that Socrates preferred type (b) definitions, but have noted that on occasion he appears inclined to take as his starting point type (a) accounts. Thus, when he proposes that 'Virtue is a type of knowledge', they conclude that he cannot take this as part of a conceptual definition since it is not known a priori by any competent user of the term 'virtue'.

---

[1] Richard Robinson, *Plato's Earlier Dialectic* (Oxford, 1953), 49–60. I. M. Crombie, 'Socratic Definition', *Paideia*, 5 (1976), 80–102. Jane Day, *Plato's Meno in Focus* (London, 1994), 19–21.

In the view of these critics, Socrates failed clearly to distinguish one good answer (*b*), one possible answer (*a*), and one impossible answer (*c*) to one reasonable question: 'What is F?' Their approach can be described in the slogan: one good question, several distinct and conflated answers. In this chapter, I shall propose an alternative way of understanding Socrates' approach to definition in the *Meno* which questions the assumption that he is asking just one question, to which he confusedly provides several different questions.

2. TWO DISTINGUISHABLE QUESTIONS IN THE *MENO*

There is evidence in the *Meno* that, from time to time, Socrates and his interlocutors consider more than one question. Socrates certainly asks his famous 'What is ...?' question. So, for example, he asks 'What is virtue?' (77b9) and seems keen to find out what virtue is (72c9–d1). In considering answers to this question he outlines a number of well-known (if somewhat ill-defined) conditions. The answer to the question 'What is F?' should have (at least) the following two characteristics:

(1) it should specify one *eidos* (form) which all virtues possess,
(2) it should specify the one *eidos* (form) by being which all virtues are virtues.

Let us call this Question 1 and answers to this question Type 1 accounts.[2] Is this the only question Socrates raises? There is some evidence that it is not, since he also poses a different question. Thus, in the case of shape, he asks 'Do you call something (*kaleis*) boundary?' (75e1)[3]. The question is naturally interpreted (in a language which uses quotation marks) as 'Do you call something "a boundary"?'

Socrates notes the kind of answer he expects as follows: 'I speak of the type of thing which is exemplified by a limit or end ...' (75e1–2). In the light of this, the original question seems to be understood as 'Do you speak of some specific type of thing as "a boundary"?' To answer this question it is not enough to say: 'Yes: I do speak of something as "a boundary"?' One needs also to go on to say what type of thing a boundary is: 'I speak of a limit as a "boundary".'[4] In this answer, one is addressing the question: 'What do you speak of as "a boundary"?'

---

[2] Question 1 vocabulary: 'What is virtue?' (77a9, see *Laches* 190d7: courage); 'What do you say (*phanai*) virtue is?' (71d5, 79e5: see *legein*: 76b1).

[3] This question, *ti kaleis* ... may be distinguished from *kaleis ti* ... in 76a1, which appears to be the existential question: 'is there something you call ...?' For similar existential formulations, see also *Protagoras* 330d3 and *Cratylos* 385b2.

[4] See *Gorgias* 454c6–d2: 'Do you call something *having learned*?' 'Yes.' 'What?' 'Having been persuaded.' 'Is this the same as having learned ...?' They then proceed to discuss whether these are the same. For a similar pattern of thought see *Protagoras* 332a4 ff. 'Do you call something folly?' 'Yes.' 'Is wisdom completely opposite to this thing?' In both cases, attempts are made to work out what is called '...'. See also *Meno* 88a6–b2.

Elsewhere he asks more generally: 'What is that of which this is the name, "shape"?' (74e11). This question, or so I shall suggest, is one which we could express as follows: 'What is it to which the name "shape" applies?'[5] To answer this question (which I shall call Question 2), Socrates needs to specify one thing which is present in all shapes (and perhaps in nothing else). Thus, he asks: 'What is it that is the same in all cases of shape?' (75a4–5). The answer to this question will be given by offering a description which is true of all and only shapes. If 'shape' signifies shape, what is being sought is something which is uniquely true of shape. The form of the answer to this question will be:

What I call by the name 'shape' is ...

where the dots are to be filled by a description of the thing which the term 'shape' signifies. I shall call such answers Type 2 answers.

Socrates' preferred answer to this question is introduced as follows: 'So now you may learn from this *o lego schema*. I say that, in every case of shape, shape is that in which a solid comes to a limit' (76a5 ff). The introductory phrase (*o lego schema*) seems equivalent to the longer phrase 'What I say is shape' or 'what I specify by using the name "shape" ...' (what I mean by 'shape'). Thus, Socrates' answer, 'I say that shape is that in which a solid comes to a limit', should be taken as equivalent to 'I use the name "shape" to specify the limit of solid'.

In the immediate context, he uses the terms *lego* and *kalo* interchangeably (75e1: *lego*, *kalo*; 75e2: *lego*, 75e3: *kalo*; 75e4: *lego*; 75e6: *kalo*; 76a1: *kaleis*; 76a3: *kalo*; 76a4: *legeis* ... *eipo*: 76a7). So, the phrase *o lego schema* seems to be treated as equivalent to *o kalo schema*. Elsewhere, when the latter phrase is used, 'they call (*kalousi*) this the diagonal', it is treated as equivalent to ' "Diagonal" is the name for this ...' (85b6–8). If so, the phrases 'they call this, the limit of solid, "shape" and 'they call shape this ... the limit of solid' should be taken as equivalent to ' "Shape" is the name of the limit of solid'. In a similar way, 'I say this (the limit of solid) is shape' should be equivalent to 'I call this (the limit of solid) shape' and to ' "Shape" is the name of the limit of solid'.

There is, therefore, some prima-facie linguistic evidence in favour of the view that Socrates asks not one but two 'What is ...?' questions in the *Meno*. One asks 'What is F?' and is answered by giving a definition of the thing. A second asks 'What is "F"?' and is answered by giving an account of what is named by the linguistic term 'F'. I shall now offer several further considerations in favour of the same conclusion.

(1) The constraints on an answer appropriate to Question 2, as understood above, are less demanding than those required for Question 1: for an answer to

---

[5] The Greek could also be interpreted to mean: 'What is the nature of the thing which is called "shape"?' I shall return to this possible ambiguity below. The possibility of ambiguity at this point strengthens the main argument of this chapter.

Question 2 need not involve reference to the essence of the object signified. All that is sought is an answer adequate to pick out all and only cases of (e.g.) shape or virtue: some feature which all and only such cases possess (*pathos*). This is clear in the first example which Socrates offers in considering shape: that one thing which always accompanies colour (75b8–11). This is clearly adequate as an answer to Question 2, but inadequate as an answer to Question 1, because it does not refer to the essence of the object in question. That this is the first example that Socrates offers in the immediate context suggests that he is, in fact, attempting to answer Question 2 and not Question 1. It his focus on Question 2 that explains why he omits all reference to his key Question 1 terminology in the present context. In 75a4–6, there is no mention of such terms as 'form' (*eidos*) or 'in virtue of' (*di'o*). These terms are replaced by the idea of a feature common to the relevant phenomenon, an idea wholly appropriate as an answer to Question 2 but not to Question 1.

(2) In answering Question 2, there is no requirement that there be one and only one correct answer. There can be several correct answers provided that all pick out the object in question. Thus, the number two could be specified correctly as

the successor of one,
the sum of one and one,
half of four,
the first even number,

provided that all these descriptions pick out the same number and nothing else.[6] By contrast, there has to be one and only one answer to Question 1 as there is one and only one essence of the object in question.

The fact that Socrates offers two accounts of shape in *Meno* 75b10–11 and 76a1–7 is easily accommodated within the present framework. For the accounts of shape as the limit of solid and as that one thing which always accompanies colour both pick out the object which 'shape' signifies. By contrast, had he been answering Question 1,

What is the nature of the object which is named 'shape'?

only one answer would have been appropriate, since the object has only one essence.

The differences noted in (1) and (2) stem from a common source. While Question 2 is a question about which object a linguistic term signifies (or names), Question 1 focuses on the nature (or essence) of the object which is signified (or

---

[6] In 75a5 Socrates requires that the answer given to Question 2 refer to something which is the same in all cases of shape or colour. But this does not require that there be just one thing that is the same in all cases. There could be several. This constraint is weaker than the request that one find one (and only one) form (*eidos*) which is the same in all cases (72c8), a request plausible for an answer to Question 1.

named). More is needed to answer Question 1 than merely giving an identificatory account of the object which is named 'A'. But this is good enough to answer Question 2.

3. ANSWERS TO QUESTION 2: SOME FURTHER DETAILS

There are three further points to be made about Socrates' answers to Question 2,

> What is the object which the name "shape" signifies?

over and above those already mentioned. The first concerns a feature they share with legitimate answers to Question 1, the second and third highlight differences between them.

(3) In answering Question 2 one is certainly required to specify the object signified in terms which do, in fact, signify the same object (75d1–2). But nothing more is demanded. In particular, the terms used need not be ones which have to be grasped by anyone who understands the concept of shape. Still less is it a requirement that no one could rationally question whether the identity

> shape = the one thing that always accompanies colour

is true. The truth of the identity claim rests solely on how the world is discovered to be, not on what is known a priori by anyone who understands the term 'shape'. Indeed, one will have a true answer to Question 2 provided that the identity statement is itself true. This seems difficult to reconcile with the contention that Socrates is looking, in answering Question 2, for a conceptual account of what shape is. Indeed, there can be true answers to this Question which are not accepted, or even grasped, by the interlocutors. If the interlocutor does not understand the account you offer, you can legitimately say: 'It is your job to grasp the account ...' (75d1–2) and imply 'It is not mine to make it comprehensible to you'.

There seems to be no general requirement on the adequacy of such accounts that they be expressed in terms which all involved in the discussion agree in advance. In this respect there is no difference between legitimate answers to Questions 1 and 2.

Socrates clearly thinks that in some contexts it is preferable to use terms which the interlocutor agrees he understands (or understands in the same way as the speaker). One should certainly proceed thus in a friendly discussion in which a more relaxed, less eristic, style is appropriate (75d3–7). But this seems to be a condition on the type of adequate answer to Question 2 to be produced in non-eristic discussion, not on what is to count as an adequate answer to that Question. For, considered as an answer to that Question, there was nothing wrong with the style of answer, suited to eristic discussion, suggested in 75c8–d2.

Further, it is not required that any competent user of the term 'shape' understands these terms. Indeed, as far as this passage is concerned, it seems permissible to use scientific terms (not understood by all) provided that they are genuinely understood and accepted by the interlocutors. The permitted answers are context-sensitive. There is no attempt to show that any competent user of the term 'shape' must understand the phrase 'limit of solid'.

(4) In answering Question 2, there is no need to latch on to what is explanatorily basic or prior in real definition (as is needed to satisfy the 'in virtue of' requirement in Type 1 definitions). In the first account of shape, as that which always accompanies colour (75b8–11), no attempt is made to meet this requirement. But the second account, offered at 76a1–7, also runs into difficulty with this condition. For, as Aristotle remarked in *Topics* 141^{b}4–8, if solid itself is be defined in terms of shape, one will not have captured the proper order of definition in defining shape in terms of solid. However, while this objection may count against representing the account offered in 76a1–7 as a real definition of shape, it makes no impact on the proposal that it is an account of what the term 'shape' signifies. And this fact should incline us to see the account offered in 76a1–7 as an answer to Question 2 rather than Question 1.

(5) There need be no worry about circularity in Socrates' account if he is addressing Question 2. As has sometimes been remarked, if one combines the two statements

> Shape is that which always accompanies colour
> Colour is the effluence of shape

one arrives at either

> Shape is that which always accompanies the effluence of shape

or

> Colour is the effluence of that which always accompanies colour.

But, from the present perspective, any appearance of circularity through combination is unproblematic. For all that is required is that each description separately picks out the object in question (perhaps using terms the interlocutors understand). Question 2 does not have to be answered in a way which avoids circularity by combination.

Interim summary

The argument so far has been favourable to Socrates. In place of one question ('What is F?') with several competing answers, some good some bad, we have found two different questions, which we can articulate as follows: 'What is F?' and 'What does "F" name (or signify)?' The second question can be legitimately answered in the three styles which earlier critics described as 'conceptual', 'factual', and 'real' definitions. For the constraints to be met in answering it are distinct from those required for a satisfactory answer to the first question. If so, it seems that Socrates is not guilty of the specific confusion which these critics claimed to detect. Unfortunately, his situation is not as good as it seems. There is no happy ending.

4. IS SOCRATES' SITUATION AS GOOD AS IT LOOKS?

Even if there are two distinct questions mentioned in the course of the *Meno*, are they properly distinguished throughout the dialogue? Do the interlocutors, Socrates included, always succeed in distinguishing them? Here there is less reason for optimism. Let me explain.

First, the language which Socrates himself uses sometimes blurs the very distinction he has drawn. Thus, while in 74e11 he appears to ask the question 'What is it of which this is the name "shape"?', he offers his first answer in 75b8 as an answer to the question 'What is shape?', where the absence of the article (*to*) may suggest that he is talking about the phenomenon in the world not the linguistic expression. Of course, he may be answering the question 'What is shape?' in the way required to answer the question 'What does "shape" name (or signify)?', but (at very least) he is not keeping the two issues clearly separate by using the linguistic resources he possesses to distinguish them.[7]

Similar problems arise in considering the second definition. For while, as suggested above, Socrates appears to be answering the question 'What do I say shape is?', understood as 'What does "shape" signify?', the answer he gives is of the form 'I'd say that shape is the limit of solid', which appears to be an account of shape as a phenomenon in the world and not 'shape' as a linguistic expression. Once again, he is not using the vocabulary which keeps the answers to the two questions clearly distinct.[8]

Secondly, the definition of colour offered in 76d4–5 is generally taken as an attempt at a real or essential definition of colour, not merely as an attempt to pick out what "colour" signifies. However, the proposed definition 'Colour is the effluence of shapes ...' is compared by both Socrates and Meno with the earlier answers given (such as 'Shape is the limit of solid'), as if they were answers to the same question (76d6–8, d9–e4). But in the account offered in the previous section this would be a mistake. For while the third definition is an attempt to provide an essential definition, the first and second aim to say what a name signifies. While these distinct types of definition could be compared along

---

[7] See also n. 4 on the possible ambiguity of the question raised in 74e11.
[8] Socrates is using Question 1 vocabulary to answer Question 2 in 76b8 (*ti esti schema*) in a context where Question 2 is being answered (see the phrase *eipein areten* ... in 75c1), without any indication that he is aware of the shift.

different dimensions, one would have expected Socrates to emphasize their different roles before doing so.

Indeed Plato's language at the point of transition from the second to the third definition is, I believe, very revealing. Meno begins by asking *to de chroma ti legeis*; (76a8), which seems to be a version of Question 2: 'What do you say "colour" is?', and in this way continues the discussion of Type 2 accounts begun at 75a3. But Socrates immediately takes up the issue by asking, in Question 1 mode: 'What does Gorgias say virtue is?' (76b1), and continues in a similar vein up to 76d5, without noting any shift of perspective from Question 2 to Question 1. It seems as if in this passage Socrates has slipped from a discussion of Question 2 to considering Question 1 without acknowledging the important differences between these two questions. Nor is it difficult to understand why this is so. The two forms of question are very similar in Greek, so that the crucial transition from what is 'A' (e.g. *to de chroma ti legeis*) to what is A (e.g. *ten de areten ti legeis einai*) could easily have escaped attention. After all, it is made simply by the addition of the apparently innocuous verb 'to be'! Plato's failure to detect it (if this is what happened) is the more readily excusable since Greek lacked the resources (quotation marks) which allow us unambiguously to distinguish between the use and mention of a linguistic expression. Nor had his philosophical predecessors formulated the technical terminology required to draw the relevant distinction. Indeed, some of their bolder claims may have been vitiated by their failure to do so.[9]

Thirdly, the place where Socrates would be expected to use his distinction between Questions 1 and 2 is in his discussion of Meno's paradox. Meno, at a loss to give an account of virtue, raises the following important question:

[A] How can you search for something (e.g. for what virtue is) if you do not know at all what virtue is? (80d5–6)

His question naturally arises in the following way: if you do not know anything about virtue, you will not know what the name "virtue" signifies because you will lack a way of specifying the referent of the term itself. But if you lack an account of what 'virtue' signifies, you cannot search for what virtue is. In terms of the distinction already drawn between two kinds of Question, he is saying: you cannot answer Question 1 until you have answered Question 2. If one does not have an account of what "virtue" signifies, one does not have an answer to Question 2 and so cannot know what it is whose essence one is seeking. If one does not know what one is seeking, one would not know that one had found it if one came across it (80d6–8).

---

[9] e.g. is Heraclitus' use of the term *account* ('logos') free from all confusion between use/mention? Does he use it to refer to the statements we make or to the subject matter of such statements (e.g. an order in the world) or does he conflate the two? A proper study of the prehistory of the use/mention distinction could profitably examine this and several other key pre-Socratic terms (such as *being, not-being*, and *truth*).

Socrates, in reply, reformulates Meno's question as follows:

[B] A person cannot search for what he knows because he already knows it nor can he search for what he does not know, since he does not know what he is searching for.   (80e2–5)

But Socrates would not have altered Meno's question in this way had he focused on his own distinction between accounts of what terms signify and accounts of the essences of the thing (at least if he was being straightforward).[10] For, with that in mind, he should have noted that one can easily come to learn something one does not know in cases where one has an answer to Question 2 but lacks one for Question 1. Thus, if one grasps an account of what the name signifies (i.e. an account that is of something found in all and only cases of virtue), one will be in a good position to go on to find out the relevant essence. For one will have secured the target which needs to be examined and will be well placed (if all goes well) to find out what the essence needs to explain. In this way, if one distinguishes Questions 1 and 2, one can easily accommodate the acquisition of further knowledge once one has knowledge of what the relevant term signifies. (There would have been no objection to Socrates' reformulating Meno's question as an 'eristic logos' and then replying to it by drawing the relevant distinction. But this is not what he actually does as the dialogue progresses.)

Socrates' striking reformulation of Meno's question is easy to understand on the assumption that he is conflating Questions 1 and 2. For if he thought that to know an account of what the term 'virtue' signifies is to know the essence of the thing signified, there are only two epistemological situations open to the would-be enquirer: either she knows both accounts and there is nothing left to discover about the kind, or alternatively she knows neither and so does not know what she is searching for (and so could not recognize it if she encountered it). As Socrates remarks in *Meno* 80e4–5: 'either one knows, in which case one cannot search, or else one does not know so cannot search for what one does not know'. Either way enquiry is impossible. In the context set by the earlier discussion of definition, the radical conclusion which Socrates draws makes sense on the assumption that he is failing to distinguish Questions 1 and 2 in the way suggested. Let me explain why this so.

If Socrates had kept the relevant distinction between these two questions in mind, he would have responded to Meno's specific concern by focusing directly on what is required to answer Question 2. There were several possibilities:

(1) we do have knowledge of what "virtue" signifies in the form of an identificatory account of virtue, or

---

[10] Charles Kahn has suggested that Plato (in effect) distinguished throughout between accounts of what terms signify and accounts of essence but conflated them in the *Meno* 'as part of [his] art' (*Plato and the Socratic Dialogue* (Cambridge, 1996), 160).

(2) we have knowledge of what "virtue" signifies but not in the form of an identificatory account of virtue. Such accounts are not required to find out what the essence of virtue is.

His goal should have been to specify more precisely (*a*) what is required to begin an investigation into the essence of virtue and (*b*) whether we in fact possess such accounts. Thus, he should have investigated what the ordinary user of the term 'virtue' knows and why this is not enough to begin an investigation into the nature of the phenomenon. Why is an identificatory account, which picks out a feature common to all and only cases of virtue, required as a preliminary to investigating its essence? These are the issues which he needed to address to engage with Meno's specific question: how can I come to have any knowledge at all if I do not possess an answer to Question 2 of the type sought, an identificatory account of what the relevant terms signify? Socrates should have left the issue of how one reaches an answer to Question 1 in the background and focused on Question 2 alone. For it might well turn out to be easier to resolve Question 1 once one has uncovered the minimum required for an investigation to begin.

It may be objected that Socrates' reformulation of Meno's question is merely a rhetorical (or eristic) exercise. Perhaps he has the relevant distinction between Questions 1 and 2 firmly in mind, and uses it as the dialogue progresses.

If Socrates had the distinction between the two questions before him, he should have turned (after his brief eristic moment) to further reflection on Question 2. However, as the dialogue develops, he appears, in fact, to turn away from consideration of this question. In his discussion with the slave, Socrates finds out that the slave knows (*gignoskei*) what a square is (82b10), first by giving an example and then by giving a general account of what a square is, and later in a similar fashion makes sure that the slave understands what 'diagonal' signifies (85b5–6). Beginning with these bits of knowledge he shows how the slave can come to possess (occurrently) other bits of knowledge. In both cases, his knowledge of Greek seems to be enough to get the discussion going. While this way of proceeding may point to an answer to Socrates' own puzzle, it cannot address Meno's question, since he was focusing on the cases where one does not know an account of what the term "virtue" signifies (and so lacks an answer of the desired form to Question 2) even though one knows Greek and can make fluent and well-received speeches about virtue (80b4–6).[11] His puzzle (how one can enquire into virtue without knowing an identificatory account of what the term "virtue" signifies) seems to have been dropped at this point in this discussion.

---

[11] Had the theory of recollection been deployed to answer Meno's specific question, Socrates should have proposed that we know dispositionally an identificatory account of what the term signifies. But instead he chooses to focus on the issue of how, granted that one knows occurrently what the term signifies, one can come to activate one's dispositional knowledge about the properties of the thing signified.

The problem, just mooted, can be developed as follows. Either the slave knows an account of what 'diagonal' signifies or he does not. If he does not, it seems that he can use the term and carry out an enquiry without possessing an account. But, if so, his procedure runs contrary to the assumption which drives the earlier part of the dialogue and is made explicit by Meno in 80d5–8. If one can proceed in this way, there can be no objection to Meno's seeking the essence of virtue without grasping an answer to Question 2. This possibility would mark a major volte-face in the dialogue. However, if the slave does possess an account of what "diagonal" signifies, we should be told what it is and when he acquired it (if there is to be an answer Meno's question).[12]

Nor is this problem confined to Socrates' discussion with the slave. Later, in employing the hypothetical method, he begins with the hypothesis that (e.g.) virtue is a good (87d2–3), while exercising proper caution over the question of whether virtue is something in the soul.[13] But the formulation of this hypothesis seems to require a grasp on an account of what 'virtue' signifies (see 71b2–6). Given his earlier contention that one may not know an account of what 'virtue' signifies even when one can make long and fluent speeches in Greek about it, he does not seem entitled to claim that he himself possesses such an account. If so, how is he entitled to propose the hypothesis that virtue has a certain property?

In sum: it is not just that Socrates fails to make use of the distinction he has suggested between Question 1 and 2 when he reformulates Meno's question in 80e1–5. Worse still, he seems to assume in the remainder of the dialogue *either* that he and the slave know an account of what the term signifies (in the case of the slave) *or* that they can engage in some form of investigation about (e.g.) virtue without knowledge of such an account.[14] But one or other of these claims was precisely what he needed to argue for if he was successfully to engage with Question 2. It is not enough, in the present dialectical context, merely to assume that one or other is correct. Had he seen the issue clearly, he would have sought to establish one or other of these possibilities.

Fourthly, at the beginning of the dialogue, Socrates claims that one cannot know what features something has unless one knows what it is (71b2–6), and then goes on to give an essence involving account of what the answer to the question 'what is ... ?' (72d5–7). Thus, it seems at the outset that one cannot

---

[12] It is significant that, in these contexts, Plato uses the term 'know' (*gignoskei*) rather than 'believe' (*doxa* ...). It seems as if the slave begins not with belief, but rather with knowledge, about what the term signifies. For the slave appears to be agreeing that he knows the terms in which the argument is to be conducted. (He seems to fulfil the condition on friendly dialectic set in 75d6–7, using the term 'know': *eidenai*.) Plato does not appear concerned to claim that the slave only has correct beliefs about what the term signifies.

[13] I am indebted to Vassilis Karasmanis for helpful discussions of this section of the *Meno*. He argues that the relevant hypothesis is that virtue is a good in 'The Hypothetical Method in Plato's Middle Dialogues' (Oxford D.Phil. 1987), 77–85.

[14] In fact, the method of hypothesis is introduced by taking the case of a specific figure, where one knows what one is talking about. Thus, this case is unlike that of virtue.

know what features a thing possesses unless one knows its essence. However, if he had used his distinction between Question 1 and 2, he should have continued as follows:

> one may need to know what an account of what the term signifies in order to know what qualities it possesses; but it less plausible to claim that one needs to know its essence to know what qualities it has.

He should not have insisted that one needs to know the essence of a thing in order to know what qualities it has. But nowhere, in this context, does he employ the distinction required for this move. This is surprising in the immediate context since an answer to the question 'is Meno tall?' does not require one to know Meno's essence, but only to have some way of identifying the man in question. Socrates should have seen, if he was using his distinction between Question 1 and 2, that one does not need to know the essence of F before one can know what qualities it has.[15]

The consequences of not employing the relevant distinction may be more unfortunate still. Socrates' attachment to the claim that knowledge of the essence is required for knowledge of a thing's properties may well have led him later to accept that knowledge always involves 'knowing the causes' (98a2–5). For knowledge of the essence is what is needed for knowledge of the cause of the thing's having the properties it has. Socrates' definition of knowledge is, of course, extremely stringent, ruling out such everyday cases of knowledge as knowledge of one's own name or knowing who Meno is. But one can see how he could have been driven to this very demanding definition of knowledge if he held that

(1) one cannot know whether (e.g.) virtue is F (for any F) unless one knows an account of what 'virtue' signifies, and
(2) knowledge of an account of what 'virtue' signifies requires (or is identical with) knowledge of the essence of virtue.

For if he had combined these claims with the further (plausible) assumption that

(3) knowledge of the essence of virtue is knowledge of the cause of virtue being F

he would arrive at the conclusion that knowledge of virtue's being F will require one to know the cause of its being F. Since he could deploy this form of argument to any claim of the form 'a is F', he would be forced to conclude that one can never know anything of this type without knowing the essence of a, the cause of a's being F. In this way, his conflation of accounts of what terms signify and

---

[15] It is perhaps worth noting that the claim in 71b3–8 that one cannot know that a is F unless one knows what a is does not require that one knows what a is prior to knowing that a is F. It is consistent with this claim that one cannot know what a is without knowing (for some F) that a is F. For all that is said here, knowledge of what a is and of what properties a has might emerge together.

accounts of the essence of the thing signified may have been an important part of what led him to his famous but implausibly demanding account of knowledge in the *Meno*.

5. IS SOCRATES CONFUSED?

The problem is this: Socrates in the *Meno* made (or gestured towards)[16] an important distinction between an account of what a term names (or signifies) and an account of the essence of the thing signified, but failed to use it as we would have expected him to do.[17] Contrast the situation with that of Aristotle in the *Analytics* who (or so I have argued elsewhere[18]) uses precisely Socrates' distinction between accounts of what the term signifies and accounts of what the thing is to develop his stage-by-stage view of enquiry. In his account, we arrive at accounts of what the essence is on the basis of accounts of what the names signify (in successful cases).

Can Socrates be defended against this criticism?

Defence 1

Socrates, it might be suggested, did draw a distinction suggested between accounts of what the names signify and accounts of the essence of the kind, but held as a matter of philosophical doctrine that the only way in which one could know an identificatory account of what (e.g.) 'virtue' signifies is by knowing the essence of virtue. For this is only thing which can demarcate all and only cases of virtue. That is, it is only if one knows that one thing in virtue of which all cases of F are cases of F that one knows an identificatory account of what 'F' signifies. There is no confusion here, only philosophical speculation (or doctrine). Further, it is because Socrates held this doctrine that he was drawn to the theory of recollection. For unless we knew at some point the essence of the kind or thing named we could not now use the name correctly. Since we do not know the essence now, we must have known it (occurrently) at some time before.

This defence does not ring true to the discussion in the *Meno*. For, as I noted above, when Socrates introduces his question 'What is it that the name, "shape", signifies?', he proceeds to give conditions noticeably weaker than those he had

---

[16] Note, once again, the possible ambiguity in the question raised in 74e11. See n. 4.

[17] In a fuller discussion one should investigate whether Socrates (or Plato) distinguished in a more consistent fashion between Questions 1 and 2 and the corresponding types of account in other earlier dialogues. If Vassilis Karasmanis is correct to represent the *Meno* as providing an overview of Socrates' approach to definition in these dialogues (in this volume), Questions 1 and 2 may be confused there also. I leave this issue for further investigation.

[18] In *Aristotle on Meaning and Essence* (Oxford, 2000), chs. 2 and 3.

first offered. For there is no reference to the 'in virtue of condition', or to the essence or form (*eidos*) of shape in this passage. (Compare 75a3–5 with 72c5–9.) Nor is this a chance omission, since the first example he offers, 'Shape is that one thing which always accompanies colour', is clearly not an example of an account which specifies the essence (or form) of the thing itself. Further, in offering two accounts of shape in this passage he appears to give up his initial claim that there is one *eidos* which all cases of shape should share, in favour of the weaker condition that there be something which is common to all cases of (e.g.) shape.

In the light of his own distinction between the two different types of account, Socrates would have needed some powerful arguments to show that the philosophical doctrine in question is correct. But this is not found in the *Meno*. Further, if Socrates (or Plato) elsewhere came to hold this doctrine, he would need to show what was wrong with the shallower type of account of what a name signifies which Socrates appears to countenance in the *Meno*. Indeed, it would be tempting to see the roots of any such doctrine as lying in the conflation of the two distinct questions which Socrates succeeded in holding apart (however temporarily) in the *Meno*.

Defence 2

Socrates, it might be suggested, identified accounts of what names signify and accounts of essence as a result of a different philosophical doctrine. If he was committed to the view that names signify essences, he could have concluded that any account of what a name signifies must specify the essence of the thing (or kind) signified. And, since there is some evidence elsewhere that Socrates (or Plato) did hold such a view, perhaps his commitment to this semantical thesis influenced his discussion in the *Meno*.[19]

Once again, for the reasons just mentioned, it is difficult to see this semantical doctrine as present in the *Meno*. At least one account of what "shape" signifies ('the one thing that always accompanies colour') does not refer to the essence of shape. Further, Socrates introduces his remarks on what "diagonal" or "square" signify without referring to the essences of the phenomena in question. These remarks suggest that, in the *Meno*, terms are taken to signify not the essence but rather the thing which has the essence: the diagonal, the square, shape, etc. There is no evidence here in favour of, and some against, the view that names signify essences.

There is a second, more general, reply. If Socrates elsewhere accepts that names signify essences, he needs to show that it is a mistake to think that they signify merely objects or kinds which have essences (and not the essences themselves).

---

[19] I am indebted to both Gail Fine and OUP's anonymous reviewer for alerting me to the possibility of this line of defence. Neither endorsed it without qualification.

But what is his motivation for this claim? It is, after all, one thing to argue that Forms (or essences) are required to answer Question 1, quite another to think that they are needed to reply to Question 2. Against the background of the *Meno*, it is tempting to see his later semantical doctrine as the result of his conflation of accounts of what names signify and accounts of the essence signified. For if he fell victim to this confusion, it would have been hard for him to avoid the conclusion that names signify essences. If Socrates had other (better) philosophical motivations for this latter, radical, semantical contention, they are not present in the *Meno*.

Defence 3

It might be said that there is nothing more to Type 1 definitions (in the *Meno*) than accounts of what the name signifies. Perhaps the difference between an identificatory account of what a name signifies and an account of what the essence of the thing is has been exaggerated. Is there more to the thought that there is one form (*eidos*), itself the essence (*ousia*), in virtue of which Fs are F than is captured by giving an account of features which all and only Fs possess? So understood, 'Being the one thing which always accompanies colour' and 'Being the limit of solid' might both be part of one nature, the nature of shape, that in virtue of which all shapes are shapes.

This defence comes with a high price since it runs contrary to the widespread assumption that the form (*eidos*) is used not to pick out any features of the object in question, but some particularly important ones, those in virtue of which bees are bees (72b3–5). What makes something a bee is not merely some feature all and only bees have (e.g. being intermediate in size between wasps and hornets, living in hives, making honey, etc.), but is the essence in question. The defence presently under review is in danger of collapsing the distinction, on which Socrates insists (e.g.) in the *Euthyphro*, between the essence of a thing and the type of features it happens to possess.

Defence 4: A plea for mitigation

Socrates may have failed to use the distinction he drew, but this does not really matter since he (and his interlocutors) failed to come up with even an introductory account of what 'virtue' signifies. So they were in no position to search for an account of the essence of virtue. Indeed, since they had not got to first base, they were not at all hampered by any possible confusion between accounts of what terms signify and accounts of what the object is. While Socrates failed to use the distinction he drew to the full, this was because he did not even get as far as an account of what the name signifies.

I partially replied to this line of defence when I argued above that, had Socrates used the distinction he has sketched, he would not have generalized Meno's paradox in the way he does, and would have focused more insistently on the very precise issue that *Meno* raises: how can you search for the essence of virtue when you do not know what it is that 'virtue' signifies? In particular, he would have examined the following issues:

1. What is needed to have an account of what the term signifies? Does one need an identificatory account? How demanding are the conditions?
2. Does one need to know an account of what a term signifies (as specified in the answer to (1) to be able to use the term in an investigation which leads to knowledge of the essence of the term named)?

Socrates' failure to engage with either of these key problems is a source of some disappointment for the attentive reader of this dialogue. He seems to lose direction at the crucial moment.

Socrates appears to have been attracted, in the *Meno*, to the following premises:

[A] One cannot come to have knowledge of the nature of A unless one knows who/what A is.
[B] One cannot know who/what A is unless one knows an account of what 'A' signifies.[20]

[A] seems to be explicit in *Meno* 71b1–8. [B] appears to be Socrates' way of spelling out what is involved in knowing who/what virtue is.

[C] One cannot know an account of what 'A' signifies unless one possesses an appropriate account, given in general terms, of what A is.
[D] One cannot possess an appropriate account, given in general terms, of what A is unless one knows some feature which all and only As possess.

[C] and [D] appear to be at work in *Meno* 75a4–6. Had he not confused the identificatory account specified in [D] with an account of the essence of A, he would have been encouraged to ask whether one must begin an investigation into (e.g.) the nature of virtue forearmed with an identificatory account of the phenomenon. It was precisely this claim that Aristotle rejected when he suggested (in the *Analytics*) that one could come to have knowledge of essences beginning with accounts of what terms signify which do not enable us to identify the phenomenon in question in the way required by [D]. In his account, one could begin an investigation into the nature of thunder (or man) while knowing only

---

[20] It is important to note that Socrates does not claim that one cannot meaningfully use the term 'A' without being able to formulate an account of what 'A' signifies. His contention is only that, without such an account, one cannot come to have knowledge of the essence of A. The issue of the type of understanding possessed by one who uses 'A' meaningfully without having at his (or her) disposal an account of what 'A' signifies is not raised in the *Meno*. Perhaps, theirs is the condition of people with belief (*doxa*) in the *Republic*? There are a number of interesting issues left open at this point.

that thunder was a type of noise in the clouds (or that man was a type of animal).[21] Indeed, this is one of the features which distinguishes his account of the route to knowledge of essences from Plato's.

6. THE CONSEQUENCES OF SOCRATES' FAILURE CONSISTENTLY TO DISTINGUISH QUESTIONS 1 AND 2

Socrates, or so I have been arguing, failed to distinguish consistently between two questions, which we could represent as follows:

[1] What is virtue?
[2] What is 'virtue'?

Indeed, because of this confusion between (what we would term) use and mention, Socrates seems to have thought that knowledge of an account of what 'virtue' signifies requires (or is identical with) knowledge of the essence of virtue. This confusion, combined with the thought that one cannot carry out a successful investigation into virtue without knowing an account of what 'virtue' signifies, had significant epistemological and metaphysical consequences. I shall mention four, in addition to the one already noted at the end of section 4. There may well be more.

1. The theory of recollection

If Socrates wished to allow for the possibility of enquiry, and held firm to the assumption that this required knowledge of an account of what 'virtue' signifies which involves a specific claim about the essence of virtue, he had to explain how we could come to have such accounts of what the term signifies. This is particularly pressing if one thinks that we have not (in this life) so far come to know the essence of the kinds around us! One obvious move, given this package, is to suggest that we must have acquired the relevant type of account (with its understanding of the essence of virtue) before we were born. If we have not acquired this account during our lives here, we must have acquired it elsewhere, without empirical experience of objects in this world. If so, he would need to devise a theory of recollection to account for our grasp on the account of what the term signifies. Indeed, if one thinks that we can carry out enquiries of the relevant type, and holds to the assumptions just noted, the theory of recollection could

---

[21] I argue for this claim in *Aristotle on Meaning and Essence*, 38–42 and 161–4. Aristotle relies partly on the presence of causal factors (not necessarily known by the thinker) to fix the reference of the term 'thunder'. Plato appears to require that the thinker have a complete identification of the object named in mind before she can begin her search for its essence.

easily seem to be the most plausible solution. For where else can we have acquired the needed, essence-involving, account of what the term signifies?[22]

2. The separability of the Forms

If (1) is correct, the essences so discovered must exist independently of this world, since they are grasped by us prior to our existence in it. If so, it cannot be essential to their existence that they are instantiated here. While Forms (or essences) may explain why contingent things work as they do in this world, it cannot be essential to their existence that they do so. As with numbers, the relevant essences could have existed even if they had not been instantiated around us.

3. The ambitions of dialectic

If it is a requirement of successful investigation that we possess a priori (at birth) essence-involving accounts of what our terms signify, one route to knowledge of essence will consist in our making explicit what we already possess. If we can bring to light and fully analyse these accounts, we will come to know the essences in question. Clarification and articulation of what we already know in grasping the relevant concepts will provide a route to knowledge of what has to be the case. Indeed, conceptual analysis, aided by dialectical discussion, may be the best way we have of gaining the type of knowledge we seek.[23]

4. The a priori knowability of essences

The essences we grasp in answering Question 1 cannot simply be basic explanatory factors in some chain of causation, grasped by a posteriori or empirical investigation. They must also be capable of being known a priori, since we have knowledge of them prior to empirical investigation when we grasp accounts of what the relevant terms signify (as answers to Question 2).

At this point several questions become pressing. How can specific essences be both basic starting points in explanation and capable of being known a priori by us? Is it a mistake to think that they have to play both these roles? Can there be essences of the type required? Is Plato's notion of essence a coherent one?[24]

---

[22] See e.g. *Phaedo* 74e8–75a3. This (unpalatable) conclusion cannot be avoided simply by substituting true belief for knowledge. For if one who believes an account of what the name signifies also needs to have true beliefs about the specific essence of the thing named, the same question arises: where do we acquire beliefs of this kind (prior to investigation of the phenomenon in this world) if not before birth?

[23] Some (in the spirit of Nietzsche) might be tempted to see here the birth of conceptual analysis from the spirit of confusion!

[24] On this issue, see G. Vlastos, *Platonic Studies* (Princeton, 1981; 2nd edn.), 410–17.

One elegant solution to these three last questions would be to propose that essences (or Forms) cannot essentially be involved in any form of explanation which has to be grasped by a posteriori investigation. Forms can only figure essentially in explanations which, like those grasped in the 'second journey' in the *Phaedo* (99c8–101c2), are known independently of all a posteriori research. It would be an important matter to discover the range of such explanations. Perhaps Plato (in the *Republic*) came to believe that (some) final as well as formal causes can be grasped independently of all a posteriori investigation. But, at the very least, he would have found it difficult (if not impossible) to encompass material and efficient causes within the preferred fully a priori understanding of the world.

My present conjecture is that Plato accepted (in some form) the four consequences just noted and built much of his distinctive metaphysical and epistemological theory around them. No doubt he modified some and had further reasons for others. But, nonetheless, there is a line of thought which leads directly from the confusion implicit in failing steadfastly to separate Questions 1 and 2 to these radical conclusions. Perhaps Plato had such confidence in Socrates' philosophical insight that he was prepared (as Socrates maybe was not) to 'bite the bullet' and accept the consequences that flow naturally from the thought that we (or some of us) actually possess a priori accounts of what terms signify which involve knowledge of the essences of things. If so, he would have seen the identification of answers to Question 1 and 2 not as a mistake but rather as a suitable foundation for some of his most ambitious and distinctive philosophical contentions.

Aristotle, by contrast, realized that Socrates had been right to separate (albeit fleetingly) Questions 1 and 2, and began to investigate in a more careful way what is actually involved in grasping an account of what terms signify (if this does not involve a grasp on the essences of the kinds involved). Thus, he aimed to undermine the assumptions involved in setting up Meno's dilemma (as reformulated by Socrates) and not to find a way of living with the radical consequences of accepting one of its horns (1–4 noted above). In this way he liberated himself from one of the motivations which led to Plato's transcendental metaphysics and super-rationalist epistemology. By developing different strands in Socrates' *aporetic* remarks on definition in the *Meno*, Plato and Aristotle were led to radically different accounts of knowledge and reality.[25]

---

[25] I am indebted to participants in the 2001 Socrates conference in Delphi for their comments and criticisms of an earlier draft of this chapter. I gained much from subsequent discussions with Lesley Brown, Jane Day, Gail Fine, Lindsay Judson, and Vassilis Karasmanis. A revised version was read in 2003 at the NEH Summer School on 'Aristotle on Thought and Meaning' in San Diego and at a workshop in the Javeriana University in Bogota. I am most grateful to participants in these events for their helpful comments.

8

Definition in Plato's *Meno*

Vassilis Karasmanis

The *Meno* is considered to be a transitional dialogue between Plato's early and middle period. Plato, in the *Meno*, goes beyond the 'Socratic' *elenchus* and proposes new theories and positive ways to arrive at knowledge. In the *Meno*, we find for the first time the distinction between knowledge and belief (together with a definition of knowledge), the theory of recollection and the hypothetical method, themes that we meet in other middle dialogues.

Scholars usually divide the *Meno* into two main parts: (*a*) 70–9 and (*b*) 80 to the end.[1] On this view, in the first part the object is to find a definition of virtue. Meno proposes three definitions, and all of them are refuted by Socrates. In the second part, the search for a definition is abandoned and the two interlocutors try to find whether or not virtue is teachable. All the new elements in Plato's philosophy, which make the *Meno* a transitional dialogue or the first of the middle dialogues, appear in the second part.

There seems to be a general agreement among scholars that the first part of the dialogue—where we find three unsuccessful attempts to define virtue—is similar to the early or 'Socratic' dialogues.[2] In this chapter I shall try to show that in this part of the dialogue we have something more. My opinion is that Plato summarizes here results from other early dialogues and proposes a—more or less—complete theory of definition. In this way, even the first part of the dialogue has to be considered more 'Platonic' than 'Socratic' in the sense that we find here a more theoretical interest and positive views about the problem of definition.

---

[1] The second part is usually divided into another four parts; see e.g. R. S. Bluck, *Plato's Meno* (Cambridge: CUP, 1961), 4.
[2] Ibid., 7; R. Robinson, *Plato's Earlier Dialectic*, 2nd edn. Oxford: OUP, 1953), 122; R. W. Sharples, *Plato: Meno.* (Warminster: Aris & Phillips, 1985), 1; Paul Friedländer, *Plato*, ii. *The Dialogues: Early Period* (London: Routledge & Kegan Paul, 1964), 276; T. Irwin, *Plato's Ethics* (Oxford: OUP, 1996), 127; J. E. Thomas, *Musings on the Meno* (The Hague: Martinus Nijhoff, 1980), 11. I am not going to discuss the problem of whether or not Plato's early dialogues reflect the philosophy of the historical Socrates.

A. THE *TI–HOPOION* DISTINCTION

The opening question of the dialogue (70a) is the following: 'Could you tell me, Socrates, whether virtue can be taught? Or can it not be taught, but is it acquired through practice? Or can it neither be acquired through practice or learned, but is it something which men possess by nature or in some other way?'[3] Socrates immediately turns the question of the teachability of virtue into that of what virtue is (70b3–4). 'If I do not know what (*ti*) a thing is, how should I know what sort (*hopoion*) of thing it is?' Plato makes here two different points. First, that the question 'what a thing is' is different from the question 'what sort of thing it is', and, secondly, that the first question is prior to the second.[4]

This distinction between *ti* and *hopoion* is not new. In *Gorgias* 448c9, Polus defines rhetoric as 'the noblest of the arts' and Socrates replies to him: 'Nobody asked you what was the quality (*poia*) of Gorgias' art but what it was (*tis*)' (448e7–8). In *Euthyphro* 9e, Euthyphro defines 'holiness' as 'what all the gods love'. Later on (at 11a), Socrates, commenting on the above definition of holiness, says:

> It would seem, Euthyphro, that when you were asked what holiness is (*hoti pot' estin*), you did not mean to make its nature or essence (*ousia*) clear to me; you mentioned a mere affection (*pathos*) of it—holiness has been so affected as to be loved by all the gods. But what it really is, you have not yet said.

As Socrates explained to Euthyphro 'the holy is loved by the gods because it is holy, not holy because it is loved' (10e). So, Euthyphro's definition does not say something about holiness itself but rather how the gods feel about holiness. Similarly, Polus' definition is rather an answer to the question 'what is your opinion—or estimate—of rhetoric?' Polus' answer does not say something about rhetoric, but about Polus.[5] Later on, in the *Meno* (72d–73c), Plato will give us some directions of what a *ti* statement must be. But he says nothing about *hopoion* statements. We have therefore to define them negatively. What is not a *ti* statement is a *hopoion* statement. Certainly *pathos* or affection (*Euthyph.* 11a8) refers to the *hopoion* question, but the evidence is very scarce to conclude that all *hopoion* statements denote *pathos*. Plato does not tell us how to distinguish *hopoion* from *ti* attributes. But he thinks that—at least in non-disputable cases—someone can easily understand if something is *pathos* or a property that

---

[3] Translations from the *Meno* are taken or adapted from Sharples, *Plato*.

[4] See also *Laches* 190b and *Republic* I. 354c: 'For if I do not know what justice is, I am not likely to know whether it is or is not a virtue, nor can I say whether the just man is happy or unhappy.'

[5] See also Thomas, *Musings*, 74. Thomas distinguishes between two kinds of *hopoion* statements: (*a*) *pathe* and (*b*) properties that do not refer to the essence of the subject. *Pathos* has the form 'Rxy' (e.g. 'gods love holiness') and property the form 'φx' (e.g. 'the rose is red'). He also thinks that 'teachability' in the *Meno* is a property. However, the proposition 'virtue is teachable' could be transformed into 'virtue can be taught to men', having now the form of 'Rxy'.

refers to 'what it is'. Meno, Gorgias and Euthyphro agree that 'teachability' etc. refer to the *hopoion* and not to *ti* question.[6]

Socrates' statement that the *ti* question is prior to the *hopoion* question seems quite strange and has created many discussions.[7] It leads directly to the Meno's paradox (80d–e) that says: 'if one does not know altogether what X is, then it is impossible for him to search for X'. The theory of recollection comes as an answer to the paradox and, in this way, Plato links the first part of the dialogue with the second. I am not going to discuss this problem, but roughly speaking, apart from a strong sense of 'knowledge' it is presupposed a weak one. So if we do not have an acquaintance or familiarity with Meno we cannot say if he is handsome or rich etc. (71b). On the other hand definition of X is epistemically prior to other statements about X (like in mathematics).

Therefore, we can conclude that (1) in any case, we have to distinguish between what is it, or *ti* statements, and what sort of, or *hopoion* statements. (2) *Hopoion* statements cannot be definitions. (3) Definitions, or *ti* statements are prior to *hopoion* statements.

B. MENO'S FIRST DEFINITION

After Socrates' insistence, Meno defines virtue (71e–72a) as follows:

But it is not difficult to say, Socrates. First, if you want to know virtue in a man, it is easy to say that man's virtue is to be capable of taking part in the affairs of the city, and in doing so to do good for his friends and harm to his enemies, and to take care that he does not himself suffer anything like that. If you want to know virtue in a woman, it is not difficult to describe it; she must manage the house well, looking after its contents and being subject to her husband. And there is another sort of virtue in a child, both female and male, and in an old man, if you like, a freeman, or if you like a slave. And there are many other sorts of virtue, so that there is no difficulty in saying what virtue is; for there is a virtue for each of us according to each activity and time of life, and for each task, and in the same way, I think, Socrates, with badness.

Socrates replies ironically that he is very lucky because although he was looking for only one virtue he has found many. And, he continues by stating the reason

---

[6] The distinction between *ti* and *hopoion* is the first effort in the history of philosophy to distinguish between two kinds of attributes of a subject. More generally, with Plato's early dialogues we have the first effort to tackle the problem of definition. Distinctions are made for the first time and the words used are not yet fixed terms. Aristotle's term for definition (*horismos*) is never used by Plato, and the words *horos* and *horizesthai* mean rather 'boundary mark' and 'delimiting'. As Charles Kahn says (*Plato and the Socratic Dialogue* (Cambridge: CUP, 1996), 172), 'Although it is irresistibly convenient to speak of "the dialogues of definition" we need to bear in mind that we come upon the concept of definition here *in statu nascendi*.'

[7] For a good discussion on this topic see Gregory Vlastos, 'Is the "Socratic Fallacy" Socratic?', in Vlastos, *Socratic Studies* (Cambridge: CUP, 1994), 67–86, and Kahn, *Plato and Socratic Dialogue*, 157–64, 180–2.

why Meno's definition is not acceptable and one of the requirements for a proper definition, which we can call the Unity Assumption.

> Similarly then with regard to the virtues; even if they are many and of all kinds, at any rate they all have some one identical character (*en ge ti eidos tauton*) on account of which they are virtues. And it is right, I suppose, for the person who is answering to fix his sight on this and to reveal to the person who has asked the question that thing which is virtue. (72c6–d1).[8]

Socrates not only states the Unity Assumption but also gives some examples as illustrations of it (bees, health, tallness, strength) and he proceeds to a kind of proof of it, in the case of virtue (73a–c).

Let us now consider Meno's definition. The first thing we can say about it is that it is a definition by enumerating and defining various kinds of virtue.[9] In the modern theory of sets, it is permissible to define a set either by listing all its elements or by stating their common property. For example, the set of natural numbers 1, 3, 5, or the set of odd natural numbers less than 6. Also, in traditional logic, we distinguish between the extension and the intension of a concept. The extension of a concept (or a predicate) is the class of objects that it describes, while the intension is the principle (usually one or more properties) under which it picks them out. When we 'define' or determine a concept by its extension we have to exhaust all the extension of it, or, in other words, to enumerate all the objects falling under this concept and only these. Meno's division is not exhaustive, although there is the suggestion that he is able to find and define all the kinds of virtue.[10]

Moreover, Meno's definition is not exactly a definition by enumeration of the various kinds of virtue qua virtue, but according to their reference, that is, according to the bearers or possessors of virtue. We do not have parts of virtue, but classes of people to which virtue applies (72a3–4). Such divisions of classes can be made in many ways according to various characteristic marks (men–women, old–young, freemen–slaves, citizens–non citizens, educated–uneducated, etc.).

According now to Socrates, a correct definition of virtue must reveal: (*a*) a common characteristic of all instances of what we call 'virtue'[11] (see 72c6, 'one identical character', d8 'the same character everywhere'); (*b*) this common

---

[8] Cf. *Laches* 191e: 'What is that common quality, which is the same in all these cases, and which is called courage?'; also, *Euthyphro* 6d: 'but about that characteristic itself (*auto to eidos*) by which all holy things are holy'.

[9] This is not a definition by examples. The 'many' virtues that Meno enumerates are types and not tokens of X. See Lesley Brown, 'Plato *Theaetetus* 145–147', in *Proc. Arist. Soc.* (1994), 231, and A. Nehamas, 'Confusing Universals and Particulars in Plato's Early Dialogues', in A. Nehamas, *Virtues of Authenticity* (Princeton: PUP, 1999), 165.

[10] See 72a: 'And there are many other sorts of virtue, so that there is no difficulty in saying what virtue is; for there is a virtue for each of us according to each activity and time of life.'

[11] Also, *Euthyphro* 6d10, *Laches* 191e.

characteristic must be exactly what makes all these things to be virtues (72c8, 'because of which they are all virtues')[12]. This characteristic not only distinguishes virtue from all other things, but it constitutes the essence (72b1–2, 'what is the essential nature—*peri ousias pot' estin*') or the explanatory cause of something's being virtue.[13] (*c*) At 72c8–d1 Socrates says that 'it is right for the person who is answering to fix his sight on this (e.g. the common form) and to reveal to the person who has asked the question that thing which is virtue'. In *Euthyphro* 6e, we are told that knowing this common character we may look at it and use it as a standard (*paradeigma*) in order to be able to judge whether or not our actions are holy.[14] We may infer then that a definition of X can also be used as a paradigm for judging specific cases, or give the rule for someone's being X.

In conclusion we can say that Meno's first definition of virtue is one by enumeration of various kinds of virtue according to the various agents to which virtue applies. The definition is refuted not because the division is not exhaustive, but because of its form. It violates Socrates' requirement that a good definition reveals a common characteristic of all instances that is also the essential one.

C. MENO'S SECOND DEFINITION

At 73c9–d1 Meno gives the following definition: 'Virtue is the capacity to govern men.' This definition is not a *hopoion* statement and is not by enumeration. Therefore, it does have the right form.[15] However, the form alone does not guarantee the correctness of a definition.

Socrates immediately replies to Meno that children and slaves cannot govern men. Therefore, the definition is easily refuted by a counterexample.[16] The extension of the definiens seems to be larger than that of the definiendum. Socrates tries to revise the definition by adding the word 'justly'.[17] After that, he proceeds to criticize this revised definition in another way. Justice is not virtue

---

[12] Similarly, *Euthyphro* 6d11 and *Hippias Major* 289d: 'The beautiful itself, by which everything else is beautified, and seems to be beautiful when that form is added to it.'
[13] From this passage it seems that Plato asks for a real definition. He does not want only to distinguish X from all other things but also to find the essence of X. If so, there is only one proper definition for X. Nevertheless in 75a–76a, Socrates gives two different definitions of 'shape' without saying that only the one of them is a good definition. For the problem of the kind of definition Plato has in mind in the *Meno*, see David Charles's contribution to this volume.
[14] In *Charmides* 158e–159a, Socrates asks Charmides to define temperance in order to discover whether he already possesses that virtue. In *Laches* 190b, Socrates is trying to find what virtue is, in order to see in what way virtue may be imparted to boys.
[15] See Meno's statement at 73d1: '*eiper en ge ti zeteis kata panton*' (if you are looking for some one thing applying to all).
[16] For refutation by counterexamples see also *Laches* 190e–191b, 192e–193b, *Gorgias* 454a, *Republic* I. 331c, *Hippias Major* 301e, *Charmides* 159c.
[17] See 73d7–8: 'Shall we not add to this that it is being able to do so justly and not unjustly?'

but one (or, a part of) virtue.[18] There are also other virtues like courage, temperance, wisdom, dignity, etc. So the definition now becomes 'virtue is the capacity to govern with justice, courage, wisdom etc.'. And Socrates comments after that (74a): 'The same thing has happened to us once again, Meno; once again we have found many virtues when we were looking for one, but in a different way from what happened just now.'

What Plato tells us in this passage is (A) that when we have a definition of the right form (one over many) we must check whether we can find counterexamples. In this case, definiens and definiendum do not have the same extension, the definition is refuted and the characteristic mark of the definition (*differentia*) is not the right one. (B) If the extension of the definiens is larger than that of the definiendum, we can revise the definition by adding to the definiens one more qualification. (C) We must be careful not to identify a part with the whole (or a species with the genus). (D) If we consider the notion to be defined as a genus, then a definition through enumeration of the species of this genus is not a valid definition, not having the correct form.

D. MENO'S THIRD DEFINITION

After the refutation of Meno's second definition, Socrates gives three examples (*paradeigmata*, 79a10) of correct definitions (75b–77a). Immediately after, Socrates asks Meno again to give a new definition. Meno defines virtue as follows (77b3–4): 'I think that virtue is, as the poet says, "to rejoice in fine things and have the power"; and I say that this is what virtue is, to desire fine things and have the power to get them.' But since 'fine things' are 'good things', and everybody desires good things (78b5–6), we conclude that the phrase 'desiring good things' does not add anything and therefore is a superfluous element in the definition. We can call this principle the Economy Principle. In a definition, superfluous elements that do not qualify the definiendum must be dropped.

The definition is now revised as follows: 'virtue is the ability to get good things' (78c1). But unjust acquisition of good things is not virtue (78d5–6). Therefore, since we find a counterexample, the definition is not valid. And since the extension of the definens is larger than that of the definiendum, we can revise the definition by restricting the extension of the definiens. So, 'virtue is the acquisition of good things with justice, or with one of the other parts of virtue' (78d8–e1).[19] But now, 'the not getting good things when this acquisition is

---

[18] Socrates insists on this point by giving an example. He wants us to be careful not to identify a part with the whole (or a species with the genus). More generally he says that inclusion relations are different from identity relations. See also *Protagoras* 350c–d, *Euthyphro* 11e–12a, 12c.

[19] In *Laches* (192b–d), Laches defines courage as 'endurance of the soul'. But because there are cases of endurance of the soul that cannot be courage (the extension of definiens is broader than that of the definiendum), the definition is revised with the addition of the word 'wise' in the definiens.

unjust, is also virtue' (e4–5). Thus there are cases of virtue that fall outside of the extension of the definiens. With this counterexample we find that the extension of the definiendum is broader than that of the definiens. Therefore the definition is restrictive and we have to revise it by dropping a qualification from the definiens. So, Socrates remarks at 78e6–79a1: 'getting good things won't be virtue any more than not-getting, but, as it seems, whatever comes about with justice is virtue, and whatever comes about without all these things is badness'. In this way we obtain the last definition (79b5): 'Doing whatever one does, with a part of virtue, that is virtue.'[20] But even this definition is unacceptable for two reasons: (*a*) because we have arrived again at a definition through enumeration of the parts of virtue (see 79a9–10: 'Because I asked you just now not to break up virtue or chop it into little pieces') and (*b*) because in this definition the word 'virtue' appears both in the definiendum and the definiens and such a definition does not define anything.[21] Finally, Socrates concludes with a remark that one cannot know the parts without first knowing the whole, that is to say, the definition of a genus is prior to the definition of the species[22] (see 79c8–9: 'and do you think that someone knows what a part of virtue is, when he does not know what virtue itself is?').

Let me now summarize what results from Meno's third definition. First of all we have the Economy Principle: predicates that do not qualify the definiendum are useless for the definition. Secondly, in a definition having the right form, it is possible that the extension of the definiens is broader than that of the definiendum or vice versa. In these cases we can refute the definition through a counterexample. If we want to correct (or to revise) such a definition, in the first case we must restrict and in the other case broaden the extension of the definiens by

---

Similarly in *Gorgias* 454a–b, rhetoric is defined as 'the art of persuasion' (453a). However, there are also other arts that produce persuasion, like arithmetic (453e). Therefore, the definition is broad and is revised by restricting the definiens: 'rhetoric is the art of persuasion in jury-courts, and in other mobs, and about the things that are just and unjust' (454b).

[20] In *Laches* (195a1–2), courage is defined as 'the knowledge of the fearful and hopeful things'. This definition is criticized by Socrates as being restrictive because 'the fearful and the hopeful, are admitted to be future goods and future evils' (199b3–4), while courage 'is concerned not only with good and evil in the future, but of the present and past, and of any time' (199b8–c1). After that Socrates revises the definition by broadening the extension of the definiens (199c3–d2): 'Then the answer which you have given, Nicias, includes only a third part of courage; but our question extended to the whole nature of courage: and according to your view, that is, according to your present view, courage is not only the knowledge of the hopeful and the fearful, but seems to include nearly every good and evil without reference to time. What do you say to that alteration in your statement?'

[21] See 79b7–c1: 'This is what I mean, that while I asked you to say what virtue is as a whole, you are far from saying what it is itself, but say that every action is virtue if it is done with a part of virtue ... So you need to start again with the same question, as it seems to me, my dear Meno; what is virtue, if every action would be virtue if accompanied by a part of virtue'. In other words, it seems that Plato rejects circular definitions, at least directly

[22] It is probably anachronistic to speak here for genus and species. Parts and wholes denote probably something more than species and genus. However, in this specific case of virtue I think that it is permissible to speak of genus and species. See also Brown, 'Plato *Theaetetus* 145–147', 236–8.

adding or dropping one (or more) qualification. Definitions in which the notion to be defined appears in the definiens do not define anything. The definition of a genus is prior to the definition of its species. This is another explanation of why definitions by enumeration are not acceptable.

E. SOCRATES' DEFINITIONS

So far, Plato has distinguished between *ti* and *hopoion* statements. The latter cannot be definitions. Later on, he has given us (kinds of) bad definitions and ways to refute them. Also, he has told us how to revise and correct a definition that is either too broad or too narrow. Moreover, he has told us about the right form of a definition and has given us rules for formulating correct definitions. But it seems that all these are not enough. In 75b–77a he gives three examples of correct or proper definitions, which I am going to examine now.

1. 75b10: 'shape is that which alone of the things that are, always accompanies colour'. This is a very strange definition, at least for the modern reader. We would expect a definition by genus and differentia and we find a totally different pattern. Meno objects to this definition, but not because of its pattern. His objection is that we define shape using an unknown (or not yet defined) term, namely colour. Therefore, if Socrates had asked Meno beforehand, 'do you agree that there is something called colour which is this and this?' then Meno should have been satisfied with the definition. Socrates believes that the definition is good and that he would be satisfied if Meno could give a similar definition with regard to virtue (75c1).

2. After Meno's criticism, Socrates agrees to give another definition of shape. However, before doing that, he agrees with the Meno on the meaning of some relevant terms (limit, plane, solid). The second definition of shape is as following: 76a 'shape is the limit of a solid'. This definition is a geometrical one (see 76a2, 'for example those in geometry') and at first sight is formulated according to the pattern of genus and differentia. Meno agrees immediately with this definition.

3. Meno now asks Socrates to give a definition of colour and Socrates says that he will give a definition in the style of Gorgias (76c4). Again they agree on some relevant terms according to Empedocles' theory of sight (c7–d3) and the definition follows (d4–5): 'Colour is an effluence from shapes which is commensurate with sight and perceptible.' Meno finds this definition very good (d6–7), while Socrates has his reservations.[23]

---

[23] In *Laches* we find also two definitions proposed by Socrates. At 192b1–2 he defines 'quickness' as 'the quality, which accomplishes much in a little time'. This definition is given as an example of what Socrates wants when he asks about one common quality, which is the same in all cases. At 198b he defines 'fear' as 'the expectation of a future evil'.

Let me now comment on the three definitions. The first definition states that everywhere we have colour shape accompanies it. Or, in other words, it states that we cannot have colour without shape. This wording allows the possibility of having shape without colour. However, in this case the definition of shape would not really be a definition because it would not include all things that fall under the name 'shape'. Therefore we have to accept that, according to Plato, 'shape' and 'colour' have exactly the same extension.[24] The definition states a relation between colour and shape and provides a distinguishing mark. Having an acquaintance with colours, we are able to distinguish shape from everything else. Is this relation an essential one? Or, in other words, is there a causal priority of colour? *Charmides* 168e, suggests this option ('and the vision? If it sees itself, it is necessary for it to have colour. Because vision cannot see anything without colour'). In this way we see only colours, and the shapes we see are due to differences of colour.[25]

On the other hand, this definition seems to rely on our sense of sight. Similarly we could define shape through the sense of touch (imagine someone being blind). In this case shape and colour are not related. Also, do abstract geometrical shapes have colour?[26] It seems then that this definition is valid only for visible shapes.[27] Another problem concerns the priority of the term 'colour'. It might be argued exactly the opposite: that 'shape is more fundamental than colour, and so should not be defined in terms of it'.[28] Plato, in *Timaeus* (67c–68d) considers that colours are secondary qualities that depend on the various kinds (namely, shapes) and sizes of the atoms.[29]

As I said, the second definition is a geometrical one and seems to have the standard pattern of a definition by genus and differentia. But is 'solid' the genus of 'shape' or 'figure'? From Aristotle and Euclid, we know that lines produce plane figures and plane figures produce solids. Similarly in the *Timaeus* (53c–54c), Plato's regular solids are constituted by plane figures (surfaces), these ones by the two well-known triangles,[30] and the triangles by lines. Therefore, it seems that 'shape' or 'figure' is the genus of solid and not the converse. But also the later history of this definition is interesting. We find it in Aristotle (see *Topics*

---

[24] Others who support the co-extensiveness of the two terms are: Sharples, *Plato*, 131; Thomas, *Musings*, 98–9; J. Klein, *A Commentary on Plato's Meno*, (Durham, NC: North Carolina UP, 1965), 59. If the two terms are co-extensive we are entitled to define colour in the same way (colour is that which accompanies shape). Therefore the one definition would be the conversion of the other. However, neither Meno nor Socrates criticizes the pattern of the definition.

[25] R. Hoerber, 'Plato's Meno', *Phronesis* (1960), 96–7, claims that this definition of shape is the 'deepest philosophically' and the only one that reveals an insight into the causes.

[26] I owe this remark to David Charles.

[27] See also Thomas, *Musings*, 100; Sharples, *Plato*, 132.

[28] See Sharples, *Plato*, 132.

[29] Of course, someone could reply that when Plato wrote the *Meno* he had not yet formed his physical theory.

[30] The one is the isosceles right-angled, and the other the right-angled which is half of the equilateral.

141ᵇ4–25;[31] also *Metaph.* 1060ᵇ14–17, *Categ.* 5ᵃ2–5) who speaks critically about it. Also, in Euclid's *Elements* we find in the list of definitions three strange statements, immediately after each of the definitions of 'line', 'surface' (*epiphaneia*), and 'solid'. These statements are the following: (1) the limits (*perata*) of a line are points (def. I. 3), (2) the limits of a surface are lines (def. I. 6), and (3) the limits of a solid are surfaces (def. XI. 2). It is certain that these three statements are remnants from an early period in geometry. These statements were the old definitions of point, line, and surface (or shape) as we see also from the above passages from Aristotle. These definitions were probably challenged by some people (including Aristotle—see the passage from the *Topics*) and were replaced by others.[32] But Euclid kept them, changing the order of the two terms. That is to say, 'the limits of a solid are surfaces' instead of 'shape is the limit of the solid' making in this way the genus species and conversely.

We saw before that, according to Plato, there is a priority of the genus with regard to its parts or species. How is it possible then to propose such a definition? The only answer I can give is that, at the time Plato wrote the *Meno*, geometry was not yet organized in a proper axiomatic and hierarchical system. Therefore, he thought of the 'solid' as the genus of 'shape' and not the converse.[33] Moreover,

---

[31] 'That the definition has not been stated in more intelligible terms can be taken in two senses, namely, that it is composed in terms which are less intelligible either absolutely or to us.... Thus absolutely the prior is more intelligible than the posterior; for example, a point is more intelligible than a line, a line than a plane, and a plane than a solid.... To us, however, the converse sometimes happens; for a solid falls most under our perception, and a plane more than a line.... Absolutely, then, it is better to aim at knowledge of the posterior by means of what is prior; for such a method is more scientific. Nevertheless, for the benefit of those who are incapable of acquiring knowledge by such means, it is perhaps necessary to frame the description by means of terms, which are intelligible to them. Among definitions of this kind are those of the point, the line, and the plane; for all these demonstrate the prior by means of the posterior—the point being called the limit of the line, the line that of the plane, the plane that of the solid. We must not, however, fail to notice that it is impossible for those who define in this way to show the essence of the subject of their definition.' (Tra E. S. Forster, Loeb Classical Library, 1960.)

[32] See also T. Heath, *Euclid: The Thirteen Books of the Elements* (Cambridge: CUP, 1926), i. 165; V. Karasmanis, 'The Hypotheses of Mathematics in Plato's *Republic* and his Contribution to the Axiomatization of Geometry', in P. Nicolacopoulos (ed.), *Greek Studies in the Philosophy and History of Science* (Dordrecht: Kluwer, 1990), 128–9.

[33] It seems that the first axiomatization of geometry takes place within the Academy. According to Proclus (*In Primum Euclidis Elementorum Librum Commentarii*, ed. Friedlein, (Lipsiae, 1873 (65–8) on the evidence of Eudemus (pupil of Aristotle who wrote the first history of geometry) all the major mathematicians of the 4th cent. were members of the Academy or associated with it. He mentions three geometers who wrote Elements of Geometry before Euclid. The first is Hippocrates of Chios who worked in Athens at the end of the 5th cent. The other two are Leon and Theudius, both members of the Academy. The first evidence that we have about an axiomatized geometry is from Plato's *Republic* 510c–d. Here, he says clearly that geometers posit at the beginning principles (for Plato they are hypotheses) for which they do not give any argument, and are considered 'plain to all'. Let's see now which *Elements* Plato had in mind when he wrote the *Republic*. First of all we have to note that when Proclus speaks of Elements of Geometry this does not necessarily mean *axiomatized Elements*. Proclus (or rather Eudemus) says for Hippocrates just that he was the first who wrote *Elements* (65. 7–8), while for Leon that 'he compiled a book of elements more carefully designed' (66. 20–2) and for Theudius (67. 14–16) that 'he produced an admirable arrangement of

this definition does not cover all cases of shapes, for example, shapes or figures drawn on a blackboard, on the earth, or on a piece of paper. It also fits better with three-dimensional shapes, although it seems that Plato has in mind two-dimensional shapes as well (see 74d–e).[34]

The definition of colour is based on Empedocles' theory of vision. It is a definition in the framework of an empirical theory related to the world of human experience. If this theory is refuted or challenged, then the definition collapses. It is rather an explanation of how we perceive colours than a definition. However, it is not a bad definition for a physical theory and I believe that even Plato in the *Timaeus* (where he considers his physics as a 'likely myth') would be able to propose such a definition.[35] We have also to note that this definition of colour uses the word 'shape'. But this is probably because shape has been already defined.

F. EVALUATION OF SOCRATES' THREE DEFINITIONS

All three definitions are examples of good definitions. They all fulfil Plato's criteria for a good definition: (*a*) the extension of the definiendum is the same as that of the definiens,[36] (*b*) we have one characteristic common to all cases (one over many), and (*c*) they reveal the cause of something's being X.[37] But not all definitions are equally good. For Meno, the best definition is the third and the worst the first. For Socrates, the worst definition is the third. But still, it is a good definition in a limited area: in the area of an empirical physical theory. But Socrates seeks probably for something more.

Therefore, our problem is which of the first two definitions is better according to Plato. In my experience, most people believe that the second definition is the best. Regarding the first definition, Socrates himself says that he would be satisfied if Meno could define 'virtue' in the same way as he defined shape (75c1–2). But he does not make any comment on the second definition of 'shape'. There are two possibilities: (*a*) both definitions are equally good, or

---

the elements'. Apart from what Proclus says, I believe that Hippocrates' Elements were not axiomatized for two reasons. First, by Plato's silence in his dialogues before the *Republic* about first principles in geometry, but mainly because of the way in which Hippocrates used the word 'principle' (*arche*). In the text of Eudemus (reported by Simplicius, *In Physics*, ed. Diels, 60–8) where he speaks about Hippocrates' quadratures of Lunes the word *arche* is used to describe not first principles but theorems useful to solve his problems. Moreover, there is no evidence that Hippocrates worked on definitions or other kind of principles. Therefore, I think that when Plato wrote the *Meno* geometry had not yet been organized into an axiomatic system.

[34] In this latter case, a definition like 'the limit of a surface of a solid' would be more appropriate.
[35] After all, Plato's theory of vision is quite close to that of Empedocles.
[36] Or, at least, nobody raises question against that.
[37] I prefer not to refer to the essence of X, because it is not clear what for Plato is the essence of something here.

(*b*) one of them is better than the other. In the first case, we would have to admit that Plato permits at least two good definitions for the same thing. But the Unity Assumption tells us that a definition must also reveal the essence of the thing defined. Therefore, we would have to admit that, according to Plato, one and the same thing might have two essences, or that he did not notice this strange consequence. If on the other hand we want to avoid this dilemma, we have to suppose that one of the two definitions of shape is better than the other.[38]

In this case, I am inclined to believe that, for Plato, the second definition is the best one, because the first refers rather to the sensible world. However, we do not have to dismiss the first definition. I say that, not only because of Socrates' statement for this definition, but also because the second definition is restricted in the area of geometry. It is a definition for geometrical shapes and not for 'shape' in general. As I said, the third definition is good only in the framework of an empirical theory. Similarly we can say that the second definition is good, but only in the framework of geometry. From this point of view we might say that the first definition is the most general.

Meno objects to Socrates' first definition because the term 'colour' is not known. It is not certain whether or not Socrates accepts this criticism. First of all he says he would be satisfied if Meno could give a similar definition of virtue. On the other hand he agrees to give another definition of shape. At 79d he says 'if you remember, when I gave you an answer just now about shape, we rejected the sort of answer, I think, that tries to give an answer in terms of things that are still being searched for and have not yet been agreed on'. From this passage one may infer that Meno's criticism was quite strong, and even Socrates believes that his first definition has been refuted. However, let us see what this agreement is. At 75e–76a, before the second definition of shape, Socrates agrees with Meno on some relevant terms:

Tell me, do you say there is such a thing as an end? I mean like a limit and an extremity—I mean the same by all these; perhaps Prodicus would disagree with us, but you at any rate I suppose say that there is such a thing as 'having been limited' and 'having ended'—this is the sort of thing I mean, nothing complicated. . . . Well then, do you say there is such a thing as a surface, and again such a thing as a solid, for example like those in geometry?

It is impossible for one to believe that the 'agreement' on the terms 'limit', 'surface', 'solid', etc. means definition of these terms. They rather agree on the meaning or the use of a term, or on the existence of a thing ('do you say there is such a thing', 'I mean like a limit', 'this is the sort of thing I mean'; or later before

---

[38] In the case that one definition is better than the other we may suppose that the best one refers to the essence while the other is an account of what the name signifies. Even in the case that both definitions are equally good, there is the possibility that neither of them refers to the essence, but we have two good accounts of what X signifies. For the distinction of these two kinds of definitions, see Charles's contribution to this volume.

the third definition: 'do you speak of certain effluences')[39] Therefore, if Socrates had asked Meno before the first definition 'do you agree that there is something called colour which is this and this?' then Meno should have been satisfied with this definition. So, we cannot accept that Socrates really believes that his first definition was rejected.

Is there any conclusion from all this discussion? The only certain thing is the advice that, before giving a definition, we ought to agree on the relevant terms and so avoid vagueness in the terms we use. But this agreement does not necessarily mean 'giving a definition'. Also, we may have 'definitions' for specific purposes, or areas, like the definition of colour. It seems that, although Plato gives techniques to refute bad definitions, and also some rules that a good definition must obey, still he does not have a method for finding definitions. We have to wait until the *Sophist* for a new Platonic contribution on this topic.

However, and apart from all these difficulties regarding definition, I hope that I have managed to support my main thesis, that in the first part of the *Meno*, Plato summarizes and presents all his findings so far on that problem. So we find in the *Meno* rather a theory of definition (more or less complete), not simply the refutation of three bad definitions of virtue. Plato is then ready to continue the dialogue by exposing his other new ideas and theories.[40]

---

[39] It is very important for the notions we use to be clear to interlocutors and not vague. See *Laches* 198b: 'And now let us proceed a step, and try to arrive at a similar agreement about the fearful and the hopeful: I do not want you to be thinking one thing and us another.' See also *Charmides* 161c–162a, *Gorgias* 453b, 451e, 489e, 491b–c, *Protagoras* 341a–c, *Republic* I. 331e.

[40] I am grateful to David Charles for his valuable comments and suggestions. For helpful comments, I am also grateful to Vasilis Politis, Richard McKirahan, and Pantazis Tselemanis.

9

Sharing a Property

Theodore Scaltsas

The Socratic discussion in the *Hippias Major* 300–303, is not a passing comment on plural reference; it is a theory of plural subjecthood. It has escaped attention because it is a small part of a larger complex argument on the topic of which pleasures are fine. Socrates' theory is further concealed by the fact that it is presented as an antithesis between Hippias and himself, whereas in fact Hippias' position shares much with Socrates' theory. I begin by examining Hippias' position, and subsequently Socrates' criticism of it. I then turn to Socrates' further proposal, and the development of a theory of plural subjects that incorporates elements of Hippias' position, and Socrates' own. At the end, I address the question of the ontology of plural subjects. I argue that the key to sharing a property between subjects is not in the way that the plural terms refer to these subjects together, or in any decomposition of the commonly owned property instance into parts distributed to these subjects. Plural subjects own a property instance together by doing just that and nothing more, namely, by collaborating in owning that property instance together. I develop an account of how this metaphysical function of collaborative ownership can be performed by the plural subjects without threatening their distinctness or their plurality.[1]

HIPPIAS' THESIS

1. Distributive plural predication

Hippias argues for the position that, if some things are f, each of them is f, too; and if each of them is f, they are f, as well. Or:

---

[1] This chapter developed from ideas in my earlier paper (Scaltsas 2003). I am grateful to many colleagues for criticisms and suggestions on earlier versions of this paper presented at the Royal Institute of Philosophy Symposium on 'Being One: A Symposium on the Nature of Unity', University of Manchester; the workshop on 'Nominalizations and Abstract Objects', University of Stirling; the philosophy colloquia at the universities of Leeds; Liverpool; Bologna; Rome—Centro Nazionale per la Ricerca; and Edinburgh. Special thanks go to David Charles for his very constructive criticisms.

[D] Some (of *a*) are *f* iff each of them is *f*.

His defence is the following:

HIPPIAS: If both of us were just, wouldn't each of us be too? Or if each of us were unjust, wouldn't both of us? Or if we were healthy, wouldn't each be? Or if each of us had some sickness or were wounded or stricken or had any other tribulation, again, wouldn't both of us have that attribute? Similarly, if we happened to be gold or silver or ivory, or, if you like, noble or wise or honoured or even old or young or anything you like that goes with human beings, isn't it really necessary that each of us be that as well? SOCRATES: Of course. (*Hippias Major* 300e8–301b1)

The examples offered by Hippias are not in themselves objectionable. All cases mentioned are recognizable and uncontroversial ways of speaking about people, and by extension, about any other entity. The problematic aspect of his position is the necessity claim. Hippias mentions the necessity in the latter case only: e.g. if we are wise, then necessarily each of us is wise. But it will be clear from his rejection of the Socratic position that he means the necessity to hold in the opposite direction too: e.g. if each of us is just, then necessarily we are just.

The necessity claim is problematic since, although it is true that if we are wise it may be that each of us is that too; it is not the case that if we are wise, necessarily each of us is wise. For instance, if we are heavy, e.g. too heavy for the elevator, it may be that only one of us is heavy. And similarly in the opposite direction, if each of us sings melodically, it does not follow that we sing melodically together.

A second problem with Hippias' position is his universality claim, namely that his theory holds for any attribute of human beings. As we shall see, Socrates will find some attributes that human beings may have, without each of them having them, and vice versa. So Hippias' examples are acceptable, but his necessity and universality claims face counterexamples.

The prima-facie way of reading Hippias' statements invites a *distributive* reading. If each of us is unjust, we are unjust; and if we are just, each of us is just too. Taking a further step, we can in fact pay justice to Hippias' necessity claim by assuming that, for him, not only is it the case that if each of us is just, we are just, too; but further, that we are just *only* because each of us is just; the instantiation of an attribute in each individual is the ground for both individual and plural predication; and if it is the only ground, there would be no other way for us to be just than each of us being just. Indeed Hippias says: 'Never shall you find what is attributed to neither me nor you, but is attributed to both of us' (300d7–8). If this is assumed, his necessity claim (301a5–7) is justified.

The reason that I am not entirely satisfied in attributing this position to Hippias is that Hippias seems to find the ground for individual and plural predications in his metaphysical doctrine of the continuous theory of being, to which I shall now turn.

2. The metaphysics of Hippias' position

To understand Hippias' position better, we need to look at the metaphysical grounding that he attempts to give to it. This is the notoriously cryptic doctrine of the continuous theory of being.

> The *continuous theory of being*, according to Hippias, does not allow it to be otherwise, but whatever both are, that each is as well; and whatever each is, both are. (301e3–5, my emphasis)

The challenge is to derive Hippias' theory of language from his metaphysics. The distributive reading of plural predications is the most straightforward way of understanding that if both then each, and if each then both. What metaphysical picture could justify such a reading, namely that attributes are attributed to many individuals only if they belong to each of these individuals, and if they do belong to each, they are true of all? Can this position be derived from Hippias' own metaphysics?

The only glimpse we get of Hippias' continuous theory of being is given in the following passage:

(1) But Socrates, you don't look at the entireties of things (*ta hola tôn pragmatôn*), nor do the people you're used to talking with. You people knock away at the fine (*kalon*) and the other beings (*onta*) by taking each separately and cutting it up with words. Because of that you don't realize how great (*megala*) they are—naturally continuous bodies of being (*dianeké sômata tês ousias*). (301b2–7)

(2) And now you're so far from realizing it [i.e. how great they are—naturally continuous bodies of being] that you think there's some attribute (*pathos*) or being (*ousia*) that is true of these both but not of each, or of each but not of both. (301b7–c2)

Hippias' position divides into two parts. Both parts derive from criticisms of Socrates, i.e. that Socrates fails to recognize the *magnitude* and *continuity* of the beings such as the fine and other attributes. In consequence, for Hippias, Socrates engages in cutting up an attribute through its definition into its constituents (corresponding to the terms in these definitions). And further, Socrates fails to realize that an attribute's being true of things individually goes hand in hand with its being true of them together.

The text of both the Hippian doctrine and his Socratic criticisms is extremely condensed, metaphorical, and rich in philosophically loaded terminology. All this makes for a multiply ambiguous text. The combinations are numerous; it would be tedious to enumerate them, and numbing to analyse and interpret them. I shall only register my conclusions, while occasionally mentioning lines of interpretation I did not follow.

What is given, or surmised, is, on the one hand, what Socrates should have realized and, on the other, the mistakes he made because he did not. The challenge for us is to see why, if Socrates had realized what Hippias was bidding him to, he would not have adopted the positions he did. According to Hippias, Socrates failed to see the entireties of things (*pragmata*), the greatness of the beings (*ta onta*) such as the fine (*kalon*), and the natural continuity of such beings. Is seeing the entireties of things the same as seeing the greatness of the beings? If yes, how is this related to cutting up the beings into components through definitions?[2] Is it that we miss out on their entirety and greatness, as well as on their continuity, when we dissect them? Is Hippias criticizing Socrates further (i.e. over and above the dissection charge) for ontologically singling out each of the beings (through its definition), cutting it off and isolating it from its instances and from the other beings, or is this not meant to be suggested by the text? If it is, could it be that the entirety of things includes the instances along with the beings, and that the greatness and continuity of the beings consists in their connectedness with these instances? More combinations are possible, with equally little textual ground to walk on.

The second Hippian criticism of Socrates is that, not realizing the greatness and the continuity of the beings, Socrates did something worse than cutting up the beings; he thought that the beings could be true of a number of individuals without being true of each of them, or be true of each of the individuals but not of them together. Hippias is clearly suggesting that metaphysics simply precludes the aforementioned possibilities. This direction in the chain of explanation is so important that it is repeated soon after in the text, in a stronger form: 'The continuous theory of being, according to Hippias, *does not allow it to be otherwise*, but whatever both are, that each is as well; and whatever each is, both are' (301e3–5, my emphasis). The challenge then is to find a way of accounting for the nature of the beings (such as the fine) so as to derive from this account the Hippian restrictions on the way these beings can be attributed to individuals singly or together.

In an ancestral version of this paper, I considered George Kerferd's and Robin Waterfield's interpretations of Hippian metaphysics, and found reasons that led me not to adopt either of them (Scaltsas, 2003).

Kerferd thought of the attributes as classes of things (in Taylor 1997: 259). Waterfield attributed a much more complex metaphysical account to Hippias, which required him to charge Hippias with many metaphysical confusions (Waterfield 2000: 252). I have, myself, tried accounting for Hippias' beings in terms of sets, mereological aggregates of instances, fusions of instances, forms supervening on instances, and even Platonic Forms, but I found none that could deliver the Hippian restrictions on how the beings belong to individuals. It is not sufficient even to restrict the Hippian world to a world of individuals only; individuals are all we need for an attribute to belong to many individuals together;

---

[2] We can assume what Hippias has in mind are attempts at explaining or defining terms through other terms, which would deliver the ontological constitution of the first entity through the latter; e.g. if a human is a rational animal, then the entity human is broken up into the constituents of rational and animal.

neither sets nor any other type of complex object are needed. Why should an *instance* of the Hippian fine not be a group of individuals, each of which is not fine? Or why should it not be the case that each individual is just, but they are not? What could block such attachments of the beings to individuals?

The difficulty I have been emphasizing is that no manner of account of the nature of a Hippian being, such as the fine, will deliver his constraint that, whatever both individuals are, each is as well, and whatever each is, both are. He offers us a cryptic description of beings as great, naturally continuous bodies of being. But why should an equivalence between plural and individual predication follow from this? A satisfactory answer has yet to be suggested.

SOCRATES' THESIS

1. Collective plural predication

Socrates argues that there are counterexamples to the Hippian Constraint. Failing to resist irony, he says:

SOCRATES: We were so foolish, my friend, before you [Hippias] said what you did, that we had an opinion about me and you that each of us is one, but that we would not both be one (which is what each of us would be) because we are not one but two. But now, we have been instructed by you that if two is what we both are, two is what each of us must be as well; and if each is one, then both must be one as well.

If each of us is one, wouldn't he also be odd-numbered?... Then will both of us be odd-numbered, being two?

HIPPIAS: It couldn't be, Socrates.

SOCRATES: But both are even-numbered. Then because both are even-numbered, on account of that, each of us is even-numbered as well.

HIPPIAS: Of course not. (301d5–302b1)

Here it is clear that Hippias does not have the distributive way out. Even if we could say that John and George are one, we could not derive from this that John is one and George is one. The predicate 'one' in these statements means something different; in the first it may mean something like 'inseparable friends', while in the latter it would mean 'one person'. Nor is the predication 'we are two' distributive either; neither I nor you are two, despite the fact that we are two.

Still, this does not mean that Hippias has no way out of these counterexamples. For instance he could try to argue that numbers are not properties of things, and do not, therefore, behave as the beings in the world, such as the fine, do. In so doing, Hippias would be in good company: Oliver quotes Frege from the *Grundlagen* (pp. 40–1):

Whereas we can combine 'Solon was wise' and 'Thales was wise' into 'Solon and Thales were wise', we cannot say 'Solon and Thales were one'. But it is hard to see that this should be impossible, if 'one' were a property both of Solon and of Thales in the same way that 'wise' is.[3]

Also, Yi reports that 'On the *standard* conception of property and relation, there is no property like being two', and argues against it (Yi 1999: 166, my emphasis). Yet, we shall see that this is not a way out of the Socratic objection. There are myriads of examples that cannot be neutralized by excising items from the attribute-ontology. So, Socrates:

> When both of anything are even-numbered, each may be either odd- or possibly even-numbered. And again, when each of them is inexpressible, both together may be expressible, or possibly inexpressible. And millions of things like that. (303b6–c1)

Socrates' initial example of 'being two persons' is the simplest to see. Each of Socrates and Hippias is a person, while they are two persons. The attribute of being 'two persons' belongs to them, but not to each of them; it is instantiated only in Socrates and Hippias together. Similarly, if we hear some birds singing and we recognize that 'they are starlings', this is something that none of these birds is on its own, but only they are, together. Such plural predications as 'are two persons' and 'are starlings' are true of all the subjects collectively, but of none of the subjects individually.

2. The metaphysics of the Socratic position

By contrast to Hippias, Socrates' metaphysical account of plural predication is explicit. In collective plural predication the attribute belongs to all the subjects together; this belonging is not reducible to, nor does it need to be grounded on, the attribute belonging to the individual subjects; as the last quotation showed: 'when each of them is inexpressible, both together may be expressible, or possibly inexpressible' (303b7–c1). Let us consider two chords. Each is harmonious and both together disharmonious. Hippias could hold that we are justified in saying that the chords are harmonious since each is harmonious. But it is also true that, played together, the chords are disharmonious. The attribute of being disharmonious belongs to them together, whereas the attribute of being harmonious belongs

---

[3] Oliver (1994: 78). In fact, one can challenge Frege's claim by imagining an admittedly rare context in which one could say 'George and Michael are one': suppose that each person comes to the dinner with or without a partner. Then one could say, counting guests, that George and Michael are one, while Dora is two. It is a strange context, but still using the predicates in a numerical sense, rather than to indicate identity or difference. Oliver (p. 78) argues that for Frege such plural predications as '... are one', or '... are two' are not meant numerically. He quotes Frege as saying in his *Collected Papers* that such a statement: 'is not meant as a statement of number. I find that it is actually used in only two cases: first, with the numeral "two", in order to express difference... and secondly, with the numeral "one", in order to express identity'. For a useful distinction relating to this use of the numerical predicates, see Yi's distinction between pure numerical properties, e.g. being two, and impure ones, e.g. being two humans, in Yi (1999: 188–90).

to each of them individually. This is what is distinctive of the Socratic position: its metaphysics allows that several individuals together can be the subjects of a single instance of an attribute, which may not be instantiated in each individual; and an attribute instantiated in each individual may not be instantiated in all of them together. A plural instantiation can coexist with instances of the same attribute in each of the subjects, as when each chord is harmonious, and they are all harmonious, too; or it can coexist with its opposite, as when chords, each of which is harmonious, are disharmonious together, in which case each possesses an attribute (harmoniousness) which they do not possess together, and they possess an attribute (disharmoniousness) which each fails to possess. This independence is just what Hippias denied when he said: 'how could that be, Socrates? That any state of being whatever could be attributed to neither, since that attribute, which is attributed to neither, is attributed to both?' (300b6–8). Whereas Socrates says that 'it was by the being that adheres to both, if both are . . . [f]—it was by *that* they had to be . . . [f], and not by what falls off one or the other' (302c4–7). But this attribute does not make each of them f: if 'that attribute adheres in both, but not in each . . . then *that's* not what makes each of them . . . [f]; it doesn't adhere in each' (302e5–10).

How does the chord's possession of harmoniousness, which it shares with another chord, differ from the chord's possession of harmoniousness all by itself? The metaphysical innovation of Socrates is that a single instance of an attribute can be shared by a number of subjects; the instance is shared between them; they co-possess it, co-own it. I do not use the term part-own, or part-possess, as it may mislead by suggesting that there are parts of the attribute, each of which is fully possessed by one of the subjects respectively. The attribute in question belongs to a single subject in the sharing-case differently from the way it belongs to it when fully possessed by that subject alone. In the case of shared ownership, only *all* the sharing-subjects together possess the attribute. It is like a statue being supported by two pillars. The statue is not partitioned so that one part of it stands on one pillar, and the other part on the second; nor does the statue stand on the first pillar, or even on the second; rather, the statue stands as a whole on the two pillars. Without both pillars, the statue would fall; the whole statue would fall, not just part of it. In an alternative circumstance, the statue could be supported by several pillars and not fall by the removal of one or more of them, but come to be fully supported by fewer of them. Similarly with the many owners of an instance of an attribute. In the case of their being 'two people', the loss of one would be detrimental to the instantiation of the attribute; in the case of their 'walking', the loss of one or more walkers may not block its instantiation.

A single instance of an attribute that belongs to many subjects together is a case of *plural collective belonging*.

As Socrates explained in the last quotation above, co-possessing f does not make x f. Co-possessing twoness does not make either of the two friends two. Co-possessing disharmony does not make any of the chords disharmonious; each of them may be harmonious on their own, and be disharmonious only with each other. Socrates' position is in fact strong. He says that the individual subject does not come to have any qualification itself on account of jointly possessing f with other subjects: if an 'attribute adheres in both, but not in each . . . then *that's* not what makes each of them . . . [f]; it doesn't adhere in each' (302e5–10) This seems to be a controversial position. In discussion of this paper, David Charles and Allan Back independently expressed the intuition that we would be justified in attributing f-ness to an individual on the basis of shared ownership of it; so, if George is carrying the piano together with Mary, one would be justified in saying that George is carrying the piano, without, of course, thereby committing oneself to George's having carried the piano by himself. On the other hand, in a more Socratic vein, Ian Rumfitt (2002) holds that if 'William and Mary reigned over England', what they did together to England neither of them did to England. (In fact they could not have, since if one of them reigned over England, the other could not have, simultaneously, nor could both of them together, at the same time as either.) Rumfitt takes it that we cannot say that William reigned over England, since he only co-reigned over England with Mary. Yi also argues (1999: 185) that in 'John and Carol carry a piano', the predicate is the same as in 'John carries a piano', which renders the latter sentence false. This is in full agreement with Socrates, in so far as co-owning and instance of f-ness does not make any one of the sharing subjects f.

THE COMBINED POSITION OF DISTRIBUTIVE AND COLLECTIVE PLURAL PREDICATION

Socrates does not reject Hippias' position on plural predication. He does argue that there are counterexamples to Hippias' thesis. But Socrates thinks that the counterexamples are special cases, different from the cases that Hippias explained in his theory. These special cases require a new account; but it does not follow from this that Hippias' examples need to be reconsidered. In fact Socrates says the following:

> We had things that come to belong to particular things in this way: if they come to belong to both, they do to each also; and if to each, to both—all the examples you [Hippias] gave. . . . But the examples I gave were not that way. (303a4–9)

So what is the final theory of plural predication for Socrates? It is that there are many sentences in language with plural terms in the subject place, such as 'we', or 'they', 'both', 'the pleasant by sight and the pleasant by hearing', etc., where the terms refer to many subjects of which the predicate is predicated. It is important to register here that, for Socrates, the question about plural predication has nothing to do with any peculiarity of plural reference. In contemporary accounts, a plural term does not refer singly to each one of the items within its extension, but only to all of them together. But there is nothing in the text to make us think that Socrates considers the way that George is referred to in 'George and John are...' different from the way he is referred to in 'George is...'. In this sense, plural reference for Socrates consists of several singular references.

According to the Socratic combined position, then, one case is provided by the Hippian examples: in some plural predications, if the predicate is true of many subjects it is also true of each of them, and vice versa. But Socrates does not follow the reductive metaphysics which I used in understanding the examples of Hippias. That is, I took it that, in the Hippian examples, attributes need belong to individuals singly only, and on this basis alone both individual and plural predications can be true of them. Instead, Socrates has attributes belong to individuals singly for individual predications, and belong to them collectively for plural predications; he holds a single model of attribute-belonging for both the Hippian examples and the Socratic ones, but explains the difference between the two sets of examples in terms of different dependencies. Specifically, the Socratic model for all cases is that attributes belong to subjects at two levels: the plural or collective level, and also at the level of the individuals. In the Hippian examples, the two belongings go always together; in the Socratic cases, they may diverge.

Thus Socrates says that in the Hippian examples the condition is that if each individual subject possesses an attribute, they all possess it too; and if they all possess it, each of them does too; so Socrates: 'If I am strong and so are you, we're both strong too; and if I am just and so are you, we both are too. And if both, then each' (303b2–4). But in the Socratic examples, this does not hold. If they all possess a property, they need not possess it individually too, and vice versa: 'it's not entirely necessary,... that whatever both and each are, each and both are as well' (302b1–3); 'when both of anything are even-numbered, each may be either odd- or possibly even-numbered. And... when each of them is inexpressible, both together may be expressible, or possibly inexpressible' (303b6–c1).

So, Socrates holds that always attributing a property to many subjects requires that they all possess it together, collectively. In the case of the Hippian examples, if they possess such a property together, they also possess it individually, and vice versa. In the Socratic ones, they may possess it together, but not individually, and vice versa.

It may seem uneconomical to require collective possession of an attribute in the cases of the Hippian examples. Socrates does insist on it explicitly: 'you agreed that they are both and each fine. That's why I thought it was by the being that adheres to both, if both are fine—it was by *that* they had to be fine, and not by what falls off one or the other' (302c3–7).[4] No reason is given for opting for this account of plural predication in the Hippian cases. If Socrates derived his

---

[4] The reasoning of this passage, consisting of the quotation and preceding sentences in the text (3032b8–c3) is this: pleasure through sight and pleasure through hearing are fine in the way of the Hippian examples, not in the way of the Socratic ones, because they are a case where plural and individual belonging go hand in hand. And in such a case, the many are f on account of the f-ness they possess together, not the f-ness each of them possesses (even though in these cases the plural belonging goes always together with the individual one).

metaphysics in the Hippian examples from a distributive reading of plural predication, which I have here attributed to Hippias, he would not have needed the collective possession of a property in the case of the Hippian examples. But for Socrates, 'we are strong' says something about us that is not reducible to statements about the individuals involved, although it may presuppose them. So, my being strong and your being strong makes us strong together; but *our* being strong together is different from, though it may depend on, *each* of us being strong.

A further question is whether a property's behaving according to the Hippian or the Socratic examples with regard to plural and individual possession depends on the type of property it is. On the Socratic side, Peter Simons has suggested a list of predicates that always generate examples of our Socratic type: they are never true of single individuals, e.g. plural number-predicates like 'seven in number', others like 'meet', 'disperse', 'surround', and those that are derived from relational predicates such as 'shaking hands', etc. (Simons 1982: 214). But there is no reason to expect a more general classification of properties or predicates which would entail if they give rise to Hippian or Socratic cases.

For Socrates, the plural phenomenon is metaphysical, rather than semantic or linguistic; the question is not how the plural term refers to the items in its extension—collectively or not; or how the predicate distributes to the subjects. Plural predication rests on the collective belonging of a property to some subjects. In some cases, collective and individual belonging go together; in others, they do not. But how can an attribute belong to a number of individuals, when this is not reducible to its belonging to each of them? To this we shall now turn.

PLURAL SUBJECTS

1. Composition and plural reference

The two most striking features of *plural collective belonging* are: first, in both the Hippian and the Socratic cases, that the subjects are not unified in any way, nor is the property partitioned, in order for the property to belong to these subjects collectively; secondly, in the Socratic cases, that there is a possibility of divergence of the collective from the individual possession of a property by the subjects.

On the first topic, much of the present discussion in the literature is aimed at establishing, against some of the tradition on the subject, that plural reference cannot be handled by singular reference to a special, higher order entity. The tradition here includes, according to Alex Oliver, Frege. Oliver argues against Michael Dummett on this. For Dummett, Frege repudiated pluralities in favour of a predicative analysis of plural terms. Dummett says that, for Frege, ' "All whales are mammals", correctly analysed, has the form "If anything is a whale it is a mammal" '[5] But according to Oliver, 'Frege understood plural noun phrases, when combined with collective predicates, as proper names for complex wholes' (1994: 80). Oliver quotes Frege as saying that 'the phrase "the Romans" in the sentence "the Romans conquered Gaul" is to be regarded as a proper name, for we are not saying of each Roman that he has conquered Gaul; we are speaking of the Roman people, which is to be regarded logically as an object' (Oliver 1994: 75–6).

Against such an account, Peter Simons argues that aggregates and groups are not the *designata* of plural terms (1982: 168–77). George Boolos argues against collections of any kind being such *designata*, urging us to 'abandon, if one ever had it, the idea that use of plural forms must always be understood to commit one to the existence of sets (or "classes", "collections", or "totalities") of those things to which the corresponding singular forms apply' (1984: 442). David Lewis argues against classes, sets, and properties in favour of plural quantification being irreducibly plural (1991: 65–70). Byeong-Uk Yi argues against plural reference being reference to a complex object (1999: 164–6). Ian Rumfitt (2002) argued against sets and fusions, and generally against a singularist account of plural reference. In the present account, no composition of the subjects referred to by the plural term is assumed.

At the same time, there seems to be agreement on the phenomenon of plural reference in the literature, namely on how a plural term refers to the many items individually or somehow jointly. The question discussed is whether a plural term can refer to several objects without referring to any one of them. Yi says, 'The plural term "Bill and Hillary" ... refers to some things, namely Bill and Hillary (as such). This does not mean that the plural term refers to Bill and also to Hillary; it refers to neither of them. A typical plural term refers to some things without referring to any one of them' (Yi 1999: 176). He is not alone in thinking so; Simons (1982: 208), Rumfitt (2002), and Hossack (2002) agree. If this is so, I do not see how this type of reference can avoid being grounded on a sort of composition of the subjects into some kind of complex object. None of the above would agree with this, and I have no argument for this claim at present. But nor do we have an explanation of how such plural reference is effected. In this chapter, I have followed a different route for understanding the phenomenon of plural predication, inspired by the Socratic position. I do not account for it through plural reference, or through composition of plural subjects, or partitioning the attribute into the subjects; rather I centre on how a single instance of an attribute is *possessed* by many subjects without presupposing any of these mechanisms. How the plural term refers to these subjects plays no role in the collective possession of a property by the subjects, while neither subject-composition nor attribute-partitioning occur in collective belonging of an attribute to subjects.

---

[5] In M. Dummett, *Frege: Philosophy of Mathematics* (London: Duckworth, 1991), 93, as Oliver points out (1994: 74).

2. The metaphysics of plural subjects

What is distinctive in the case of plural subjects is that a single instance of a property is jointly owned by several subjects. If we think of a book being commonly owned by two siblings, then we get the sense in which a single instance of a property is commonly owned by some subjects. The book is not divided between the two siblings so that one of them owns the first half of the book and the other the second half. Rather, each of the siblings owns the whole book together with the other sibling; but neither of them owns the book fully by himself or herself. Similarly, if Socrates and Prodicus are two, or the chords are harmonious, it is not the case that each of these subjects possesses either part of the twoness, or part of the harmoniousness. They possess these properties wholly only together.

Nor do the subjects become one in order to manage co-possession, any more than the two pillars become one when they hold a statue together, or the wheels of a car become one when they sustain a car. When we say that Socrates and Prodicus are two, it would undermine the truth conditions of this statement if the attribution of twoness to the siblings turned them into one entity, or even one subject. We saw that Yi has argued convincingly against the generation of such an entity in such cases of predication, and so have Boolos, Lewis, Simons, and Rumfitt, examining various candidates of abstract entity that might be thought to be generated from the siblings, such as classes, sets, ordered pairs, etc.[6] So, then, how do Socrates and Prodicus achieve sharing the ownership of a property instance between them?

To understand the metaphysics of the co-possession of an instance of a property by some subjects, we will begin with the question of what the ontology of a subject is, and then see how this can help us understand what the ontology of plural subjects is. The prominent contemporary conception of how a subject comes to be is derived from Aristotle's theory of substantial forms: here, a subject is born along with a substance, when a substantial form is instantiated. For example, when the form of an elm tree is instantiated, a subject is created, the elm tree itself, possessing the properties of the generated substance. This is reflected in current theories of the analytic tradition of the past four decades in the use of sortals when explaining the generation of things in the world. For example, Eli Hirsch follows David Wiggins (*Identity and Spatiotemporal Continuity* (Oxford: Blackwell, 1967), 29–30) in defining a substance sortal as follows:

'F is a substance sortal' means: F is a sortal, and it is a conceptual truth that if S is a continuous succession of F-stages, and S is not a segment of a longer continuous

---

[6] Boolos (1984) says: 'Abandon, if one ever had it, the idea that the use of plural forms must always be understood to commit one to the existence of sets (or "classes", "collections", or "totalities") of those things to which the corresponding singular forms apply' (442); 'in the absence of other reasons for thinking so, we need not think that there are collections of Cheerios, in addition to the Cheerios' (449).

succession of F-stages, then the beginning and end of S correspond to the coming into existence and going out of existence of an F-thing. (Hirsch 1982: 49)

Here, the instantiation of sortal F results in the generation of substance which is the F-thing, namely the thing that is F. The creation of a substance is the creation of a subject of properties. And in this case, the creation of a subject of properties goes hand in hand with the creation of a single substance. This is achieved by the instantiation of a sortal because the sortal brings with it the individuation and persistence criteria for substances of that kind, providing a count principle for such objects.

But sortals are not the only metaphysical package for the individuation of entities. The instantiation of a property corresponding to a mass term like 'water' or 'porridge' is the instantiation of a kind of stuff (maybe a natural kind) that brings with it individuation and persistence criteria for the kind. But the instantiation of a mass-property is not in itself the generation of a substance, since it does not carry with it individuation and count principles for substances of any kind. Nevertheless, it does lead to the creation of a subject, that stuff, which possesses the properties of that kind of stuff. Comparing the instantiation of a sortal to the instantiation of a mass-property we find that the latter involves some, but not all, of the metaphysical functions of a sortal (lacking e.g. individuation and count principles). So, the package of metaphysical functions comprising the instantiation of a sortal is not an all or nothing affair; mass-properties bring with them some but not all the metaphysical functions that accompany the instantiation of a sortal.

Material substances or stuff are not the only types of subject. Aristotle, for example, finds reason to individuate further entities, such as the genera and the species in his categories, and other abstract entities such as numbers. In all the above cases, the entity involved is either a concrete or an abstract entity. The metaphysical functions associated with their individuation vary depending on the type of entity they are. But in all cases, it is an entity that is individuated, concrete or abstract, which is the subject bearing the properties of that entity. There is therefore a very strong association between being a subject and being an entity, across the ontological spectrum. It is this association that needs to be challenged with plural subjecthood. We need a metaphysical package for plural subjecthood that does not bring along with it the unifying functions resulting in the individuation of an entity, as in all the cases above, which would undermine plurality.

The metaphysical function of plural subjecthood consists in some things possessing an instance of a property in common. 'In common' does not mean as one. It means that the subjects possess the single instance of a property as many, but jointly together. They each enjoy ownership of the instance of the property, partly owning it, although not owning any part of it. The requirement is that the metaphysical function of property *co-ownership* not bring with it any attendant metaphysical functions which result in the composition of the many subjects into a complex object.

The common ownership of an instance of a property can be seen in two ways: top-down, there is one instantiation of the shared property; the property does not become fragmented into partial-instantiations in the many subjects; it belongs to the many subjects intact, as wholesome as when it belongs to a single subject. But bottom-up, there is fragmentation of ownership of this instantiation of the property; none of the subjects enjoys the whole of the property instance to itself. Where and how do the two directions meet?

The solution I propose is the separation of subjecthood from entity-hood. This is required since the function of owning a property does not unify anything ontologically; property co-ownership is not an ontological glue, any more than co-owning an apartment is. But this is a negative ontological description, in terms of what does not happen in cases of co-ownership of an instance of a property. What *does* happen? How does the single instance come to rest on, and belong to, the many subjects, without unifying them and without itself being partitioned?

The key to the solution is the realization that when some things share a property instance, what comes to be is not a subject, but, putting it simply, engagement in a function: the metaphysical function of co-owning an instance of a property (putting it ungrammatically, what comes to be is not a subject but 'subject-ing'). The performance of this function is grounded on the properties and activities of each of the many co-owners of the property instance. Thus, what grounds the chords' being harmonious together is exactly what grounds the metaphysical function of their co-ownership of that property, namely the properties and relations of the chords. Their metaphysical collaboration is a function that supervenes over these subjects. But its obtaining is not the instantiation of any entity. Plural subjecthood is, so to speak, an activity of the subjects involved ('subject-ing'), not an entity that comes about from them.

There is an asymmetry between the subvening and supervening levels: the circumstances and organization of the collaborating subjects ground the co-ownership of the property instance, but not vice versa. The relation of supervenience is not specifically designed to express this asymmetry. David Charles has argued in favour of composition rather than supervenience, to capture this asymmetry: 'The relations of *being explanatorily* prior, and *being the ontological basis* of, are stronger than the one expressed by any member of the supervenience family' (1992: 275). The collectively owned property instance belongs to its subjects because of the properties they possess, and the activities they are engaged in, which are explanatorily and ontologically prior to the common metaphysical function of the subjects. The relation of composition is more faithful to the asymmetries between subvening and supervening levels than the relation of supervenience. But here caution is required not to misunderstand what it is that is being composed. It is not a new complex object that is being composed from the many; it is not even a new subject that comes to be composed from the many. What is new, what is *composed*, is a function performed by the many objects: their co-ownership of the instance of the property.[7] And this is all that collective plural subjecthood comes to.

REFERENCES

Boolos, George (1984). 'To be is to be a Value of a Variable (or to be Some Values of Some Variables)', *Journal of Philosophy*, 81/8: 430–49.

Charles, David and Kathleen Lennon (1992). *Reduction, Explanation and Realism* (Oxford: Clarendon Press).

Hirsch, Eli (1982). *The Concept of Identity* (New York: Oxford University Press).

Hossack, Keith (2002). 'Plural Logic, Vector Logic', presented at the Royal Institute of Philosophy Symposium on 'Being One: A Symposium on the Nature of Unity', University of Manchester, 14 Dec.

Lewis, David (1991). *Parts of Classes* (Oxford: Blackwell).

Morris Cartwright, Helen (1996). 'Some of a Plurality', *Philosophical Perspectives*, 10: 137–56.

Morton, Adam (1975). 'Complex Individuals and Multigrade Relations', *Nous*, 9/3: 309–18.

Oliver, Alex (1994). 'Frege and Dummett are Two', *Philosophical Quarterly*, 44/174: 74–82.

Rumfitt, Ian (2002). 'Understanding Plurals', presented at the Royal Institute of Philosophy Symposium on 'Being One: A Symposium on the Nature of Unity', University of Manchester, 14 Dec.

Scaltsas, Theodore (2003). 'If Each then Both: and if Both, then Each', in V. Karasmanis (ed.), *The Philosophy of Socrates* (Athens), 289–94.

Simons, Peter M. (1982). 'Three Essays in Formal Ontology', in Barry Smith, *Parts and Moments* (Munich), 111–260, p. 214.

Smith, Barry (1982). *Parts and Moments: Studies in Logic and Formal Ontology* (Munich: Philosophia Verlag).

Taylor, C. C. (ed.) (1997). *Routledge History of Philosophy*, i. *From the Beginning to Plato* (London and New York: Routledge).

Waterfield, Robin (2000). *The First Philosophers* (Oxford: Oxford World's Classics, OUP).

Woodruff, Paul (1978). 'Socrates and Ontology: The Evidence of the Hippias Major', *Phronesis*, 101–17.

Yi, Byeong-Uk (1999). 'Is Two a Property?', *Journal of Philosophy*, 96/4: 163–90.

---

[7] What the subjects instantiate is the co-owned property instance, e.g. twoness or harmoniousness. They do not instantiate 'co-ownership', for the same reasons that a chord possessing harmoniousness does not instantiate 'possession'—only 'harmoniousness'. Possession of a property, or ownership of it, or co-ownership of it, are alternative descriptions of a thing's being such and such, or of several things being such and such. Talk of the metaphysical function of co-ownership makes explicit the difference between a chord being harmonious and two chords being harmonious with each other: it describes the collaboration between the two chords in being harmonious with each other.

10

Socrates the Sophist

C. C. W. Taylor

In his speech against Timarchus, delivered in 345, Aeschines asserts baldly that 'You, Athenians, killed the sophist Socrates because he was seen as having educated Critias, one of the Thirty who overthrew the democracy' (*Tim.* 173). So a little over fifty years after Socrates' death, an orator can take the description of him as a sophist for granted, as something which his audience will accept as uncontroversial. Now it is commonplace that Plato regarded the perception of Socrates as a sophist as having contributed to the hostility which led to his being accused and his death, and that it was consequently central to his apologetic programme to distance Socrates from the sophists. Together with many others I have maintained that thesis in print,[1] and I see no reason to recant my adherence. So is the perception of Socrates which Aeschines takes for granted in his hearers simply testimony to the failure of Plato's apologetic efforts? In this chapter I suggest that the situation is not so simple. While Plato did think that characterization as a sophist had helped to create hostility to Socrates, and that it was therefore necessary to correct that characterization, he nonetheless himself presents Socrates, not merely by implication but avowedly, as sharing some of the characteristics which define a sophist. His presentation of the aims and activity of sophists is not wholly negative, but includes the attribution to them of some activities which have positive intellectual value, and which they share with Socrates. Nietzsche famously said of himself that he was always fighting with Socrates because he was so close to him; it can justly be said of Plato's Socrates that he is always fighting against the sophists because he is so close to them.

While several dialogues represent Socrates engaged in discussion with one or more sophists, in the only dialogue devoted to the attempt to define what a sophist is, the *Sophist*, Socrates appears only in the introductory conversation, his

---

This paper was originally delivered at the Sixth Annual Colloquium in Ancient Philosophy, on 'Socrates, Plato and the Presocratics', held at the University of Arizona, Tucson, in Feb. 2001. The commentator on that occasion was Professor Julia Annas. I am grateful to Professor Annas, to my commentator at Delphi, Dr Pavlos Kalligas, and to the participants in the discussions in both venues for their helpful suggestions.

[1] C. C. W. Taylor, *Socrates* (Oxford and New York, 1998), 68–73.

place as leader of the substantive discussion being taken by the Eleatic Stranger.[2] Socrates' role in the introduction is to pose the question to be investigated in the trilogy of dialogues *Sophist*, *Statesman*, and (unwritten) *Philosopher*, namely, whether these three names pick out three distinct kinds of person, or only one or two (217a6–8), while the answer, that the three kinds are indeed distinct, but not easy to distinguish from one another (b1–3), is given by the Stranger, who leads the investigation from that point. The question of the distinction, or lack of it, between the sophist, statesman, and philosopher, was introduced by Socrates in the highly enigmatic passage 216c–d, where he says that real, as opposed to bogus, philosophers wander from city to city looking at the affairs of men like gods in disguise, taking on all kinds of appearances 'through the ignorance of the others', including sometimes appearing as sophists and sometimes as statesmen. 'Through the ignorance of the others' (c4–5) is particularly puzzling. The Homeric analogy of the gods wandering about the world in disguise (*Od.* 17. 485–7) would suggest that people's failure to recognize them is the result of their disguise, but Socrates seems to reverse the causation; philosophers 'appear as all sorts of things' (*pantoioi phantazontai*), including sophists and statesmen, because people fail to see what they really are. This implies that some of those who are ordinarily taken to be sophists are in fact philosophers; and this suggestion on Socrates' part is reinforced by the description of these philosophers as 'going from city to city' (*epistrōphōsi poleas* c5: *Od.* 17. 486), a description which suggests the conspicuously peripatetic sophists.[3]

Socrates, then, is restricted to posing the question for discussion, which it is left to the impersonal figure of the Stranger, whom I take to be a more direct representation of philosophical authority, and therefore of the author's own position, to answer. Moreover, the terms in which Socrates raises the question indicate not merely that it is difficult to distinguish the sophist from the philosopher (an epistemological thesis on which all agree), but that as far as Socrates is concerned there is at least an overlap between the extensions of the concepts. I suggest that Plato is here signalling that his own portrayal of Socrates

---

[2] In her comments made in Tucson Julia Annas emphasizes the significance of this feature of the dialogue. She writes: 'In the *Sophist* we find Plato distancing himself from Socrates in a way which is not unrelated to the fact that in this dialogue Socrates yields to the Eleatic Visitor as leader of the discussion. In this dialogue Plato is doing something for which he found Socrates an inappropriate spokesperson, and this is reflected in the dialogue's account of sophistry, which of course presupposes a conception of philosophy against which it is defined ...'

[3] In the discussion at Delphi Professor David Gallop made the intriguing suggestion that Socrates' description might be intended to recall the beginning of the poem of Parmenides, where the 'knowing man' travels through the world in the chariot of the daughters of the sun. The designation of the Eleatic Stranger as himself a god (216a5–c3) would make an Eleatic reference especially appropriate, while the description of the genuine philosophers as 'looking from above on the life of those below' (c6–7) might suggest the heavenly journey of the sun-chariot. There is an even more direct echo (in *epistrōphōsi poleas*) of Parmenides if Diels's reading *kata pant' astē*, 'through all cities', is adopted in Parmenides 1. 3, but A. H. Coxon has shown ('The Text of Parmenides fr. 1.3', *Classical Quarterly*, NS 18 (1968), 69) that that reading has no manuscript authority.

and the sophists leaves the boundaries between the concepts of the philosopher and the sophist unclear, and that in that portrayal Socrates himself is presented as both a philosopher and in some respects a sophist. It is the role of the Stranger, not of Socrates, to provide that more rigorous characterization of the sophist which will definitively discriminate the latter from the philosopher.

This characterization is approached via a series of definitions, using the method of division. As these divisions make more or less explicit reference to the presentation of sophists in earlier dialogues, they can be seen as summing up the results of those discussions. In the first (221c–223b) the craft of the sophist is defined as a certain kind of hunting, namely the hunting of rich and prominent young men (*neōn plousiōn kai endoxōn . . . thēra*, 223b5–6). This might remind us of the picture of Protagoras (*Prot.* 315a), surrounded by the followers whom he has collected from all the cities which he has passed through, 'charming them with his voice like Orpheus'; as Orpheus charmed the beasts by his singing and made them follow him, so Protagoras has collected a menagerie of followers. But in that same dialogue, the person who is expressly described as a hunter of rich and prominent young men is not Protagoras but Socrates, whose anonymous friend describes him in the opening sentence of the dialogue (309a1–2) as having come straight from the hunt (*apo kunēgesiou*) for Alcibiades. Now we might think that this merely attests a popular and mistaken perception of Socrates as the *erastēs* of Alcibiades; after all, we (having read the *Symposium*, which Socrates' unnamed friend presumably has not) know that it was Alcibiades who pursued Socrates erotically, not the other way round. But first we should observe that the stimulus to Socrates' visit to Protagoras is the insistent pursuit *of* Protagoras by Hippocrates, who chases after the sophist with all the uncritical enthusiasm of a groupie pursuing a pop star. The roles of hunter and hunted are interchangeable; so even if Socrates is hunted by Alcibiades, he may be a hunter himself none the less. And that in effect is how he describes himself in his opening speech in the *Theaetetus* (143d):

If I were more concerned with affairs in Cyrene, Theodorus, I should ask you if any of the young men there are keen on geometry or any other kind of learning. But since I care less for them than for people here, I am more eager to know which of our young men are thought likely to become distinguished. I keep an eye on this myself as far as I can, and I enquire of others with whom I observe the young men keeping company.

So Socrates is not merely the passive object of Alcibiades' affections; he actively seeks out young men who are keen on learning, as indeed we see him doing at the opening of the *Charmides* (153d ff.). Nor was the erotic relationship with Alcibiades totally one-sided in Plato's portrayal (*Symp.* 217a, 218c, *Alc.* 1. 103a–104c), while we may recall Aeschines' Socrates, who ascribes his influence over Alcibiades to the power of his (Socrates') love for him:

Through the love which I felt for Alcibiades I had had the same experience as the Bacchae. For the Bacchae, when they are inspired, draw up milk and honey from the wells from which other people cannot even get water. And so I too, though I have no science with which I could help a man by instructing him in it, nevertheless felt that by being with him I could make him better through my love for him. (fr. 11 (c) Dittmar)[4]

Socrates is, then, a hunter of young men, prompted by his love for them to associate with them for their intellectual and moral good. This combination of themes occurs in a striking passage from the *Symposium*, Diotima's myth of the birth of Love, in which Love is described as

always poor, far from soft and beautiful as generally thought, but tough and unkempt and shoeless and homeless ... always in want ... going for what is fine and good, courageous, full of initiative and eager, a skilful hunter, always thinking up schemes, desirous of knowledge and capable of acquiring it, a lover of wisdom throughout his life, a skilful magician, sorcerer and sophist. (203d)

It is hard not to read this combination of physical attributes and traits of character and intellect as a portrayal of Socrates,[5] who is thus treated as a personification of the *erōs* which is his standing motivation. If that is correct, then it is particularly striking that he is described not merely as a hunter, but as a magician and sorcerer and (explicitly) a sophist. (On the implications of 'magician' (*goēs*) and 'sorcerer' (*pharmakeus*) see below.)

The account of the sophist as a hunter of rich and prominent young men is thus one which Plato largely accepts as characterizing Socrates as well as the sophists. There is, however, a qualification. Alcibiades was rich, but there is no suggestion in Plato's account of his relations with Socrates that that was why Socrates sought him out, while Socrates' self-description of his hunting out promising young men at the beginning of the *Theaetetus* indicates that he is interested solely in their intellectual promise. The sophist's hunting, by contrast, is a way of making a living, specifically that in which the hunter charges his quarry a fee (as opposed to mere board and lodging, *Soph.* 222e5–223a5). But whether a given activity is done for a fee or gratis is not a distinction internal to the activity itself; playing the cello is the same activity, whether the player is an amateur or a professional. So the characterization of the sophist as a professional hunter, as contrasted with the amateur Socrates, tells us nothing about what, if anything, differentiates the content of their respective activities. It remains open that Plato believed, and intended to convey to his readers, that Socrates' activity had substantial similarities to some activities of some sophists.

The commercial theme continues in the second and third definitions (223c–224e) of the sophist as a travelling merchant or stationary salesman of learning, specifically learning about *aretē* (224c1–2, d1–2). This elaborates Socrates' description at *Prot.* 313c4–6 of the sophist as 'a travelling merchant (*emporos*)

---

[4] H. Dittmar, *Aeschines von Sphettos* (Berlin, 1912).
[5] The terms 'shoeless' and 'unkempt' (*auchmēros*, lit. 'dry, unwashed') make a pointed contrast with Socrates' initial appearance on his way to Agathon's dinner-party (174a), washed and wearing shoes, which, the narrator Apollodorus comments, 'he rarely did'.

or dealer (*kapēlos*) in goods by which the soul is nourished'. The two kinds of salesman casually mentioned in the *Protagoras* passage are carefully distinguished in the *Sophist*, with particular emphasis on the fact that the *emporos* buys foreign goods and hawks them from city to city (224a–b), whereas the *kapēlos* stays at home, selling a stock which includes goods of his own manufacture as well as things which he has bought (224d). The travelling merchant who deals in learning about *aretē*, moreover, is a special instance of a more general type, whose stock includes all kinds of *mousikē*, as well as painting and *thaumatopoiikē*, conjuring or perhaps more generally showmanship (224a). The theme of *thaumatopoiia* recurs in the culminating definition of the sophist as a sort of image-maker (see below). For the present we may observe that the contrast between *emporos* and *kapēlos* appears to offer a point in favour of the latter, namely, that his stock, unlike that of the former, includes some items of his own making. Applied to learning generally and more specifically to learning about *aretē*, that suggests a contrast between, on the one hand, someone with his own views and, on the other, someone whose expertise is restricted to retailing the views of others. At *Rep.* 493a–b the *polis* itself is the 'greatest sophist' in that it is the norms and educational influences of the community which are decisive in moulding people's moral views; professional sophists merely echo the prejudices of the multitude, calling good whatever wins popular favour and bad whatever the crowd dislikes. Similarly in his 'Great Speech' Protagoras presents himself as in effect a spokesman for conventional morality, claiming that goodness of character is transmitted from one generation to another by the moral norms and educational traditions of the *polis*, and that he is simply 'a little bit better than others at helping people to attain it' (i.e. *aretē*, 328a8–b1). The stay-at-home *kapēlos*, on the other hand, has some of his own ideas to impart, though nothing is said about their content, except that they concern *aretē*, or about their truth. I am very far from clear why Plato here distinguishes the travelling salesman from the stay-at-home variety, and attributes a degree of originality only to the latter. But Socrates' unusual attachment to his native city is emphasized by the Laws at *Crito* 52b (especially b2–3, *ou gar an pote tōn allōn Athēnaiōn hapantōn diapherontōs en autei epedēmeis*) and even more emphatically at *Phaedrus* 230c–d, where Phaedrus says that Socrates hardly ever sets foot outside the city walls. Is it possible that the description of the stay-at-home *kapēlos* is intended to suggest Socrates? I find the idea tempting, but would not wish to go further than that. If it is, then presumably the point is the same as in the case of the first definition; as Socrates and the sophists are both hunters of young men, professionally in the case of the sophists, disinterestedly in the case of Socrates, so both Socrates and the sophists are purveyors of ideas about *aretē*, but the transaction is a commercial one only in the case of the sophists. In each case the reader has to supply the crucial difference from his or her background knowledge of Plato's portrayal of Socrates.

The same is obviously true of the fourth definition of the sophist as an eristic, a verbal combatant in individual discussion of matters of right and wrong

(225c7–9) (as distinct from the forensic orator, b5–7). The dialogues frequently portray Socrates in this role, e.g. in the discussions with Thrasymachus and Protagoras, and the *Protagoras* is rich in competitive imagery. In insisting that he can't cope with long speeches, so that Protagoras will have to stick to question and answer, Socrates compares himself to a slow runner who can't compete with the Olympic champion Crison (335e–336a), and when the discussion gets under way and Protagoras points out an apparent contradiction in the poem of Simonides, Socrates compares himself to a boxer who has taken a heavy punch and has to resort to some delaying tactics to gain time for his head to clear (339e). Once again, the crucial difference is that the sophist is a professional eristic (*to chrēmatistikon genos*, 226a1).

Professional eristic is actually distinguished from another kind, which is 'undertaken for the pleasure of this kind of discussion to the neglect of one's own affairs' and which, since it is unpleasing to most of those who hear it, can properly be called 'chattering' (225d7–10; the word rendered 'chattering' (*adoleschikou*) is assumed to be equivalent to *aēdoleschikou*, 'speaking unpleasantly'). 'Chattering' (*adoleschia*) is what Socrates ironically accuses himself of at *Tht.* 195b–c when he fears that he may have dragged out the question of the possibility of false beliefs to unnecessary length, and it appears in a number of contexts as an abusive term applied by the ignorant to serious discussion and intellectual enquiry. At *Parm.* 135d Parmenides advises the young Socrates to practise dialectical exercises 'using what is regarded by most people as useless chattering' (*dia tēs dokousēs achrēstou einai kai kaloumenēs hupo tōn pollōn adoleschias*), while in the myth of the ship of state in the *Republic* the captain, who alone possesses the knowledge of the Good necessary to steer the ship, is reviled by his mutinous crew as a 'useless, star-gazing chatterer' (*meteōroskopon te kai adoleschēn kai achrēston*, 488e4–489a1). The latter passage is unmistakably recalled in the sequel to the *Sophist*, *Statesman* 299b–c, where the Eleatic Stranger ironically describes a situation in which the state is run according to rigid laws which rulers, however expert, are forbidden to challenge:

> if anyone is found looking into steersmanship and seafaring, or health and truth in the doctor's art ... above and beyond the written rules, and making clever speculations (*sophizomenos*) of any kind in relation to such things, in the first place one must not call him an expert doctor or an expert steersman but a star-gazer, some babbling sophist (*meteōrologon, adoleschēn tina sophistēn*); and then that anyone ... should indict him and bring him before some court or other as corrupting other people younger than himself (*hōs diaphtheironta allous neōterous*) ... and if he is found guilty of persuading anyone, whether young or old, contrary to the laws and the written rules, that the most extreme penalties must be imposed on him.[6]

---

[6] *Plato: Statesman*, ed. with introduction, translation and commentary by C. J. Rowe (Warminster, 1995).

Here we also have an explicit reference to the trial and death of Socrates, with a loose quotation from the indictment (*adikei de kai tous neous diaphtheirōn*, DL 2. 40). Socrates is thus the paradigm intellectual whose activities are dismissed by the ignorant as mere useless chattering. The association in the last two passages of star-gazing with chattering fixes the Socratic reference even more firmly, recalling as it does Socrates' statement (*Apol.* 18b7–c1) of the picture of him which people had got from Aristophanes' *Clouds*:

> there is a certain learned man called Socrates, an inquirer into things in the heavens (*ta te meteōra phrontistēs*) and an investigator of everything beneath the earth, someone who makes the inferior argument superior.

The person who goes in for eristic for the pleasure of it seems then to be Socrates seen through hostile eyes; since most people don't like that style of argument he can appropriately be called (as Socrates and people like him actually were called) 'a chatterer'. That he does so 'neglecting his own affairs' looks like a reference to Socrates' conspicuous poverty.

The first four definitions thus present the sophist under various descriptions which apply with appropriate qualifications to Plato's portrayal of Socrates. In the latter Socrates too appears as a hunter of young men, a sort of purveyor of views about *aretē*, and an eristic combatant. The crucial difference is that Socrates does none of these things for money (and indeed he neglects his own affairs in his enthusiasm for debate about *aretē*), and there is the further point that at least some of the views about *aretē* which he purveys are his own. All four definitions are instantly recognizable as applying to the sophists portrayed in earlier dialogues, and then can be shown to be applicable to Socrates via hints and allusions in various dialogues. But when we come to the fifth definition there is an abrupt change of gear (226b). The previous definitions all depend on a purportedly exhaustive division of human activities into creative and acquisitive (219a–c), and are all reached by subdivision of the latter category. But the fifth takes household tasks as the basic genus, identifies a species of such tasks as those which proceed by separating one thing from another (e.g. filtering, sifting, and combing) and then places a certain kind of sophistry within that species. One species of separation is getting rid of impurities, whose sub-species include washing and purging, respectively the separating off of external and internal impurities. Medicine purges the body, and there is a corresponding task of purgation of the soul (227d). The evils to be purged from the soul are now dichotomized into psychological conflict as described in *Rep.* 4 on the one hand and ignorance on the other, and the latter in turn into ignorance in specific arts and crafts, to be remedied by technical education, on the one hand, and on the other general ignorance, which we may think of as moral ignorance or ignorance of values, which is the province of *paideia*. The latter appears to be conceived as springing from a particularly pervasive and problematic kind of ignorance, namely, thinking that you know what you do not in fact know; this is described as 'a great and difficult sort of ignorance, equal in influence to all the other kinds' (*pasi tois allois autēs antistathmon meresin*, 229c1–3), which the Stranger suspects is responsible for all mistakes in thought (c5–6). Conventional methods of *paideia* such as chastisement and exhortation are ineffectual; since all wrongdoing springs from the mistaken conviction that what one is doing is right (230a5–10), that conviction has first to be got rid of before the wrong-doer is prepared to listen to exhortation. And the method of purgation is Socratic *elenchus*, in which the mistaken beliefs are questioned and compared with one another and shown to contain contradictions (230b4–8). This is the most important and most effective of all purgations; the person who has not undergone it, no matter if he has attained the heights of earthly felicity, is uneducated and wretched, since this purgation is necessary for genuine well-being (230d–e).

The elevated tone of this last passage recalls the *Gorgias* (e.g. 479–81), and there are also some affinities with that dialogue's parallel classification of crafts caring for the body and for the soul (464–6). The references to anger and shame as the effect of the *elenchus* on the person subjected to it also recall such instances as Socrates' effect on Alcibiades (*Symp.* 216a–c) and on Thrasymachus (*Rep.* 350c–d; cf. Aeschines' *Alcibiades*, frr. 9–10 Dittmar). There can be no question that the Socratic reference of this definition and of the discussion which leads to it is primary. Indeed, the question is whether this is a definition of any sort of sophistry at all, rather than of something different, namely, philosophy. The classification of household crafts does not fit the fundamental division into creative and acquisitive, and this section reads at first sight like an importation from another dialogue. Might one indulge the flight of fancy that it was actually part of a preliminary draft for the unwritten *Philosopher*, inserted here because Plato thought it too good to lose? But that is too fanciful; the section is carefully crafted into the dialogue. The Stranger is hesitant about calling such practitioners sophists, since that would be giving sophists too much credit, and in response to Theaetetus' saying that all the same there is a similarity he replies that that is why one must be particularly careful not to confuse the kinds (231a). 'Yet', he says, 'let the designation stand; for if people are sufficiently careful I do not think that there will be a dispute about small matters of terminology' (a9–b1); and he goes on immediately to say that the craft of the elenctic practitioner should be given no other name than that of 'the noble kind of sophistry' (b7–8). There can be no doubt that, in the Stranger's view, granted that it is of the highest importance to differentiate the elenctic practitioner from the sophist as ordinarily conceived, as important as distinguishing the most gentle dog from the most savage wolf (231a6), nevertheless Socratic *elenchus* is properly conceived as sophistry of a kind; a very different kind, clearly, from that practised by Protagoras or Prodicus, but a kind of sophistry for all that. That is to say, when it comes to classifying the activity of *elenchus* with respect to the dichotomy between philosophy and sophistry, it is more illuminating to place it on the sophistic side than on the philosophical. While this is indeed consistent with the results of our examination of the four earlier definitions we do not yet have an explanation of why the Stranger takes that view of *elenchus*.

In the above discussion *elenchus* is described via a medical analogy, as a kind of purgation of the soul. The Socratic 'noble sophist' is thus a sort of doctor of the soul, the only kind of person who can tell whether the sophists' merchandise is good or bad for you (*Prot.* 313d–e). The medical analogy picks up the description of the Socratic *erōs*-figure in *Symposium* 203d as a *pharmakeus*. A *pharmakeus* is an expert in the use of drugs, and also in the use of spells and charms which, in some traditional Greek medicine, accompanied the administration of drugs. We see Socrates depicted in this role at the beginning of the *Charmides*. He is struck by the good looks of the young Charmides, and wants to find out whether he is as fine in soul as in body (154b–d; cf. *Tht.* 143d–145b). Charmides has a headache, and at Critias' suggestion he is brought over to speak to Socrates on the pretext that Socrates knows a cure (*pharmakon*) for it (155b–c). The cure is the application of a certain leaf, accompanied by the recital of a spell (*epōidē*), and when Charmides asks Socrates to tell him the spell Socrates obliges in a most unexpected way. He explains that, just as the body forms a connected system, in which the cure of any part requires that the whole is in a sound state, so body and soul are connected in such a way that all the good and ill of the body depends on the soul. So the spell to cure Charmides' headache is a spell to put the soul into good condition, and such spells are in fact the 'fine words' (*kaloi logoi*) which engender temperance in the soul (155e–157a). Socrates is then a *pharmakeus* precisely in that he is a teacher of virtue. The passage itself gives no information on the nature of the instruction which engenders temperance; the rest of the dialogue suggests that it may involve a correct account of what temperance is, reached by means of *elenchus*.

The Socratic *erōs*-figure of the *Symposium* is also described as a *goēs*, a magician or illusionist, and that term takes us back to the definitions in the *Sophist*. After the definition of 'noble sophistry' Theaetetus and the Stranger resume the discussion, recapitulating the definitions proposed so far and instigating a further attempt, which identifies the sophist as a controversialist and teacher of controversialists in all subject-matters, including religion, natural science, metaphysics, law and politics, and the practical crafts. Since the universal knowledge which they thus pretend to is actually impossible, they succeed by producing in their hearers an illusion of such knowledge, as painters can deceive children into thinking that painted cows and trees are real. The sophist is then 'a sort of illusionist, an imitator of real things' (*tōn goētōn esti tis, mimētēs ōn tōn ontōn*, 235a1), and hence a showman or conjurer (*tōn thaumatopoiōn tis heis*, b5–6),[7]

---

[7] The terminology is suggestive of the image of the cave in the *Republic*, where the prisoners are in fact watching a shadow-play produced by a number of puppeteers, who cast the shadows of their puppets onto the wall which the prisoners are facing. The puppeteers are concealed behind a wall, just as actual showmen (*thaumatopoioi* 514b5–6) are concealed from their audience by a screen (e.g. a Punch and Judy man). As the showman attempts to create the illusion that his puppets are moving

and the imitations which he produces are further specified as being misleading or deceptive, i.e. as appearing F without actually being F (235d–236d).[8] In the concluding section of the dialogue (264–8), where the definition of the sophist is completed after the metaphysical digression to establish the nature of non-being and falsehood, the sophist is finally defined by the addition of the further specifications that he is aware of the deceptive character of his illusions and that he produces them by making his interlocutors contradict themselves by question and answer (268a–b). This leaves us with two related questions: (*a*) what are the features common to sophistry proper and 'noble sophistry' which make it more appropriate to class the latter with sophistry than with philosophy? (*b*) given that the sophist is a *goēs* in the sense of a *thaumatopoios*, a showman or illusionist, what kind of *goēs* is the Socratic *erōs*-figure of the *Symposium*?

The answer to the first question emerges from the final characterization of the sophist just cited; what is distinctive of the sophist is the method by which he produces his illusions of universal knowledge, namely, the use of question and answer to make his interlocutor contradict himself. But that is precisely the method by which the practitioner of 'noble sophistry' purges the soul of his interlocutor of his false pretensions to knowledge. The method is identical, the aims diametrically opposed; the sophist uses the method to produce false beliefs about knowledge, namely the false beliefs that the sophist is expert in this or that sphere, whereas the practitioner of 'noble sophistry' uses it to get rid of false beliefs about knowledge, namely the false belief that the 'patient' already knows what is best for him. But why should the Stranger not draw the conclusion that this method is common to philosophy and sophistry? In general, philosophy and sophistry both involve the use of argument, but it would be absurd to conclude that therefore every enquiry which uses arguments, including philosophy itself, is a form of sophistry; why is that inference any better in the specific case of elenctic arguments leading to contradictions? Of course it isn't, but nothing in the text obliges us to suppose that the Stranger commits that fallacy. Rather his argument must be that 'noble sophistry' is more like sophistry *tout court* than it is like philosophy, since it shares one of the most distinctive marks of sophistry, the

---

of themselves and speaking, so these puppeteers succeed in creating the illusion that the shadows of their puppets are real things which move and some of which speak. The picture of the prisoners strongly suggests that they are the victims of a conscious piece of trickery or illusion-making. In the final classification in the *Sophist*, images of the products of human art (of which misleading images are a sub-class) are the counterpart (265–6) of divinely produced (i.e. natural) images of real things, among which images, shadows and reflections are specifically mentioned (265b–c). Thus a shadow is an excellent pictorial representation of a semblance, and mistaking a shadow for the thing whose shadow it is is a good representation of being taken in by a semblance, i.e. of taking it for the reality which it impersonates.

[8] In their comments both Prof. Annas and Dr Kalligas emphasize that this is essential to the definitive characterization of the sophist, and that it has no counterpart in the characterization of the noble sophist. I fully agree. Hence the most that I can claim is that noble sophistry shares one of the distinctive marks of sophistry, while lacking the most distinctive mark of philosophy (see below).

production of contradiction by questioning, while (presumably) it does not share the most distinctive mark of philosophy. What, then, is that most distinctive mark? Since Plato did not write the *Philosopher*, he does not tell us explicitly, but I take it that the answer must be that philosophy is comprehensive knowledge of the nature of reality, which the practitioner of purgative *elenchus* depicted in the dialogues, i.e. Socrates, by his own confession lacks. Purgative *elenchus* is not a method of achieving that knowledge, but a propaideutic to it, since it has the wholly negative function of getting rid of false beliefs whose presence in the soul prevents the acquisition of knowledge (230c–d). That *elenchus could*, of course, be undertaken by a genuine philosopher, i.e. by one who has mastered the dialectical investigation of reality exemplified in the later dialogues, but as depicted in Plato's presentation of Socrates' elenctic practice, it is not in fact undertaken by a genuine philosopher so understood.

This brings us to the final question, what kind of *goēs* was Socrates in Plato's depiction? Not a charlatan or illusionist, since the latter creates false beliefs, whereas Socrates' characteristic skill lies in getting rid of them. I should like to suggest, following a suggestion of Alexander Nehamas,[9] that Plato intends to depict Socrates as a *goēs* in the sense of a magician, of someone possessed of unaccountable powers. Though he disclaims expertise in matters of good and bad, he systematically claims not merely to reveal inconsistencies in the thinking of his interlocutors, but to free them from false beliefs. But that presupposes that he can reliably identify which of those beliefs are false, and since he lacks expertise it is mysterious how he does it. Again, he argues that virtue is knowledge, and is reliably virtuous, while disclaiming knowledge; in his own terms, the source of his virtue is mysterious. In the concluding section of the *Meno* Socrates argues that what is commonly recognized as virtue comes about not through knowledge but by 'divine dispensation without intelligence, unless in the case of a *politikos* who could make someone else a *politikos*' (i.e. someone who could reliably pass on his expertise in matters of good and bad, 99e–100a). Such a person would be like Tiresias in *Odyssey* 10, a living man among ghosts (10. 494–5), a passage which recalls Socrates' first encounter with the sophists in the *Protagoras*, where he presents himself as a living man in Hades (in this case Odysseus himself) meeting the shadowy figures of the sophists (315b9, c8). In the *Meno* Socrates does have a reliable method of imparting knowledge, namely, critical questioning whose aim is to stimulate the recollection of truths eternally known. But unless the person guiding the recollection has active knowledge of the truths to be recollected, the success of the method is mysterious. In writing the *Meno* and *Protagoras* Plato does, I believe, intend to depict Socrates as a genuine philosopher in contrast to the sophists, who are mere simulacra. But if, as I think probable, he abandoned the theory of recollection, and developed his own

---

[9] Alexander Nehamas, *The Art of Living: Socratic Reflections from Plato to Foucault* (Berkeley, Calif., 1998), ch. 3, esp. pp. 85–91.

view of philosophy as a systematic investigation of the fundamental structure of reality to which Socrates had never aspired, he had to abandon the view of Socrates as a systematic philosopher. Socrates' success in guiding self-critical thought to the elimination of false beliefs had then to be ascribed not to philosophy as he had previously believed but to a special sort of 'divine dispensation'. Socrates is then a magician, an individual with an unaccountable power of divining the truth and leading others to it, and by the same token no longer, by Platonic standards, a philosopher, but a very special, and very noble, sophist.

11

Arcesilaus: Socratic and Sceptic

John M. Cooper

I

At least since the time of Cicero the interpretation of what we call Academic scepticism has been uncertain and subject to dispute. For us today the central disputed question, or related set of questions, concerns the relationship between the philosophical views of the Academics, and their argumentative practices—from the time of Arcesilaus, when Plato's Academy first 'went sceptical',[1] down through his successors Carneades and Clitomachus in the late second century—to the self-styled Pyrrhonism inaugurated by Aenesidemus in the first half of the first century. This is a question that Cicero never raises, and may not have been in a position to raise: he seems to have had no inkling of any such new Pyrrhoneans, though the first of them were his contemporaries.[2] But it was certainly raised by the new Pyrrhoneans themselves—by Aenesidemus, and by Sextus Empiricus,

---

[1] This is Malcolm Schofield's phrase, at the beginning of 'Academic Epistemology', in K. Algra, J. Barnes, J. Mansfeld, and M. Schofield (eds.), *Cambridge History of Hellenistic Philosophy* (Cambridge, 1999), 323–51.

[2] In his surviving works and letters Cicero never names Aenesidemus, or shows any knowledge of scepticism in his own time beyond the teaching of Philo (Clitomachus' successor as head of the Academy)—his own boyhood teacher at Rome. Nor does Cicero seem to know of Pyrrho himself (*c*.365–275 BC) as any sort of sceptic. He never refers to Pyrrho in connection with doubts about the possibility of knowledge, or the propriety of suspending judgment, or related issues—the staples for him of the Academic philosophy. Indeed Cicero never associates any epistemological views at all with Pyrrho's name. He assigns him only views in ethics: Pyrrho held that virtue is the only good, and that any other thing (such as the 'preferred' and 'counterpreferred' indifferents of the Stoics—health, wealth, pleasure, or pain, and so on) is not only neither good nor bad, but there is nothing about any such thing that gives a reason or even, for the right-thinking person, so much as an *incentive*, for or against them. For Pyrrho, the wise man is unmoved, unaffected one way or another, by any of them, or the prospect of them—he is 'apathetic' (see *Academica* 2. 130). Now a modern reader may perhaps see lying behind this 'apathy' a Pyrrhonean sceptical 'life without belief', in which, never believing that things are any one way rather than some other, you only move, if at all, randomly or capriciously (some later testimony, e.g. Diogenes Laertius 9. 62, says this is the sort of life Pyrrho himself led); but Cicero clearly does not see that (for him the apathy rests specifically on the refusal to find any value in anything except virtue, and vice). Cicero associates Pyrrho repeatedly with Aristo and Herillus, early 'unorthodox' Stoics who thought virtue the only good and refused to accept Zeno's distinction between preferred and counterpreferred indifferents. All three, he says,

our principal exemplar and source of testimony for the new school.[3] Recently a strong current of opinion (not unopposed, of course) has favored the view that these earlier and later ancient sceptical movements were in fact in agreement on all important matters of philosophical substance (relatively minor details aside). Thus, they should be treated as having put forward a single set of ideas, a single approach in philosophy, that we can call 'ancient' or 'classical' scepticism, and where necessary contrast with late Renaissance and modern sceptical thought— the scepticism developed by Montaigne and Descartes, presupposed by Locke and Berkeley and Hume and Kant, and made a standard topic in twentieth-century epistemology.[4]

It is worth noting that it was apparently only the new Pyrrhoneans who called themselves sceptics—*skeptikoi*—and were so called by others in antiquity. Cicero,

---

held long-exploded and disregardable theories about value (see *Tusc. Disp.* 2. 15, 5. 85, *De Off.* 1. 6, *De Fin.* 2. 35, 43, 3. 11–12, 4. 43, 5. 23). Thus, it appears, 'Pyrrhonism' would not indicate to Cicero either a predecessor or a successor view similar in any way to the Academics'.

[3] Aenesidemus notoriously said that the Academics of his own time held in a dogmatic way (as no proper sceptic should) that knowledge (i.e. knowledge as the Stoics defined it) was unattainable; they were no better than Stoics fighting Stoics (Photius, *Library* 169b38–9, 170a14–17 Bekker). Sextus (*Pyrrhonean Sketches* [*PH*] 1. 3) distinguishes his own Pyrrhonism from the Academic philosophy of 'Clitomachus and Carneades and other Academics' by saying that the latter held that the matters investigated by philosophy are 'ungraspable' or unknowable (*akatalêpta*), whereas the Pyrrhoneans keep on investigating so as to find out whether any such thing can be known (and do so without being convinced yet either that it can or that it cannot). It is noteworthy that Sextus does not name Arcesilaus here; on that, see below s. V. He distinguishes (*PH* 1. 220) between a 'middle' Academy (Arcesilaus) and a 'new' one (Carneades and Clitomachus) and makes only the 'new' Academy just the sort of 'negative dogmatists' that he describes in this passage of 1. 3 (compare *PH* 1. 232–3 and 226–30). I return to this distinction below, s. V.

[4] See esp. M. Frede, 'The Sceptic's Two Kinds of Assent and the Question of the Possibility of Knowledge', in R. Rorty, J. B. Schneewind, and Q. Skinner (eds.), *Philosophy in History* (Cambridge: CUP, 1984), ch. 11, repr. in his *Essays in Ancient Philosophy* (Minneapolis: University of Minnesota Press, 1987), 201–22, 201; also G. Striker, 'On the Difference between the Pyrrhonists and the Academics', in her *Essays on Hellenistic Epistemology and Ethics* (Cambridge: CUP, 1996). 135–49: the differences that Striker does draw attention to are real and important, but as she says at pp. 147–8 the two schools 'do not in fact seem very far apart from one another' and are 'very close' 'as far as skepticism itself is concerned'. (She fails to see the very significant difference, precisely so far as scepticism itself goes, between Arcesilaus and Sextus which I develop below, s. V: see her comments on 'the skeptical Stoic', p. 141.) M. Burnyeat's 'Can the Sceptic Live his Scepticism?', in M. Schofield, M. Burnyeat, and J. Barnes (eds.), *Doubt and Dogmatism* (Oxford: OUP, 1980), 20–53) begins with Hume's claim that the Pyrrhonean sceptic cannot live his scepticism, but proceeds to discuss ancient scepticism more generally (though with special reference to Pyrrhonism); he brings Academic 'sceptics' frequently into his discussion, and applies to them the same analysis, concluding that ancient sceptics in general cannot live their scepticism. However, in 'The Sceptic in his Place and Time', repr. in *The Original Sceptics* (Indianapolis: Hackett Publishing, 1997), 92–126, Burnyeat registers the view (n. 7, p. 95), without explaining what he may have in mind, that there is a real and fundamental difference between Pyrrhonism and the 'dialectical arguments for sceptical conclusions put forward by Arcesilaus and Carneades'. In 'Antipater and Self-Refutation', in B. Inwood and J. Mansfeld (eds.), *Assent and Argument* (Leiden: Brill, 1997), 277–310 n. 76, he suggests that there might be some difference between the way Academics and Pyrrhoneans understand the crucial idea of an 'appearance'; if this is the basis for the real and fundamental difference he had in mind in the earlier article, it appears that Burnyeat too has not taken note of the crucial difference between Arcesilaus and Sextus that I develop below.

Arcesilaus: Socratic and Sceptic 171

Sextus, and (so far as I know) all our other ancient sources never refer in that way to the Academic (as *we* say) 'sceptics'.[5] They always refer to the Academics only as Academics, and to their philosophy as the 'Academic' one, not any sort of 'sceptical' philosophy. As Sextus makes clear,[6] to be a *skeptikos* philosopher means to be one who constantly inquires about or considers questions of philosophy, and keeps on inquiring about and considering them. That is, a sceptic is one whose stock in trade is precisely that—taking philosophical questions up, inquiring into them, considering the matter at issue, without however ever coming to any conclusion, one way or the other, neither (1) by deciding that some given answer or theory is correct, nor even (2) by judging that one or more given proposed answers are definitely incorrect, nor, yet again, (3) by concluding that on the matter in hand there is no correct answer at all, either in the nature of things or anyhow available to us.[7] Of course, even though in

---

[5] A potential exception is found in Aulus Gellius, *Attic Nights* 11. 5. 6 (late 2nd cent AD). In reference to the much-discussed question whether Pyrrhoneans and Academics really differ at all and if so in what way, Gellius says (perhaps on the authority of the 2nd-cent. Academic Favorinus, whose *Tropes of Pyrrhonism* he has just cited), that Academics, just like Pyrrhoneans, are called (*dicuntur*) *skeptikoi, ephektikoi, aporêtikoi* (sceptics or people who inquire, ephectics or people who suspend, and aporetics or people who raise difficulties). H. Tarrant, *Scepticism or Platonism?* (Cambridge: CUP, 1985), 22, claims that this passage is evidence that 'those descriptions were regularly used of Academics' in discussions about whether Academics differed from Pyrrhoneans at least as far back as the 1st cent. AD. Two points should be noted, however. First, we have here a whole list of terms, in fact three of the four with which Sextus characterizes the Pyrrhoneans in his chapter on the names used for his school and its members (*PH* 1. 7: Aulus Gellius omits only *zêtêtikoi*)—not just 'sceptics'. Second, we should expect Favorinus, as an Academic concerned to preserve and win adherents for his Philonian heritage against the upsurge of the new Pyrrhonism, to want to appropriate for the Academics as much as he could of the more attractive aspects of the new Pyrrhonism, and there is a very solid basis from what we know of Arcesilaus and Carneades for claiming that Academics are ephectics and aporetics (on Arcesilaus in this regard, see the heavy emphasis laid in Cicero's evidence about Arcesilaus' Socratic heritage on withholding assent and on raising questions about views positively put forward by others, below ss. II–III). When, then, he throws in 'sceptics' as well, we should take this not as evidence of general philosophical and scholarly usage at the time but as part of Favorinus' own—motivated—back-appropriation for the Academics of attractive Pyrrhonean self-characterizations. When Gellius says that Academics, like Pyrrhoneans, 'are called' by these names, we should understand that merely as reflecting Favorinus' insistence that they are equally entitled to them all. In fact, Gellius himself elsewhere uses the term *skeptikos* as a name *specifically* for the Pyrrhoneans (11. 5. 1). I don't know of any ancient text which unambiguously refers to Academics as *skeptikoi*. It is noteworthy that even as late as in the *Anonymous Prolegomena to Platonic Philosophy*, ed. L. G. Westerink (Amsterdam: North Holland Publishing Co., 1962), which Westerink dates to the second half of the 6th cent. AD, the author, in defending his characterization of Plato as a 'dogmatic' philosopher, and rejecting e.g. Arcesilaus' claim that in his dialogues Plato never advances any philosophical opinion as his own, five times uses the term *ephektikos* (never *skeptikos*) both to express the rejected alternative description of Plato and to characterize those sceptics who claim Plato as their model, whether these *ephektikoi* are to be distinguished from the Academics (7. 10–14, 10. 1–6) or the latter are to be included under the same heading (10. 10, 11. 20, 12. 2). He felt quite comfortable describing Academics and Pyrrhoneans alike as ephectics; apparently not so for 'sceptics'.

[6] See *PH* 1. 7; see also Diogenes Laertius 9. 70.

[7] One slender piece of possible evidence suggests that already Pyrrho might have been known during his lifetime or not long after for having given himself over to the activity of *skepsis*. In his *Lampoons* (apparently in the second book where he takes Xenophanes as his guide in pointing out

antiquity the Academics were never called sceptics, it might still be that they were just as much entitled to this name—meaning by it, with Sextus, 'ones who keep on inquiring, without reaching any conclusion'—as the official and self-proclaimed sceptics, the Pyrrhoneans, themselves were. In what follows I will pursue this question, so far simply as concerns Arcesilaus. I leave aside Carneades and other later Academics. My question, then, is whether Arcesilaus was a sceptic, where being a sceptic is understood Sextus' way—as one who keeps on inquiring into all sorts of philosophical matters, without reaching any conclusion of the sort just specified on any of them.

II

Cicero in the *Academica* gives us by far the most extensive and detailed account of Arcesilaus as a philosopher that we have. In fact, each time through himself as speaker, Cicero presents two separate accounts of the history of the Hellenistic Academy beginning with Arcesilaus but including its philosophical forebears. Cicero presents the first account in *Ac.* 1 upon the invitation of Varro, who has just completed an exposition (15–42) of Antiochus' view that the original Academic philosophy beginning with Plato (but harking back to Socrates'

---

the errors and arrogance of all other philosophers besides the modest, serene Pyrrho) Timon of Phlius, Pyrrho's pupil and publicist, has Xenophanes lament his own going off on treacherous dogmatizing ways, from age and lack of care for all *skeptosunē* (Sextus, *PH* 1. 224 = frg 833, Lloyd-Jones/Parsons = 59 di Marco). Perhaps this archaic term indicates Xenophanes' own failure to philosophize in the way Pyrrho did. In that case, perhaps Aenesidemus, if he like Sextus called himself not only a Pyrrhonean but also a sceptic, affixed this name to his philosophical movement by way of reviving or anyhow drawing on a special emphasis on the importance of continued *skepsis* in the reports about Pyrrho. However, Tarrant, *Scepticism or Platonism*, 23–4, points to Philo of Alexandria, writing in the first decades of the first century AD as the earliest author we know who used *skeptikoi* (sometimes) as a label specifically for Pyrrhoneans. From the fact that within his report of Aenesidemus' Ten Tropes Philo uses this term in its broader meaning simply of 'inquirer' (including those who, after inquiring, reached definite conclusions), Tarrant infers that Aenesidemus must not in fact have used it as a label for himself and other Pyrrhoneans. On the other hand, as Tarrant notes, Diogenes Laertius in the introduction to his own exposition of the Ten Tropes, just after citing Aenesidemus' book as his source for the tropes, mentions (9. 78) as the goal of Pyrrhonean argumentation to bring out 'the oppositions inherent in inquiries' (*tas en tais skepsesin antitheseis*)—a conception of 'inquiries' that reflects the more restricted, specifically sceptical, understanding of the term. So even if Aenesidemus himself did not appropriate the term *skeptikos* in the way that Sextus does as a label for his own school, he seems to have laid the ground for that appropriation by giving special emphasis to the centrality of ever-unfinished *skepsis* in Pyrrhonean philosophizing. That may be one, perhaps the principal, reason why (see n. 5 above) once the term *skeptikos* began to be used as a label for what we call sceptical philosophers, it was reserved for Pyrrhoneans and was not applied equally to Academics: the latter could easily be, and were, described as ephectics or aporetics (and even zetetics) but, it seems, the associations of 'sceptic' were too strongly with specifically Pyrrhonean constant inquiry. (On the question when the term *skeptikos* came to be generally used as a label for Pyrrhoneans, see also G. Striker, 'Sceptical Strategies', in Schofield *et al.* (eds.), *Doubt and Dogmatism* (Oxford OUP, 1980); repr. in her *Essays* (Cambridge: CUP, 1996), n. 1.)

discourses praising virtue and exhorting men to its zealous pursuit) was a single, complete, and comprehensive system, adhered to in all essentials by Aristotle, by Plato's immediate successors in the Academy down to Polemo and Crantor, and again by Zeno the Stoic, whose many innovations did not however make his Stoicism anything but the same 'system' of philosophy that Plato introduced. It is then Cicero's turn, being as he and Varro say (see 1. 13–14) a pupil and adherent of Philo of Larissa, to explain how and why, beginning with Arcesilaus, the Academy abandoned that philosophy for (what we call) scepticism. Cicero's account (1. 43–6) starts with pre-Socratic alleged proto-sceptics, and proceeds to Socrates and Plato and then to Arcesilaus before our manuscripts break off in the midst of a first mention of Carneades. Cicero's second account comes in the *Lucullus* (*Ac.* 2. 72–8). Lucullus, in beginning his exposition of Antiochus' detailed objections to Arcesilaus' and Carneades' new philosophical opinions and practices, had himself objected strenuously to the way the Academics, and Cicero in his first account (or rather its lost first edition version), twist and misinterpret the views of various pre-Socratics, Socrates, and Plato, in seeking to enlist respectable authorities to provide cover for Arcesilaus' sedition in departing from the 'old system' so that his departure will look less vainglorious and less simply malicious (*Ac.* 2. 13–15). Cicero's second account consists of his rebuttal of this charge of Lucullus'.

The two accounts are in general, but not total, agreement.[8] In *Ac.* 1 Cicero presents Arcesilaus as having been impressed, to begin with, just as Democritus, Anaxagoras, Empedocles and 'almost all the old philosophers', *and Socrates as well*, had been, with the insuperable obstacles that stand in the way of anyone's ever coming to know any truth ('limited senses, feeble minds, short lifespan, truth sunk in an abyss,... all things wrapped in darkness', 1. 44).[9] On these grounds, says Cicero, all these predecessors of Arcesilaus had denied all possibility of cognizing, grasping, knowing anything. Arcesilaus reached this same conclusion from the same considerations: *on these grounds*, he denied that anything can be known (*negabat esse quicquam quod sciri posset*, 1. 45)—but, taking his denial one step further, he went on to say that even that which Socrates had exempted (his own knowledge of this universal ignorance) was itself not knowable. Thus, Cicero tells us in *Ac.* 1, Arcesilaus, following Socrates, became persuaded by certain pre-Socratic arguments to accept the conclusion that nothing is either known or knowable, not even the truth of this conclusion itself. But that is not all. Cicero adds: *for these reasons* (*quibus de causis*) Arcesilaus further concluded that no one ought ever to assent to any proposition. If nothing

---

[8] Charles Brittain, *Philo of Larissa* (Oxford: OUP, 2001), 175–8, usefully reviews the contents of the two passages; his purposes do not lead him to address the differences in the two accounts, as I do below.
[9] 'angustos sensus, imbecillos animos, brevia curricula vitae, et... in profundo veritatem esse demersam.'

can be known it would be the most disgraceful thing you could do (something than which nothing is *turpius*)—in fact a disgraceful misuse of the mind—to affirm or deny anything at all. (Why so, we are not told.) Armed with these convictions, according to Cicero, Arcesilaus practised the old Socratic method of arguing against other people's opinions, with a view to making the reasons against them equally weighty as those advanced by their proponents, so that his hearers might be persuaded to follow his advice and suspend judgement.

On this account, it seems clear that Arcesilaus cannot deserve the title of a 'sceptic' (*skeptikos*), if that is understood as one who inquires about everything and keeps on inquiring without reaching a conclusion one way or another on any question inquired into. Arcesilaus *has* inquired into the possibility of knowledge, and he has concluded that none is possible for a human being. (So that question is settled; it is not something open that is still being inquired into.) Even if he has further concluded that he does not *know* that, his yet further conclusion that it is a disgrace to assent to any proposition is itself based on assent to a proposition— the proposition that it *is* a disgrace to assent to anything in the absence of knowledge. We must presume that Arcesilaus has inquired into what is and is not disgraceful to do with your mind, and has reached the conclusion, after inquiry, that it is a disgrace to assent if you don't actually *know* the truth of what you are assenting to. So on Cicero's account in *Ac.* 1. 43–6, Arcesilaus is no sceptic.[10]

Cicero's second account, in *Ac.* 2. 72–8, is not so forthright. Here he does not say that either Socrates or Arcesilaus based their idea that nothing can be known on pre-Socratic arguments about the weakness of the mind, the narrowness of the senses, truth's being sunk in the abyss, and so forth. About Socrates Cicero only says that, after reading so many Socratic discourses of Plato and others, it is impossible for him to doubt that it *appeared* (*visum sit*) to Socrates that nothing is known by anybody (2. 74). About Arcesilaus he only says that it *appeared* to Arcesilaus that it was true that the wise person would not to assent to anything

---

[10] As Cicero presents him, he also grossly contradicts himself. First Cicero says that Arcesilaus reached the conclusion that nothing can be known, i.e. that he accepted and assented to the proposition that nothing can be known. (But he did not assent as to an item of knowledge—the result of his assent would have to stand, according to the universally employed Stoic terminology of the time, as a mere 'opinion', understood as such.) Then Cicero says that Arcesilaus further concluded that, therefore, no one ought ever to assent to any proposition. Thus he assents (more than once) while holding that no one should ever assent to anything. Perhaps Cicero means (he says nothing about this) that Arcesilaus exempted from his condemnation of assents, first, the proposition that nothing can be known, and, second, the proposition that it is a disgrace to assent to any (other) proposition (than these two). That would preserve logical consistency. But what possible principled ground could Arcesilaus, on Cicero's account in *Ac.* I, have offered for these exemptions? His general principle, which does I think have its attractions (I come back to this below, s. III) is that the *only* ground on which you should ever assent is if you *know* the proposition that you are assenting to. So it's impossible to see how Arcesilaus could provide any decent basis that would license even these exceptions: he certainly did not think that either of these could be *known*. (See n. 15 below on one possible revision to Cicero's account that would restore logical consistency.)

not actually *known* by him (as, it is implied, it appeared to Arcesilaus that nothing would be), and that it is worthy of the wise person not to do so (2. 77). This might seem to leave open the possibility that Socrates, and Arcesilaus mimicking him, did not base their ideas that no one knows anything and that no one ought to assent to any proposition, on the pre-Socratic considerations mentioned in 1. 44 (and expanded upon in 2. 72–4, with the addition of Xenophanes and Parmenides to the previous trio of Anaxagoras, Democritus, and Empedocles), but perhaps on something else.[11] Furthermore, it might leave open the possibility that they may not be correctly interpreted as holding these 'views' on the basis of *any* inquiry that yielded these results as their reasoned conclusions, but on some other sort of basis altogether. In that case, one might still perhaps hold open the possibility that Arcesilaus (and Socrates, too, for that matter) was a sceptic.

Those are possibilities I do wish to hold open, and indeed to argue positively for as actualities. But it does not seem promising to argue for them (at all) on the basis of Cicero's account of Arcesilaus in *Ac.* 2. 72–8. As I mentioned, Cicero's second account is a rebuttal of Lucullus' attack on his first one—a rebuttal that certainly gives no indication that it incorporates any alteration of the view there presented. Cicero seems clearly to intend just to restate and reinforce that earlier account.[12] So we should not take Cicero in 2. 72–8, with his language of 'appearance' and his neglect to link these appearances to the pre-Socratic arguments as their grounds, to be giving a different account of the historical facts from that in 1. 44–6. In fact, in both places, but most explicitly in the first book, he claims to be speaking for Philo, to be presenting Philo's account of the history of the Academy.[13] So we should interpret Cicero as having in mind in both accounts that Arcesilaus had concluded that nothing is knowable on the basis of the pre-Socratic arguments he alludes to in both contexts.

However, the Philonian origin of this history should alert us to the need to tread carefully here. During the time when Cicero heard him at Rome, before the radical change of view recorded in his 'Roman books' that gave rise to such outrage among Antiochus and others associated then with the Academy in Athens, Philo held that it was perfectly acceptable to conclude inquiries into philosophical matters with definite assertions—provided that one did not hold that such conclusions had been definitely, once for all, established as the truth,

---

[11] It is noteworthy that, even in expanding the list of pre-Socratic proto-sceptics in 2. 72–4, Cicero only claims to be arguing that Arcesilaus was perfectly entitled to point to these distinguished philosophers as predecessors in holding that nothing is or can be known. He does not repeat the earlier claim that either Socrates or Arcesilaus reached their own conclusion to this effect *through* the same considerations as led these predecessors to it.

[12] I think Brittain, *Philo of Larissa*, is absolutely right about this.

[13] See *Ac.* 1. 13–14, and the implications of 2. 7–8, 2. 17 (*Philo vester*), 2. 66, 2. 69, 2. 73 (*atque hic [Democritus] non dicit quod nos [namely Cicero and Philo], qui veri esse aliquid non negamus, percipi posse negamus,* 2. 73).

and that one only assented to them as *opinions*, not knowledge.[14] On such a view, it would be perfectly acceptable for Arcesilaus, and Socrates too for that matter, as a hero and presumed precursor of the later Academics, to have investigated along with the pre-Socratics the possibility of knowledge (for humans) and to have concluded that it was not possible; also, for Arcesilaus to have considered what a mind should do so far as assenting to propositions goes if it could not reach knowledge, and to have concluded that it would be disgraceful to assent.[15] Thus on Philo's and Cicero's views it would make perfectly good sense to present both Socrates and Arcesilaus in the way that Cicero does present them: they inquired into the possibility of knowledge, concluded that it was not possible, and then Arcesilaus inquired into what a mind ought to do if it could not attain knowledge, and concluded that then it would be a disgrace to assent to anything. Arcesilaus would not be a sceptic (on my understanding, derived from Sextus, of what that means), but he would be a bona-fide Academic nonetheless, in Cicero's and Philo's view of the Academic philosophy.

III

But why should anyone think that Socrates, whatever might be true of Arcesilaus, reached the conclusion that no one knows or can know anything, in whatever sense and with whatever force he did reach it, by arguing from those pre-Socratic considerations? The suggestion is perfectly fantastic, and no one nowadays would give it any credence at all.[16] If we formed our ideas about Socrates from Plato's

---

[14] See *Ac.* 2. 18, and Brittain, *Philo of Larissa*, 11–17.

[15] That Philo and Cicero themselves thought you *could* reasonably and not disgracefully assent without knowledge does not affect this point, except in so far as it might permit Arcesilaus as presented by Cicero to evade the obvious objection (see n. 10 above) that on Cicero's own account he must be (disgracefully) assenting to the claim that it's disgraceful to assent to anything. This could now be interpreted as the thought that it's disgraceful to assent to anything *as known*, whereas a weaker and more tentative assent is rationally and morally acceptable. Thus on Philo's and Cicero's own philosophical principles there is a way of interpreting what Cicero says about Arcesilaus so that Arcesilaus comes out not self-contradictory after all. (That does not mean, of course, that it is at all a reasonable interpretation of Arcesilaus' views or of how he arrived at them.)

[16] Richard Bett (basing himself on the passage of Aristocles of Messene's work *On Philosophy* preserved in Eusebius *Praeparatio Evangelica* 14. 18. 1–5, which presents itself as reporting what Timon of Phlius said about him) has argued that Pyrrho came to the conclusion that we cannot know anything from considerations about how things themselves are, namely, 'equally indifferent and unstable and indeterminate' (*Pyrrho: His Antecedents and his Legacy* (Oxford: OUP, 2000), ch. 1). This looks very close to the sort of thing Cicero reports as having convinced various pre-Socratics (and Socrates) of the same conclusion. If this is right, one might suspect that Philo simply transferred to Socrates, as Arcesilaus' model for his own 'scepticism', this basis for the early 'scepticism' of Pyrrho. Or, conceivably, if indeed Philo had read, remembered, and taken seriously what Plato says at *Phaedo* 96a ff. about Socrates' early interest in pre-Socratic investigations into nature, and in particular pre-Socratic theories about the causes of things, Philo might have thought he had some basis therein for attributing the allegedly Pyrrhonean and pre-Socratic sort of view about the possibility of knowledge to Socrates too. However, the *Phaedo* passage only attests

and others' dialogues, as Cicero at *Ac.* 2. 74 suggests Arcesilaus did, we would never think that Socrates held that nothing can be known on *that* sort of basis. Rather, we would think, his ground was his own experience of examining others who claimed or were reputed to have knowledge who however always failed to stand up satisfactorily to his questioning of them on the subjects on which they were supposed to have it. The allegedly wise could not explain their allegedly knowledgeable views, when questioned for the grounds of those views and about their consequences, without contradicting themselves, or else having to assert quite implausible things—without, again, being able to argue away the appearance of implausibility. And these were failings that, Socrates assumed, knowledge itself, if anyone actually possessed it, would necessarily preclude. If we go by the Socratic dialogues, *these*, not the limitations of the senses or the feebleness of the mind (in some other respect) or the truth being buried in the abyss, were Socrates' grounds for thinking that no one knows anything, and perhaps that no one can know. You might think, then, that if, as Cicero in *Academica* 2 says he did, Arcesilaus took up his stance as a philosophical questioner by following Socrates, with some sort of conviction of the impossibility of knowledge, and aiming at inducing in his hearers suspension of judgement, he would have done so on *this* sort of basis, not the one Cicero in fact attributes to him in *Ac.* 1.

Now in fact in other works, where he is not bound to Philo's account of Arcesilaus' philosophical views or practices, Cicero does suggest just such a view. I have in mind particularly a passage of *On Ends* 2, and one of *On Oratory* 3. As he begins his criticism of Epicurean ethics in *On Ends* 2, Cicero explains why he is not going to proceed as Torquatus had done in book 1. Torquatus expounded and defended Epicurus through a single, long philosophical set piece, which, as Cicero says, even in the Academy of his own day (namely, that of Philo) would be the accepted way to proceed (*On Ends* 2. 2). Cicero however wishes to preserve some of the virtues of Socrates' (and Arcesilaus') procedures, by pausing at each juncture to see what in his counterargument an Epicurean would or would not be prepared to grant, and to argue accordingly. Socrates' way, Cicero says, was to

use thorough inquiry and questioning to draw out their opinions from those with whom he was conversing, so that he could say anything that he thought in response to the

---

Socrates' early interest in the natural philosophy of the pre-Socratics, not at all anything to do with their only tenuously related epistemological views. The suggestion remains fantastic and totally unsupported by our evidence from Plato and elsewhere about Socrates. Astonishingly, Schofield ('Academic Epistemology', 329) does however give it credence; he accepts Cicero's testimony in *Ac.* I as accurate for Arcesilaus, but since that evidence presents Arcesilaus as having followed Socrates in accepting the pre-Socratic arguments for the conclusion that nothing is known (while having gone further than Socrates did, in that Arcesilaus held that it was also not *known* that nothing is known), Schofield presumably accepts at least that Arcesilaus accepted the same story for Socrates. In fact, as I show below, as soon as one notices, as Schofield does not, and takes seriously, the fact that Cicero's history of the sceptical Academy in *Ac.* is a report of what he had heard from Philo, it becomes quite plain that this aspect of it is a fabrication, of no evidentiary value whatever, both as a report on Arcesilaus and as one on Socrates.

answers they gave. This way was not held to by his successors, but Arcesilaus revived it, and made it a practice that those who wished to be his pupils should not inquire from him but should themselves say what they thought; when they had done so, he would argue against them. But his pupils defended their own opinion so far as they could, whereas with the rest of the philosophers the person who has asked something then keeps silent.[17]

In *De Or.* 3. 67 Cicero reiterates that Arcesilaus made it his practice (a peculiarly Socratic one) not to put on show any opinions of his own but to argue against what each person had said that *they* thought.[18] But before that he adds the very important information, or suggestion, that Arcesilaus was the first to 'absorb from various books of Plato and the Socratic discourses this point above all others: there is nothing certain that can be grasped either by the senses or by the mind.'[19]

Here Cicero presents Arcesilaus as having reached his conviction that no certain knowledge can be attained (in whatever way it was a conviction) through his reading of Plato's and others' Socratic dialogues.[20] On this view, it had nothing to do with pre-Socratic worries about our sensory limitations, etc., but rather was the cumulative effect of full exposure to Socrates' practice of elenctic dialectic. It is easy to see how this might have happened. Socrates is such a skilful and resourceful dialectician that you could easily get the impression that no matter what opinion anyone put forward on any matter of ethical theory or any other theoretical question, even if it *were* quite true, Socrates could find something quite persuasive and unsettling question to ask on the other side, which moreover the other person would not be quick or good enough at argument to find any means of disarming—or, if he was, Socrates could always find something else relevant and unsettling to ask that *would* stymie the interlocutor in his effort to explain and defend it adequately, even to his own satisfaction. In displaying his talent, however, Socrates also holds up a certain ideal of what knowledge is and what it accomplishes for anyone who has it. It consists in the ability to stand up successfully to the most searching examination of the Socratic kind that the best dialectician (Socrates, in fact) could dish out—so that your announced opinion survives ultimately unscathed. If that is what knowledge really is, then what we see displayed in the Socratic discourses of Plato and others leaves the reader with

---

[17] 'Is enim percontando atque interrogando elicere solebat eorum opiniones quibuscum disserebat, ut ad ea quae ii respondissent si quid videretur diceret. Qui mos cum a posterioribus non esset retentus, Arcesilas eum revocavit instituitque ut ii qui se audire vellent non de se quaererent sed ipsi dicerent quid sentirent: quod cum dixissent, ille contra. Sed eum qui audiebant quoad poterant defendebant sententiam suam; apud ceteros autem philosophos qui quaesivit aliquid tacet.'

[18] See also *De Or.* 3. 80, *Nature of the Gods* 1. 11, *On Laws* 1. 39.

[19] 'Arcesilas primum ... ex variis Platonis libris sermonibusque Socraticis hoc maxime arripuit, nihil esse certi quod aut sensibus aut animo percipi possit.'

[20] I don't mean to suggest here that Arcesilaus made any distinction (of the sort that modern scholars do) between 'Socratic' dialogues of Plato (the 'early' ones) and the rest (or, at any rate, the rest in which Socrates is the principal speaker). Still, it is reasonable to interpret these passages of Cicero as presumably having in mind principally such Platonic works as *Apology, Protagoras, Euthyphro, Laches, Charmides*, etc.

a vivid and persuasive impression that no one has it, even that no mere human could possibly get it, so demanding are its standards.[21]

Now, if this is how Arcesilaus was affected by his reading of the Socratic discourses, then of course he did not arrive at a conviction of the impossibility of knowledge on the basis of any *arguments* at all to such a conclusion. After all, Socrates himself nowhere *argues* at all for any such conclusion.[22] Arcesilaus just got a deep foreboding and suspicion that no one has ever turned up, or will ever, who can pass Socrates' test: certainly not Socrates, as presented in the dialogues—through his profession of ignorance he denies having the ability himself to stand up to the sort of searching examination on any question to which he so expertly subjected others. So it would be quite wrong to say that Arcesilaus learned or drew from the discourses any philosophical doctrine or opinion to that effect. Here it is important to recall the other main claim that Cicero makes in the passages from *On Ends* and *On Oratory* that we are examining. This is that Arcesilaus never taught, never argued for, anything at all on his own behalf: like Socrates, he listened to others and questioned them or their opinions, *exclusively*, and never entered the philosophical arena on the answerer's side on *any* point.[23] This means that, in whatever way Arcesilaus did hold that knowledge is never attainable by human beings, this is nothing he would ever conceivably have

---

[21] Here we need to pay close attention to Socrates' exegesis of the poem of Simonides in the *Protagoras*. There Socrates argues (344b–c, cf. 341e) that when Simonides said that 'God alone can have this privilege', namely, that of *being* good, he meant that the 'best' human being there can be is one who at most sometimes 'becomes' good by acting the way a being that *is* good would act (by default, this would have to be a god), but inevitably he like everyone else will thereafter fail to do what is morally required and so, later, 'become' bad again. It seems clear that this is just another case, of which there are several, where in interpreting the poem the character Socrates insinuates views of his own. Further, he himself has just before insisted (342a–343b) that the Dorians in general and the Spartans in particular were the greatest repository of ancient wisdom, and that this wisdom was in fact what lay behind their valorous and more generally all their virtuous actions. Socrates' moral, then, is that what the gods have which makes them *be* good is wisdom (i.e. knowledge); that wisdom is denied to human beings, who even at their best (namely, according to Socrates' account, the Spartans) only can 'become' good from time to time, by doing good actions, the acts that wisdom if you had it would lead you to perform.

[22] The *Protagoras* passage cited in n. 21 is perhaps the closest Socrates comes to arguing for this thesis: one must bear in mind that if 'wisdom' is unattainable except by a god, as Socrates proposes and more or less argues there, it follows that (Socratic) knowledge is also unattainable, since he treats it as the same thing. However, by formally attributing these views only to Simonides Socrates preserves his stance of one who inquires only and does not reach conclusions which he is then prepared and obligated to defend if pressed. So Socrates does not put forward these views as his own philosophical conclusions, conclusions reached through philosophical argumentation or to be defended by it.

[23] If Cicero is right about this, and Arcesilaus never argued for, or presented as something that he would even consider arguing for, either his view that knowledge is not attainable by human beings or his view (see below) that it was a disgrace to assent to any proposition in the absence of knowledge, or indeed any other proposition, then Striker must be right in her analysis of Arcesilaus' 'argumentative strategies' as always involving 'dialectical' argument only. In philosophical argument he never reached conclusions to which he was himself committed on the basis of any commitment to the premises he used to reach them. (See her 'Sceptical Strategies'.) Striker does not refer to these passages of Cicero in support of her view, so the success of her direct account of Arcesilaus' reported arguments against the Stoics on how the wise man is rationally obligated to suspend on all questions

enunciated as an opinion of his own. Indeed, if some pupil or opponent turned up who was clever enough to begin his conversation with Arcesilaus by announcing: 'You know, I am convinced that no human being has ever known anything for certain', fully prepared to back this up with various reasons for so thinking— and surely that ploy must have occurred to *someone* during all the years that Arcesilaus was before the public—Arcesilaus would surely have argued against it. Cicero says that Arcesilaus *always* argued against *any* opinion that was announced to him. And it is not in the least difficult to think up lots of counterarguments he might have rolled out. After all, even in *Ac.* 1. 44–6 Cicero says Arcesilaus did not think he *knew* it to be true that no one knew anything. Thus the view that no one knows or can know anything is with Arcesilaus a sort of heuristic principle, governing his practice, but laying no claim of its own to objective truth. It stands inaccesible to critical evaluation because Arcesilaus never asserts it, and would indeed at any time have argued against it if anyone else had asserted it to him.

If, then, we remove from Cicero's account in the *Academica* all suggestion that Arcesilaus' (and Socrates') attitude to the unattainability of knowledge amounted to an opinion based on reasoned argument of any sort, it might begin to seem that, after all, Arcesilaus did deserve the title of sceptic—meaning by this term an inquirer who keeps on inquiring and never reaches any conclusions. Cicero says in the *Academica* that Arcesilaus spent all his philosophical time presenting equally weighty considerations on the opposed side of any question, so as to induce suspension in his interlocutor. Isn't that essentially to say, now that we have made that removal, that Arcesilaus constantly inquired into various questions on which others had opinions, always reaching a balance of reasons on both sides, and as a result suspending his own thought, while encouraging others to do the same? Doesn't that amount to inquiring and keeping on inquiring, without ever reaching any conclusion of whatever sort, on any question? So Arcesilaus would be a sceptic, according to Sextus' understanding of what being a sceptic means.

(Cic. *Ac.* 2. 77, Sextus Empiricus *M.* 7. 155–7) and on how it is possible for a person to act even without assenting to anything (Sextus, *M.* 7. 158), can serve as strong confirmation of the correctness of Cicero's view (pp. 97, 100–1, respectively, in the repr.). In his account of Arcesilaus' views Schofield, 'Academic Epistemology', pays no heed to these passages of Cicero (he does not refer at all to the relevant part of *De Orat.* 3. 67, and refers to *On Ends* 2. 2 and *Nature of the Gods* 1. 11 only in a grudging footnote, 325 n. 8). He also does not accept Striker's analysis of these Arcesilean arguments as wholly dialectical (but why not?—unfortunately the format of the *Cambridge History* does not allow authors to go into such details). As a result, Schofield gives a weakly defended and (in the light of *all* the evidence) entirely unacceptable account of Arcesilaus, as having been committed to accepting on his own behalf the proposition that the wise man will refuse assent to everything (326), and apparently also the proposition that one can act even without assenting to anything (333–4; Schofield's account of this argument is too filled with qualifications to allow the reader to be sure what his final position on this second 'commitment' is)—as well as the proposition that no one knows anything (327). As I argue below, there *is* in fact a way that Arcesilaus is committed to the righteousness of suspension (but not to unknowability), but that way turns on implications of Arcesilaus' Socraticism, of which Schofield, like Striker, seems oblivious. So, ironically, Schofield's conclusions are half-right—not entirely mistaken, as you would have to conclude if you simply followed his own analysis and the grounds he actually gives in support of it.

IV

Before we can accept that verdict we must attend to the second step in Cicero's argument in the *Academica*. Cicero argues that, from the premiss that knowledge is unattainable by human beings, Arcesilaus used the further premiss, that it would be a great disgrace to assent to any proposition in the absence of knowledge of its truth, to conclude that one ought never assent to anything. Where did this further premiss come from? Cicero does not say. But now that we see the source of his first premiss (the unattainability of knowledge), it should strike us that the same source, his reading of the Socratic discourses, must have provided him with the second as well. I mentioned above that in those discourses Socrates puts forward a certain ideal of knowledge. But no one who reads them could fail to see that Socrates also endorses this ideal, in that he passionately aspires to achieve knowledge, believes that human beings can only live their lives really well if they possess it, and holds that by questioning and refuting others he comes progressively closer to that goal—even if he has not yet reached it, and presumably never will. His refusal to announce anything as his own opinion is plausibly thought to reflect his feeling that to do that is to betray your commitment to this goal and to settle for something less than knowledge as your guide in life—mere opinion. Right-thinking, morally serious persons will withhold assent until they have attained knowledge—knowledge being understood in Socrates' ideal way.

If these ideas of Socrates are the source of Arcesilaus' second premiss, then we have to attribute to Arcesilaus a second idea derived from his devoted attention to Socratic discourses, besides the suspicion that knowledge is unattainable by human beings. Inspired by Socrates' fervour for reason's ideal of knowledge, he too accepts that reason should be our guide in life, and its perfection in knowledge our goal. When he always suspends, and thinks one *ought* to suspend, and encourages others to suspend, because considerations on the two sides of a given question are equally weighty, he thinks of himself simply as following reason where it leads. *It* leads to suspension, so *he* suspends—because reason says one *ought* to—and that is why he encourages others to do the same. It is, he thinks, a very great disgrace to assent without knowledge, because he follows Socrates' fervent example of a life devoted to reason. Socrates refused to assent to anything, that is, to put anything forward as his own view, because he thought you should not do that unless you could back it up by the ability to withstand the most resourceful and unrelenting Socratic examination of it. What, then, is the status in Arcesilaus' thought of this second idea—that you should never assent except with knowledge?[24]

---

[24] It is worth emphasizing that for Arcesilaus the ban on assent without knowledge has much stronger implications than the similar-sounding ban contained in Stoic doctrine about wise people.

I suggested that the first idea is best regarded as a sort of heuristic principle, and certainly not a philosophical opinion for which Arcesilaus would ever agree to argue (or to accept examination on before he acted upon it). Likewise, it might seem, with this second one. It is not something which Arcesilaus arrived at as the conclusion of any arguments; he came to it through his fascination with Socratic discourses and by admiring Socrates and accepting him as his model. If some pupil or clever but malicious opponent came to him and announced, 'It is my opinion that no one should ever assent to anything without being in the position to explain and defend his view successfully in the face of a Socratic examination—to do so would be the greatest disgrace for any rational being', Arcesilaus would surely argue on the other side, as he always did, seeking to balance whatever reasons the pupil or opponent could muster in support of their view with equally weighty ones against it. And again, it would not be difficult to think up arguments that Arcesilaus could roll out for this purpose. So Arcesilaus does not put this forward as a philosophical view of his own, for which he has to or intends to claim that there are good and sufficient, completely irreversible arguments to support it. Thus it might seem that it's just an idea (an inspiring one) that he has and follows in doing philosophy, as he just has the suspicion that no one knows anything or, it would seem, ever could—but does not *maintain* that that is so. If so, then, it continues to look as if Arcesilaus can legitimately be

For the Stoics, wise persons' minds are so disposed that they will never assent except to an (allegedly) 'cognitive impression' (*katalēptikē phantasia*), i.e. to one that is true and could not be false; 'weak' assents, assents to impressions other than cognitive ones, yield only 'opinions' and the wise never have any mere opinions. Whenever they do assent, the result is a 'cognitive grasp' (*katalēpsis*) of the fact that is its content or object. According to a not unreasonable conception of knowledge, such a 'grasp' would actually amount to knowledge; on such a view, the Stoics would be restricting the wise person's assents to impressions that when assented to do yield knowledge. However, in fact the Stoics (as part of their own Socratic heritage) agree with Arcesilaus in reserving the name 'knowledge' (*epistēmē*) for a mental state that achieves the very demanding Socratic ideal I have been discussing: e.g. Sextus tells us that for the Stoics 'knowledge is a cognitive grasp that is secure and firm and unalterable by (further) reasoning' (*Against the Theoreticians, M* 7. 151). Thus when they permit and indeed insist on the propriety of assents to (mere) cognitive impressions, yielding true, 100% reliable 'grasps' that, however, might or might not be thus 'irreversible', they are permitting assents that might very well not constitute knowledge. Cicero tells us (and all our other sources are in agreement with this or anyhow in no way contradict it) that 'it was against Zeno that Arcesilaus began his whole struggle' in (as Schofield puts it) 'going sceptical' (*Ac.* 1. 44). In the light of Arcesilaus' Socraticism as I explain it here, it seems right to understand his all-out attack on the very existence of cognitive impressions and cognitive grasps as motivated by a wish to defend the full-strength Socratic ideal. If there *are* no cognitive impressions then there can be no temptation (of the sort Zeno gave in to) to think that any lower standard for assent can be accepted than the original Socratic one—to assent only to propositions that are irreversible, because you could give a full and successful dialectical account of them. What must have outraged and offended Arcesilaus most in Zeno's proposals was the very idea that one could responsibly and respectably assent on the basis of anything less than full Socratic knowledge. In any event, when we read accounts in Cicero, or Sextus, or Plutarch, of Arcesilaus' insistence, in arguing against Stoics, that *on Stoic principles* one must never assent, but must always suspend, it will follow a fortiori that on his own much stronger principles one must do the same. (Of course, as I am arguing, with Arcesilaus this insistence is no philosophical doctrine, as it would be with Zeno, for which one might give philosophical arguments.)

counted a sceptic in Sextus Empiricus' usage of that term: on any and all questions of philosophy he is an inquirer who keeps on inquiring and never reaches a conclusion in which he assents in any way on any side of those questions. Neither as to the non-existence of knowledge nor as to the disgrace involved in assenting without it does Arcesilaus make any philosophical claim.

But this second view functions for Arcesilaus as more than the mere suspicion that the first one is. He doesn't just have the idea (or suspicion) that when you don't know you shouldn't assent; if Cicero's report is right he thinks it is a *disgrace* (indeed the greatest disgrace) to do that. So he is committed to a certain idea and ideal of reason—Socrates'—to violate which, he thinks, would be something really awful. In fact, his commitment to follow reason where it leads seems to be absolute, as it was with Socrates: he will suspend for just so long as reason does demand it (because there are equally weighty considerations on both sides of the question), but as soon as someone comes along to show, or he himself sees, that they are not equally weighty, and that every consideration on one side can be adequately dealt with and no longer stands against the opposed conclusion, he will follow reason in declaring that that is how things actually do stand. (He will then be in a position to *know* it, so he won't violate his principle about not assenting except with knowledge.) In fact, he only suspends because reason, to which he adheres, keeps on indicating, inquiry after inquiry, that that is what he ought to do. And, it would seem, he recommends suspension to others on the same ground, as what reason, which should be the supreme guide in all our lives, tells them they ought to do.[25] The existence, and apparent depth, of this Socratic commitment to reason and to following wherever it leads must be taken into account when answering my guiding question, whether Arcesilaus should be counted a sceptic at all, in Sextus' sense of that term. This commitment is also a crucial distinguishing feature of Arcesilaus' philosophy as compared with Sextus' Pyrrhonism.

V

In fact, Sextus' comments on Arcesilaus' philosophy support in a very precise way the interpretation that I have been developing. As is well known, at the very beginning of the *Pyrrhonian Sketches* Sextus decisively separates the 'Academic' philosophy from any sceptical one, on the ground that the Academics have declared, after investigating philosophical questions for some time, that the answers to them are not graspable (by us). They have, in other words, brought their inquiries to a definite conclusion, rather than keeping them ongoing and

---

[25] Or does he? Cicero cagily suggests in *Ac.* 1. 45 that he thought it would simply be 'easier' for people to suspend if they thought the considerations on each side were equally balanced—not that they would then be led to by reason or reasoning to do so.

open, as sceptics do. Although here the simple term 'Academic' would surely be taken by any reader to include all the Academics, beginning with Arcesilaus and going on down at least to Philo, it is noteworthy, though so far as I know scholars have not taken special notice of this, that in indicating whom he has in mind Sextus says simply 'Clitomachus and Carneades and other [not: *the* other] Academics' (*hoi peri Kleitomachon kai Karneadên kai alloi Acadêmaïkoi*), thus leaving open the question whether, in his opinion, this classification applies in fact to Arcesilaus and other Academics before Carneades. The possibility that it does not is confirmed when we read his treatment later in book 1 first of Carneades' philosophy and then of Arcesilaus'. The first thing he says (1. 226) about what he calls the 'New' Academy (that of Carneades and Clitomachus) is that, unlike the sceptics, its adherents firmly state as an established fact (*diabebaiountai*) that all things are ungraspable. With Arcesilaus (the 'middle' Academy, cf. 1. 220), however, he says no such thing; indeed, the *first* thing he says (1. 232) is that Arcesilaus does very much seem to have things in common with Pyrrhonean ways of arguing (*panu moi dokei tois Pyrrhoneiois koinônein logois*). In fact, he adds, Arcesilaus does not make *any* assertions, but 'suspends about everything', and even makes 'the ultimate end' of his philosophizing be suspension. This last point aligns Arcesilaus closely with what Sextus himself has said (1. 25) about the Pyrrhonist's ultimate end.[26] Thus Sextus takes Arcesilaus, as I have argued Arcesilaus in fact did, not to have adopted any philosophical views (views for which you are obliged, and prepared, to argue), not even the view that nothing can be known or that it is a disgrace to assent when you don't know. As to unknowability, Sextus does not indicate how it is that he thinks (as presumably

---

[26] Sextus says the 'end' for sceptics is 'unperturbedness' (*ataraxia*)—not, as he reports for Arcesilaus, suspension. But he also says that on suspension unperturbedness follows like a shadow on its body. David Sedley, 'The Motivation of Greek Scepticism', in M. Burnyeat (ed.), *The Skeptical Tradition* (Berkeley, Calif.: U. of Calif. Press, 1983), 9–29, draws on Sextus' remark about Arcesilaus' 'ultimate end' in weaving his account of the importance of the ideal of unperturbedness (through suspension) to Greek scepticism, allegedly including Arcesilaus (pp. 11–14). However, as I just noted, Sextus explicitly says that Arcesilaus made suspension itself, not unperturbedness, the 'ultimate end'. The Pyrrhoneans are firmly decided that unperturbedness is the end, and we have no evidence at all that Arcesilaus might have agreed—as if he was *hinting* that unperturbedness is the end while *saying* only that suspension is. I agree with Striker, 'On the Difference', 148 n. 11, that for a Socratic the importance of not presuming to have knowledge when one does not have it is sufficient motivation for making suspension the ultimate end of one's philosophy (if one strongly suspects that no one can attain knowledge). In fact, it is quite easy to see how a report like Cicero's in *Ac.* 1. 44–5, if corrected as in s. IV above, could lead a later figure like Sextus to conclude that, in fact, the avoidance of assent, i.e. suspension, was the ultimate goal of all Arcesilaus' efforts in philosophy, both for himself and his interlocutors—not unperturbedness. I also agree with Sedley that Sextus' basis for attributing suspension to Arcesilaus as an ultimate end was not the mere fact (if this was a fact—we have no indication of any such thing) that somewhere or other in the reports of Arcesilaus' arguments he was found to have argued (perhaps from Stoic assumptions about ends, see Sedley, 'Motivation', 13) that suspension *is* the end. Suspension as the end was a further expression of his deep Socraticism. He did not need to come upon it through dialectical encounters with Stoics, and surely he did not do so: he got it from reading and reflecting on Plato's and other Socratic discourses.

he does think) that Arcesilaus nonetheless maintains it. But it is noteworthy that he says that *Carneades* says that all things are non-graspable in a way that *differs* from the way sceptics say the same thing (1. 226). So perhaps Sextus thinks Arcesilaus says all things are non-graspable in just the same way as Pyrrhonean sceptics do. If so, I think Sextus has Arcesilaus exactly right on this point.

Where Arcesilaus differs from the Pyrrhoneans, however, according to Sextus, is in the *way* he suspended—the thoughts with which he suspended, and the motivations he had for doing so.[27] According to Sextus, Arcesilaus said that each act of suspension is really good, good in the nature of things, and each act of assent really bad, bad in the nature of things (1. 233). For Pyrrhoneans, however, suspensions and assents are accepted as good and bad respectively (things that you ought and ought not to do) only in so far as they appear that way to themselves (*kata to phainomenon hêmin*)—Pyrrhoneans do not say firmly, as a matter of established fact (*diabebaiôtikôs*), as Arcesilaus does, that suspensions are good and assents bad; they only have some impression of that sort. Now, as I will show, for this too we can find a solid basis in Arcesilaus' Socraticism as I have interpreted it. So, if my interpretation is correct, Sextus has Arcesilaus exactly right on this point too.

On my account, Arcesilaus is a Socratic in that like Socrates he is passionately devoted to reason; reason, he thinks, is our highest faculty, the one and only thing in us with which we should in the strongest and deepest sense identify ourselves.[28] This is not a philosophical doctrine for Arcesilaus, in that he will never announce it as his opinion, and he does not hold it in a way that places a burden on him to defend it with arguments of his own or against its denial by anyone. Nonetheless this is a very deep conviction of his. His identification with reason is the ground for his thinking it the *extreme* of turpitude to assent when we don't have actual Socratic knowledge—to do so would abuse the very essence of our being. Hence it is a morally good act of the highest order not to assent, but to suspend, just so long as we do *not* have that knowledge—suspending preserves and strengthens our very being. It is with that thought, and out of that motivation, that Arcesilaus suspends whenever he does, and stays away from assent. And, probably, that is why he recommends the same practice to others. In other

---

[27] I leave aside the further and final point in Sextus' account of Arcesilaus (1. 234), which in any event he introduces cautiously ('if we should trust the things that are said about him'—in the rest of his account he stands personally behind what he says, reporting straight out that Arcesilaus said or did this or that). This is that really Arcesilaus was a Platonic dogmatist all along, who merely used his method of arguing on the other side of his pupils' opinions in order to test their mettle, and if they seemed philosophically adept and capable enough, then he would drop the pretence and start teaching them the dogmas of Plato. Lucullus in Cic. *Ac.* 2. 60 makes what seems to be the same bizarre suggestion. See the same idea in Anonymous, *Comm. on Plato's Theaetetus* 54. 14, Numenius *apud* Eusebius *Prep. Evan.* 14. 6. 6, and Augustine, *Against the Academics* 3. 38.

[28] This seems to me a much more central and important aspect of Arcesilaus' indebtedness to and revival of Socratic thought than (what is uniformly appealed to by scholars) his adoption of Socrates' method of elenctic cross-questioning as the basis for his own philosophizing.

words, his suspensions are themselves *acts* of reason, expressions of his passionate acceptance of reason as a guide to life and of reason's inherent standards, one of which (he thinks) is expressed in the principle that one should always suspend when one does not actually *know*. So, he supports suspension, as Sextus says he does, *diabebaiôtikôs*—firmly, assertively, as something one *really* ought to do.

For Sextus, as he implies in distinguishing the Pyrrhonean's suspensions from the Arcesilean's, this is anathema. There is not room here to explain fully why that should be so for him. Briefly, however: almost the very goal of scepticism, for the Sextan Pyrrhonist, is to rid us totally of any such ideal, of the thought that reason, as a critical faculty with standards for judging truth and falsehood and with self-recommending procedures for deciding what to think and what to do, has any authority whatsoever for our thought or for any of our actions. Getting rid of that ideal is the essential—both necessary and sufficient—condition for living an unperturbed life. For him, the fully fledged sceptic regularly suspends and thus lives an unperturbed life, simply by going by how things appear to him, not by following reason at all;[29] such a person keeps on suspending each time, in recognition, to be sure, of the fact that critical reason, if it were to be followed, would demand this—but not *because* it does. He suspends only (by now) because, happily, that is what he feels like doing.

So we can conclude that Arcesilaus does indeed deserve the title of a sceptic, meaning by that a philosopher who inquires, and keeps on inquiring, into philosophical questions, but without ever reaching a conclusion of any sort on any of them. However, there is a very great difference between the scepticism of Arcesilaus and that of Sextus, precisely in regard to the role of reason in the acts of suspension that are common to the two. Both promote a life without assent, a life that renounces the typical Greek philosopher's ideal of knowledge as the basis for a well-lived human life. Arcesilaus, like Sextus, lives without knowledge and does so with satisfaction. As David Sedley has said, 'What above all characterizes Hellenistic scepticism is... its abandonment of [the] desire [for knowledge]—its radical conviction that to suspend assent and to resign oneself to ignorance is not a bleak expedient but, on the contrary, a highly desirable intellectual achieve-

---

[29] I speak advisedly only of the fully fledged Pyrrhonean sceptic here: as Sextus explains (*PH* 1. 12, 1. 26 ff.), the sceptic starts out in philosophy with a committed belief in the power and value of reason as a faculty for critically deciding what to believe and how to act. His hope is to use rational scrutiny to discover what is true and what is false, so that he can then live his life on the basis of what reason decides. Hence, when during that phase he suspends (as, according to Sextus, he inevitably must—so equally balanced are considerations on both sides of all questions), those suspensions are undertaken through reason itself, because reason and its standards dictate them. It is only once he has unexpectedly found that unperturbedness follows on his regular and constant reason-directed suspensions, and he has formed the habit of expecting and welcoming suspension when he next inquires into something, that he is what I call a fully fledged sceptic. From then on he has (lightly, easily, unperturbedly) renounced reason and does not follow it any longer, even in his acts of suspension. His suspensions from then on simply express how things appear to him. It then just keeps on appearing to him that suspension is the thing to do in the face of the balance of reasons, and he suspends following that appearance.

ment.'[30] But for Arcesilaus this stems from a deep and abiding commitment to another ideal, one shared not with Sextus but rather with the mainstream of Greek philosophy—that of reason itself as our guide. Arcesilaus is satisfied, and feels fulfilled, by always suspending, just because reason, his guide, keeps on telling him to suspend. Sextus suspends because in his life he follows not reason but appearances—the way things strike him. So Arcesilaus suspends thinking *diabebaiôtikôs* that suspension is good (that is the source of his self-satisfaction), while Sextus suspends expressing thereby no opinion at all about whether what he is doing is good or bad. *He* claims self-satisfaction from the fact that he *has* no such opinion, but only suspends because that is what he feels is appropriate, given his experiences. That difference seems to me more fundamental than anything the two sceptics have in common. So it is a mistake, I think, to speak of 'ancient scepticism' as a single thing—as if Pyrrhonian scepticism was in all major ways simply a revival and continuation of Academic scepticism under another name. Arcesilaus' scepticism is the expression of his Socratic commitment to living according to reason as our life's guide; Sextus' is the expression of a complete renunciation of reason altogether.

---

[30] Sedley, 'Motivation', 10.

12

The Early Christian Reception of Socrates

Michael Frede

This book commemorates Socrates' death some 2,400 years ago. Socrates plays a pivotal role in the history of philosophy. This role is reflected by the fact that scholars have come to distinguish between the Presocratics, as we now call them, on the one hand, and Socrates and the philosophers who followed him, on the other. This distinction is not as clear cut as one might wish when it comes to the details, but it does capture the enormous difference in character between the sort of philosophy we find in the Presocratics and philosophy as it emerges in the fourth century under the influence of Socrates and his immediate followers. It seems to be mainly due to Socrates that philosophers came to see themselves, and came to be seen by others, as forming a distinct group of persons engaged in a distinct enterprise to which they devote their life, namely the pursuit of wisdom conceived of in a certain way. Wisdom by these philosophers is understood in the sense of the mastery of a certain body of knowledge and an understanding of things, primarily of human beings and their affairs, in the light of which one has the right attitude towards things and knows how to go about one's life in such a way as to have a good life, to live well. It was Socrates and his immediate followers who, in their pursuit of wisdom thus understood, largely determined the agenda of philosophy in antiquity, but also the way one thought wisdom had to be pursued, if one was to attain the desired knowledge and understanding.

It is a matter of controversy what precisely Socrates' own contribution was to the shape and form philosophy came to take in antiquity. Socrates had gathered around him a remarkable number of younger philosophers. Some of them were going to play an important role in the further history of philosophy, first and foremost, of course, Plato, but also men like Antisthenes, Aristippus, or Euclid of Megara. What is striking about this rather large group of immediate followers of Socrates, many of whom for us are just names, is that they radically disagreed with each other on particular philosophical questions even of fundamental importance, but nevertheless were united in their admiration for, and devotion to, Socrates. Hence it would seem that what attracted them so powerfully to Socrates was not a specific set of philosophical theses, but rather the philosophical enterprise itself as Socrates understood it and the seriousness and clear-mindedness with which Socrates pursued it. Of course, this enterprise itself was based on certain convictions. It was based on the conviction that human beings have a mind, or a soul, as Socrates put it, which guides them in what they are doing. They act the way they do because they are minded to act in this way. How they are minded depends on how they view things, or which assumptions they make about things. Hence, if we turn our mind or reason to anything at all, we should, first of all, turn it to the assumptions or beliefs which guide us in the way we go about our life. A sound-minded person, a person with a healthy mind or soul, a soul which is not retarded, damaged, or deformed, will view things in such a way as to go about his life in such a way as to have a good life, to live well. Hence our first effort should be to make sure that we are sound of mind or wise.

Hence Socrates made wisdom thus understood the overriding aim of his life, which he pursued with a remarkable single-mindedness, clarity of mind, persistence, and consistency. The example Socrates set with his actual life, not just in what he said, but also in what he did, must have been a crucial part of what amazed and attracted his immediate followers, in spite of their widely diverging views. But Socrates also continued to be seen as the paradigm of a philosopher by later philosophers who had not personally known him, by as different groups of philosophers as the Academic Sceptics, the Stoics, and the Cynics. Socrates soon became a legendary figure.

Socrates apparently thought of philosophy as practised by himself not as a private, but a public affair, an affair which not just concerned him and those of his friends who shared his personal interests, but concerned all citizens. For how can the citizens attain a good life and contribute to the flourishing of the city, if they, and among them in particular politicians, do not in the first place give serious thought to the question what does and what does not matter in life, which assumptions and beliefs one should be guided by in one's private life or in one's public life as a citizen. Correspondingly Socrates conducted his philosophical inquiries in public. In the course of this he exposed the ignorance, confusion, and thoughtlessness of his fellow-citizens on such basic questions as what virtue, justice, benefit, or harm are. This provoked a great deal of resentment, since it was generally accepted that a respectable citizen would, and should, know the answers to such questions. For citizens in general believed that their traditional upbringing had provided them with the right answers to such questions, and at least democrats believed that what qualified a citizen to participate in the running of the affairs of his city was precisely his knowledge and understanding of such matters. But Socrates by his artful questioning showed them to be utterly confused in their understanding. As a result of the resentment generated by his elenctic practice, Socrates was indicted for impiety and corruption of the young, condemned, and sentenced to death. It seems that he could have avoided indictment in the first place, then condemnation, and finally death by escaping from prison. But Socrates accepted death in order not to compromise what he took to be his vocation or even his mission, the public pursuit of wisdom. Hence Socrates came to be remembered not so much for his role in the history of philosophy or for any specific philosophical views he may have held. He rather came to be remembered as a paradigm of a philosopher who even in his death had set an example of a life devoted to the pursuit of wisdom, to the truth which matters in life, both private and public, but at the same time a life in accord with what he perceived to be the truth which matters. It is for reasons like this, then, that it seems only fitting to remember Socrates.

Now it so turns out that this year we also are entering the third millennium of the Christian era. And this coincidence invites all sorts of reflections and comparisons, in particular in societies which see themselves as indebted to both their classical heritage and their Christian tradition. Comparisons on this occasion have been drawn between Socrates and Christ. One could also reflect on the relations between philosophy, as it emerged under the influence of Socrates and his followers, and Christianity. Or one could reflect on the way ancient society, once Christianized, tried to come to terms with its pagan philosophical heritage.

The topic I want to deal with here, though, is much more modest. I just want to consider what ancient Christians had to say about Socrates. For one might expect that Christians would take a certain sympathetic interest in Socrates and his teaching. After all, they shared his view that what it takes to attain a good life is to have the right view of things, to be right-minded. Hence the shared concern for the soundness and integrity of the soul and for orthodoxy. The Christians, we expect, will have insisted that Socrates was unable to attain the right view of things, since revelation and the teaching of Christ is needed for this. They will not have denied that Socrates, in one crucial regard, did have the right understanding of things. For they almost invariably thought that Socrates did believe in one God and rejected idolatrous worship. They knew that Socrates had stood trial for impiety or atheism and had been condemned to death. Their understanding of this was that Socrates had suffered death because he did not believe in the traditional gods and rejected public idolatrous cult. So in this regard they saw themselves as being in the same situation as Socrates, persecuted and killed for their belief in God and their refusal to participate in public idolatrous worship. Given all this, we might expect that ancient Christians managed to develop their own specifically Christian interpretation of Socrates, which might reveal aspects of Socrates which otherwise are overlooked.

This expectation that the ancient Christians might show a particular interest in, and understanding of, Socrates at first sight seems to be encouraged, if we look at the Acts of the Martyrs.[1] These acts purport to be accounts of the proceedings in court against Christians who as a result of these proceedings suffered martyrdom. In at least three of the extant acts the martyr himself in the course of the trial evokes the example of Socrates and his trial. Of course, there is the question

---

[1] For the texts see H. Musurillo, *The Acts of the Christian Martyrs* (Oxford, 1972).

to what extent the acts faithfully reflect what actually was said at the trial. Many of them clearly have undergone redaction, and some of them are extant in various versions. But in all three of our cases, a reference to Socrates seems to be entirely in line with the rest of what the accused has to say in the course of the trial. Even if the acts cannot be relied upon to preserve the actual words of the martyr, they at least do reflect the way their pious redactor thought that the martyr had argued.

The first of our three cases is that of Apollonius who in his defence before Tigidius Perennis, praetorian prefect from 180 to 185, refers twice to Socrates. There is independent reason to think that Apollonius was a person of considerable social standing, and perhaps thus an educated person. In §19 he derides the Athenians of his time who, we are told, do not even worship their traditional gods, but the Τύχη of Athens in the form of a brazen bull's head. And he suggests that it was in contempt of the idolatry in Athens in his day that Socrates swore by the plane-tree and the like. In §38 he says about Jesus that he gained a great reputation for virtue, but for this very reason provoked the resentment of the uneducated, as the just men and philosophers before him had done. He goes on to quote from Plato's *Republic* (2. 361E) how the just man will be tortured and killed. He then turns to Socrates who was unjustly condemned and killed, just as Jesus was. Here, then, an analogy is drawn between Socrates and Christ, but also, implicitly, the Christian martyrs.

The second case is that of Pionius which seems to be presented as a case at the time of the Decian persecution, though Eusebius (*HE* 4. 15. 47) dates it to the time of Marcus Aurelius. In the course of the proceedings Pionius is interrupted by a man called Rufinus who is said to be a person of some distinction in rhetoric. Rufinus tells Pionius: 'stop being conceited' (μὴ κενοδόξει). Pionius answers:

Is that your rhetoric? Is that your learning? This even Socrates did not have to suffer from the Athenians. But now everybody is an Anytus or a Meletus. Were Socrates and Aristides and Anaxarchus and all the rest in your view just conceited, when they practised philosophy and justice and steadfastness?

The third case is that of Phileas, bishop of Thmuis. According to the Latin version, though not the Greek version, of his acts, Phileas pointed out that not just Christians, but also some gentiles, are more concerned for their soul than their life, as for instance Socrates was. Phileas clearly is referring to Socrates' trial. All three martyrs, then, compare their trial and the death they expect to the trial and death of Socrates.

But if, thus encouraged, we go on to look for further Christian texts which mention or discuss Socrates, we soon notice that almost without exception all these passages occur in an apologetic context, that is a context in which Christians refer to Socrates either to defend themselves against pagan accusations or to attack the pagans. All these references rely on the fact that in late antiquity, in Roman imperial times, an educated person can hardly afford to brush aside the example of Socrates. For philosophy enjoys a privileged position in late ancient culture. Philosophy is supposed to be a crucial part of the education of any respectable person, and Socrates is supposed to be a paradigm of a philosopher. This, then, makes it rather awkward for an educated person, for instance, to accuse and condemn the Christians for something for which Socrates had been accused and condemned, especially given that it was generally agreed that Socrates had been accused and condemned unjustly. One can somehow see an underlying dialectic emerging. If Socrates, indeed, was condemned unjustly, how could it be just to condemn the Christians on the same grounds on which Socrates had been unjustly condemned? If, on the other hand, Socrates had been justly condemned for a capital crime, it is difficult to see how the pagans can present him as a paradigm to be followed. In either case the pagans seem to be in an awkward position.

Hence one begins to wonder to what extent these Christian references to Socrates do reflect a deep admiration for, and understanding of, Socrates, to what extent they show that even for Christians Socrates remained a paradigm or an exemplum which still had real moral force, or whether these apologetic references did not primarily have a dialectical or rhetorical force, because pagans were committed to accept Socrates as a moral paradigm. And one must wonder about this all the more so as, contrary to a common view, Christians by no means as a rule referred to Socrates in support of their case against the pagans in a positive way. It turns out that often enough they referred to Socrates in a negative way as part of their attack on paganism. It is by no means true that, as for instance S. Lilla says,[2] among early Christians only Tertullian shows no good will towards Socrates. There are a considerable number of ancient Christian authors who show remarkably bad will towards Socrates. This is particularly puzzling, given that, as I said at the outset, almost all Christians were agreed that there were remarkable similarities between the case of Socrates and the case of the persecuted Christians, for instance in that both Socrates and the Christians refused to worship the traditional pagan gods. That at least is what the Christians thought.

In order to understand this negative attitude, we have to remember that ancient Christians, for a variety of reasons I will turn to in a moment, had very ambivalent feelings about pagan philosophy, which only increased in the course of late antiquity. Hence, given that Socrates was the paradigm of a pagan philosopher, any attack on Socrates would be regarded as an attack on pagan philosophy in general. Moreover, given the central role of philosophy in late ancient culture, any attack on Socrates would be regarded as an attack on pagan culture. It would have dialectical or rhetorical force precisely for the same reason that a Christian defence drawing on Socrates as a positive example would be effective. And as in the positive case, so also in their criticism of Socrates we do not have to assume that the Christians necessarily showed any particular interest

---

[2] In his article on Socrates in the *Encyclopedia of the Early Church* (Cambridge, 1992).

in Socrates as an individual. He was criticized as a representative of pagan philosophy and of pagan culture, because of the standing he had among pagans.

Now to understand why Christians would be so ambivalent about pagan society, pagan culture, and pagan philosophy, we should perhaps briefly go back to the very beginnings of Christianity. Christianity started out as a community of Jews centred in Jerusalem but, mainly under the influence of St Paul, it soon opened itself up to the gentiles or pagans. The question arose how Christianity should define itself in relation to Judaism. There were those who thought of Christianity as a form of Judaism. Well into the third century and beyond there were Christian communities which insisted on the acceptance not only of Jewish scripture, but also on the observance of the Jewish law. But there were soon also influential groups within the Christian communities, sometimes into the third century, who advocated a complete rejection of Judaism, both of the law and of scripture. They claimed that the God of the Old Testament, the creator of the world, was not God, but an inferior being, perhaps even malevolent. Mainstream Christianity came to reject Jewish law, but to accept Jewish scripture. The very beginning of the Nicene-Constantinopolitan Creed involves a reaffirmation of the belief that the God of the Christians is the God of Jewish scripture, the creator of the world ($\pi\iota\sigma\tau\epsilon\acute{u}o\mu\epsilon\nu$ $\epsilon\grave{\iota}s$ $\H{\epsilon}\nu a$ $\theta\epsilon\acute{o}\nu$, $\pi a\tau\acute{\epsilon}\rho a$ $\pi a\nu\tau o\kappa\rho\acute{a}\tau o\rho a$, $\pi o\iota\eta\tau\grave{\eta}\nu$ $o\grave{v}\rho a\nu o\hat{v}$ $\kappa a\grave{\iota}$ $\gamma\hat{\eta}s$; ... *factorem coeli et terrae*). With this commitment to Jewish scripture also came the commitment to the injunction of scripture not to worship any god but the God of the Old Testament. This injunction was now understood as involving the belief that there is just one God and that all the other so-called 'gods' in reality are just demons or fabrications of demons. But with the acceptance of Jewish scripture also came the acceptance of the injunction against idolatry.

Now these two commitments were bound to bring Christianity into deep conflict with the pagan society within which Christianity had started to spread, producing an ever increasing number of Christians who were of gentile origin. For the public cult, involving idols, of the traditional gods of the community was a crucial part of pagan culture. Its maintenance was regarded as essential to the preservation of the fabric of the community or the society. Somebody who conspicuously or even demonstratively refrained from participating in the public cult publicly distanced himself from the community, excommunicated himself, as it were.

It also brought the Christians into conflict with the law. If the Christians had had their own political community with their own traditional god which they worshipped in public in their traditional way without the use of idols, they might have been tolerated. Jewish traditional worship was tolerated, and the Jews had gained an exemption from the obligation to participate in the cult of the Roman state and thus, for instance, were exempt from the imperial cult. Judaism was a legally recognized religion. But Christianity was not. Christians, in particular Christians of gentile origin, did not worship the gods of their ancestors, and they refused to participate in the state cult. They were illegal, not legally recognized as exempt from the religious obligations of the citizens of the communities of the Empire.

What made matters worse was that the Christians were not content to abstain from the public cult and to worship in private in their own way. They thought of themselves as having the mission to convert everybody in the society to the belief in and worship of the one God who did not tolerate the worship, let alone the idolatrous worship, of other gods. Christianity, like Judaism, came with a claim to exclusivity. But it also, unlike Judaism, came with a claim to universality. Hence, when Christianity quite conspicuously began to spread in the second century, pagan society began to fear for its cohesion, for its traditional order, for its traditional culture.

The way pagan philosophy entered the picture was this. In order to succeed in their missionary efforts Christians also had to convert the well-established and educated part of the society. As mentioned above, an educated pagan in this period was at least supposed to be philosophically educated, to have views about the world, about the role of human beings in it, and about human life, which were philosophically enlightened. The whole society of the time, and its educated class with it, had a growing interest in theological questions, in questions of the afterlife of the soul, in demonology. And philosophy catered for these needs. In particular Stoicism and Platonism offered what we might call religious views of the world and of human life. For an educated person there was a more or less clear distinction between civic religion and public cult, on the one hand, and one's own private philosophical beliefs in religious matters. Hence to convert the educated one had to address their more or less articulate philosophical beliefs about matters divine, perhaps by trying oneself to articulate Christian belief in philosophical terms. This obviously was a matter fraught with difficulties, some of which go back to late Judaism, some of which have something to do with St Paul's experience, as, for instance, reflected in the Acts of the Apostles or the Letter to the Colossians. But whatever the difficulties, there was a sense in which pagan philosophy of some form or other was a rival.

Now, as Christians knew only too well, pagan philosophy did not stand at all in the way of the belief in one God or the rejection of idolatrous worship. They knew that philosophers like Antisthenes, one of Socrates' followers, had said that in reality there is just one God and that the many gods of popular religion are just conventional (νόμῳ; Cic. *De nat. deor.* 1. 13; Philodemus, *De pietate*, P. Herc. 1428 fr. 21). Clement of Alexandria (*Protr.* 6. 71. 1–3) reported that Antisthenes had said that God is not in the likeness of anything and that human images of God were of no use, and Clement added as an explanation 'for he was a companion of Socrates'. I think that most philosophers in late antiquity were monotheists. But it is also the case that most philosophers tolerated or even encouraged civil religion, the public cult of the traditional gods, as Aristotle did, for reasons of social utility and because they thought that theological truth could only be grasped by the uneducated in a mythologized form. And once pagan cult came to be attacked by Christians, Platonist philosophers in particular were ready to theoretically justify the cult of images. Hence pagan philosophers in the eyes of Christians naturally seemed compromised by their support of idolatrous worship.

What is more, once the struggle between Christianity and paganism had come to take the form of a public debate at an intellectual level, it was philosophers who were attacking the Christians, supporting their persecution, claiming that the Christians were trying to destroy the traditional, divinely ordained order of things. These attacks culminated in Porphyry's work 'Against the Christians' in fifteen books. Porphyry's work, hardly by accident, was published at the time of the last great persecutions of the Christians under Diocletian. Even when Christianity at the beginning of the fourth century began to be tolerated and then became the official religion of the Empire, pagan philosophers were still crucially involved in trying to preserve and defend the pagan tradition.

So it was not surprising that Christians felt extremely ambivalent about, or even hostile to, pagan philosophy which had become closely associated with Hellenism in the sense of the religious ideology of the cultural pagan elite which had been slowly emerging since the second century. Christians came to write whole treatises against pagan philosophy, like the lengthy 'Contra Philosophos' transmitted among the works of Augustine (CCSL 58A). It became common to blame pagan philosophy for any number of heresies, like Arianism. These enormously complex relations with pagan philosophy for most Christians made it almost impossible to think in a detached and fruitful way about the relation between Christianity and philosophy. And they also account for the fact that a good number of Christian authors could not resist the temptation to attack Socrates in order to thereby attack pagan philosophy and pagan culture.

It is, then, for reasons along these lines that some Christians, even if they thought that Socrates had been condemned unjustly, and hence also were willing to argue that, since Socrates had been condemned unjustly, the Christians should not be persecuted, nevertheless were not prepared to grant that Socrates, with his life and death, had set an example of any positive relevance to Christians. To have granted more to Socrates would have undermined their case against pagan philosophy.

Let us look at all of this by considering some representative Christian authors with their views on Socrates. It is hardly by accident that the ancient Christian who takes the most positive attitude towards Socrates is also the earliest Christian author we know of who talks about Socrates. It is Justin the Martyr who before 161 wrote two apologies; the first is addressed to the Emperor Antoninus Pius and to his sons 'Verissimus, the philosopher' (that is Marcus Aurelius) and 'Lucius, the philosopher', the second is addressed to Antoninus Pius and Marcus Aurelius. Justin the Martyr himself originally had been a Platonist philosopher who had converted to Christianity. According to his own testimony (*Dial.* 1. 9; cf. Euseb. *HE* 4. 11), he continued to present himself in the garb of a philosopher. He thought of Christianity as the true philosophy.

In addressing the Emperor, Justin is trying to defend the Christians against prosecution. The Emperor could revoke the legal ban against Christianity. In the *First Apology* Justin argues that it is unjust and against all reason that persons should be prosecuted for the mere fact of being Christians, rather than for anything specific they have done. What they specifically are charged with is atheism, moral corruption, and disloyalty to the state: Justin is defending the Christians against these charges.

But before Justin begins with the defence against the specific charges, he utters a sentence which would strongly resonate in the mind of any ancient, philosophically educated, person, but particularly in the mind of a Stoic like Marcus Aurelius. Justin says (2. 4): 'You have the power to kill, but not to harm' (ὑμεῖς δ' ἀποκτεῖναι μὲν δύνασθε, βλάψαι δ' οὔ). It is a piece of Stoic doctrine that people can kill you, but that only you can harm yourself. For life and all such other things over which others may have power are in themselves of no significance, are completely indifferent. All that matters is how you deal with them, how you deal, for instance, with life or death. And the only harm which can arise for you arises out of the fact that you do not deal with these things properly and thus harm yourself, harm your mind or soul. The only way harm can arise for you is that you yourself give others power over you, by becoming attached to things you should not put your heart into, like your earthly life, and thus become corrupted. This is a piece of Stoic doctrine. The Stoics believed that it was Socrates' view. And the reason for this was that Socrates in Plato's *Apology* 30 C 6 ff says: 'For know well that, if you kill me, you will not harm me any more than you will harm yourselves. For neither Meletus nor Anytus could possibly harm me, for they would not have the power to do so' (... ἐάν με ἀποκτείνητε ... οὐχ ἐμὲ μείζω βλάψετε ἢ ὑμᾶς αὐτούς ...). Justin obviously means to allude to Socrates' remark in the *Apology*. Thus Socrates and his trial are in the background of Justin's *Apology* right from the beginning.

Only some paragraphs later, in 5. 3, Socrates makes his first explicit appearance in the *Apology*. Justin is trying to explain why the Christians are persecuted. There are evil demons who have corrupted human beings, and thus have power over them, manipulating them into believing that they (that is, the demons) are gods and into worshipping them (5. 1–2). The demons obviously would lose their power over us if they were unmasked as evil demons. Hence they try to destroy every person who tries to unmask them, by manipulating the corrupt and vicious and uneducated in such a way as to agitate against him and have him killed. This is what happened to Socrates when by reasoning he tried to bring people to their senses and to realize that these so-called gods are not gods. This is why Anytus and Meletus indicted Socrates for atheism and impiety and brought it about that he was killed (5. 3; cf. also *II Apol.* 10. 5–8).

Similarly, Justin argues, it is the demons who make base and uneducated people agitate against the Christians and accuse them of atheism and impiety, for the same reasons that they did in the case of Socrates. For Christians try to convince people that they should not worship the demons who just pretend to be divine, but rather should worship the one true God. Thus Justin is trying to establish an extended parallel between Socrates and the Christian martyrs.

Now one thing which needs some comment here is that Justin obviously assumes that Socrates refused to worship the many so-called 'gods', because he believed that there is only one true God. For the first part of this he could rely on the fact that, for instance, according to Plato's *Apology* Socrates was accused of impiety, because he refused to worship the traditional gods of the city. But why would Justin think that the reason for this was that Socrates only believed in the one true God? To justify this claim Justin in *II Apol.* 10. 6 attributes to Socrates the words: 'It is neither easy to discover the father and demiurge of all there is, nor safe (ἀσφαλές) to talk of him to everybody, once one has discovered him.' Where does Justin get these words from? Obviously they are derived from the famous lines 28 C 3–5 in Plato's *Timaeus*, except that Plato does not attribute them to Socrates, but to Timaeus, and that Timaeus is made to say, not that it is not safe to talk of God to everybody, but that it is impossible. As far as the latter point is concerned, it is to be noted that there is a whole tradition, represented by the Jewish author Flavius Josephus (*Contra Apionem* 2. 224), but also the Platonist authors Alcinous (27. 36–7) and Apuleius (*De Plat.* 1. 5), of understanding Plato's text in the way Justin does, namely as talking about its being unsafe to talk about, or to explain, the one true God to everybody. Justin obviously interprets this in the sense that one exposes oneself to grave risks by talking about the one true God. That he attributes words allotted by Plato to Timaeus to Socrates clearly rests on the assumption that what Timaeus in the dialogue says reflects Plato's view and that Plato's view basically just is Socrates' view. He was encouraged to do this by his Middle Platonist background, if, for instance, we think of Numenius. So Justin thinks that Socrates, like the Christians, believed in the one true God and for this reason refused to worship the traditional so-called gods, and that it is for this reason that he got killed, like the Christian martyrs.

In *II Apol.* 10. 7 Justin takes the parallel or analogy one step further. He introduced a comparison between Socrates and Christ. But the comparison is twofold: on the one hand it establishes an analogy between Socrates and Christ; Christ died, like Socrates, because he wanted to free man from the demons by making them recognize the Father; but there also is a fundamental disanalogy: Socrates, using human reason, did not manage to persuade anybody else to suffer death for this belief (δόγμα) in the one God; by contrast, Christ by the power of Divine Reason managed to convert people in great numbers, not just philosophers and scholars (φιλόλογοι), but humble craftsmen and ordinary persons (ἰδιῶται). What Justin here by implication is also saying, though, is that Socrates, like the Christian martyrs, suffered death for his belief in the one God.

In fact, it emerges from another passage in *I Apol.* 46. 1–4 that Justin assumes that Socrates was a Christian. It also emerges that he believes that in persecuting

Socrates and men like him, his persecutors were persecuting Christ himself. This is a rather remarkable view. It is based on Justin's metaphysics and theology, in particular his Christology. He identifies Christ as the Reason (the λόγος) of God which at the same time is the Truth, the truth as to how things are and why they are like this, how they are going to unfold and why they will do so. Each human being is given a seed of reason on the basis of which he can at least understand the Truth or Divine Reason to some extent. Those who live with reason (μετὰ λόγου) or are guided by reason, gain some knowledge of the Truth, and hence come to know Christ. Socrates, Justin explicitly says, partially knew Christ, and was following Christ in following reason. Socrates partially knew Christ, because he, for instance, knew that there is just one God, the Father and Creator.

But we should not overlook the word 'partially' here. Socrates and the pagan philosophers at best only had a partial knowledge of the Truth. The complete truth only becomes available to human beings through the incarnation of Christ. This is why pagan philosophers were always contradicting each other. They each had seen only part of the truth, and mistook this for the whole truth. This is why a philosophy based on the teaching of the incarnated Christ is immeasurably superior to pagan philosophy.

What matters here for our purposes are not the details of Justin's Christology, but rather the fact that Justin clearly is not just using Socrates in a dialectical or rhetorical way. He does believe that Socrates gave his life for his belief in the one true God. He thinks of Christian doctrine as the true philosophy, and he thinks that pagan philosophy, though inherently limited, does offer at least a partial understanding of the truth, that is of Christ. This is why he can take a genuinely positive attitude towards Socrates which goes so far as to declare him a Christian.

It is perhaps worth remarking in passing that Justin seems to have been denounced as a Christian by a pagan philosopher, the Cynic Crescens, that he suffered martyrdom under the Emperor Marcus Aurelius, a Stoic, and that according to the acts of his martyrdom the trial was presided over by Rusticus, the prefect of Rome from 163 to 168. Rusticus was known for his knowledge of Stoic doctrine, and the way he was trying to follow it in life. And he is piously remembered by Marcus Aurelius at the outset of his *Meditations* as the man who impressed on him the need to reform his character, who made him move away from rhetoric and who introduced him to the *Diatribes* of Epictetus (*Med.* 1. 7; cf. also 1. 17. 5 and 7).

Next I want to turn to Origen. Origen has a much more distanced attitude towards philosophy, towards pagan philosophy, and hence also to Socrates, than Justin does. He had extensive training and some reputation as a philosopher. Just possibly he had been, like Plotinus, a student of Ammonius Sakkas. He insisted on teaching his students philosophy. But in spite of the great importance he attributed to philosophy, he was unusually clear, in a way Justin, for instance, presumably was not, and the Gnostics obviously were not, about the limitations of philosophy from a Christian point of view. He clearly distinguished between the simple faith which saves, and the philosophical clarification, elucidation, and defence of this faith. It is not philosophy which saves, but the faith. Much of Origen's work is directed against Gnosticism of any kind. Yet philosophy does serve an important purpose, and as far as this purpose is concerned, pagan philosophy is as good as any. In fact Origen's own views in crucial respects are very close to those of pagan philosophers, something which puzzled and irritated pagans as much as Christians.

Around 248 he wrote an apology, the *Contra Celsum*, responding point for point to Celsus' attack on Christianity. Not surprisingly it is full of references to Socrates. The whole writing stands in the shadow of the trial and death of Jesus to which Origen refers in the very first sentence of his preface. But very much on Origen's mind throughout the writing also is Socrates' trial and death. One reason why this is so is that Celsus at the very beginning of his treatise had referred to Socrates' death (cf. 1. 3). He had threatened the Christians, saying that they ran the risk Socrates had been willing to run for the sake of philosophy. So here it is the pagan Celsus who introduces the comparison between Socrates and the Christian martyrs, though qualifying it by saying that Socrates died for the sake of philosophy. Obviously in his view Christians died because they were obstinate and unreasonable.

Celsus also again and again refers to Jesus' trial and death. This throughout the ancient debate between pagans and Christians was a fundamental point of disagreement. Pagans could not understand and accept that a reasonable person, let alone a divine man, let alone a god, could be thought to be willing to suffer the ignominious death of a criminal. For no reasonable person would suffer the death of a criminal if he could help it. This is a point to which Celsus comes back again and again. And so Origen has to return to it, repeatedly. In 2. 17 he points out that Socrates did willingly take death upon himself, since he could have escaped from prison. In 2. 41 he counters the claim that Jesus was not free from evils by pointing out that, if Celsus is thinking of Jesus' poverty, his persecution by absurd persons, and his crucifixion, surely Socrates was not free from evils either. When later Celsus again complains about the miserable death of Jesus, Origen retorts that Socrates and Anaxarchus equally died a miserable death.

Now these and a number of other remarks by Origen about Socrates might just be regarded as dialectical remarks which gain their force from the fact that for Celsus Socrates should be the paradigm of a philosopher, of a virtuous person, of a reasonable man. But that Origen's remarks should not be regarded as merely dialectical or rhetorical becomes obvious if we have a closer look at them. Origen explains why Socrates died willingly, obviously something beyond the comprehension of Celsus. The explanation Origen gives (2. 17) is that Socrates chose to die philosophically rather than to live unphilosophically. And later Origen, like Justin, will quote Plato's *Apology* 30 C, according to which Socrates said that Anytus and Meletus perhaps can kill him, but that they cannot harm him.

Throughout Origen speaks of philosophers, but in particular of Socrates and of Plato, in a way which is highly respectful, but also measured and restrained. Even confronted with the most offensive remarks on Celsus' part, at most he will indicate that a person of bad faith or ill will might respond quite differently. When, for example, Celsus complains that Christians trust the Jewish prophets, but disregard the oracles of Zeus or Apollo, for instance the oracle in Delphi, Origen invites us to consider what Aristotle, the Peripatetics, or Epicurus have to say about oracles (7. 3). And he criticizes the Delphic oracle for saying that Socrates is wisest among men. But he does not criticize it as being a patently absurd claim. He rather points out that the oracle in saying that Sophocles is wise, that Euripides is wiser, but that Socrates is wisest of all did not seem to have based its response on an estimate of Socrates' philosophical achievements (6. 6). When in 6. 8 Celsus complains that, unlike for instance Plato, Christians tell incredible stories, Origen responds that persons of bad character who want to speak ill of the visionary experiences of those who are morally superior to the ordinary person will have a lot to say, and to ridicule, about Pythagoras or Socrates or Plato, for instance about Plato's third eye, or Socrates' δαιμόνιον, or the swan which Socrates dreamt of who turned out to be a young man he came to meet.

Origen does not extol the virtues of pagan philosophers, but he carefully tries to do justice to those among them who deserve it, and refuses to denigrate or ridicule those who like Socrates deserve respect. But many Christian authors could not resist the temptation to do precisely what Origen refused to do. Thus, for instance, Tertullian (*De am.* 46. 9), ridiculing pagan dream interpretations, turns the swan Socrates had been dreaming of into Plato who in the arms of Socrates allures men. And needless to say, Socrates' claim to be watched over by a δαιμόνιον is interpreted by Tertullian (*Apol.* 22. 1), Minucius Felix (38. 5) and Cyprianus (*Quod idola* 6) as showing that Socrates let himself be guided by an evil demon. Many criticisms refer, or allude, as Origen had done, to the oracle according to which Socrates was the wisest among men, then try to show sarcastically what sort of wisdom pagan wisdom was. Thus Ps. Justin in his *Cohortatio* (36), who tries to persuade us that Socrates thought that ignorance was wisdom. Or Clement of Rome (*Homil.* 5. 18. 147), who suggests that this wisdom consisted in hedonism, sexual promiscuity, both heterosexual and homosexual, and the advocacy of sexual promiscuity. Or Cyril of Alexandria who similarly accuses Socrates, this summit of pagan wisdom and virtue, of sexual promiscuity and the most sordid desires (*Contra Julianum* 7. 226).

Some Christians in their eagerness to prove pagan philosophy to be empty conceit tried to undermine the very idea that Socrates and the martyrs may have anything of importance in common. Thus John Chrysostom (In *I Corinth. homil.* 4. 4), in response to the remark that also among the pagans there were many who despised death, tries to explain that there is nothing remarkable about Socrates' death. He did not drink the poison willingly, but because he had no choice. If you have no choice, but die of necessity, this cannot be said to be a matter of courage, and in any case he had already reached an extreme age, and so one can hardly talk of despising death. To this he adds later in the homily (4. 5) that the great Socrates had to die because he was suspected of a small innovation in theology. I take it that John Chrysostom is referring to Socrates' δαιμόνιον. But surely this is a rather disingenuous way of referring to the suspicion that Socrates did not believe in the traditional gods, because he believed in God.

Tertullian was a master in this sort of criticism. Socrates, he says, did have some wisdom. He knew that the gods do not exist. This, of course, did not prevent him from having a cock sacrificed to Asclepius. Presumably he did this to honour Apollo, Asclepius' father, to whom he owed his reputation as the wisest man. But it was not very clever on Apollo's part to attest through the Delphic oracle the wisdom of a man who denied the existence of gods and thus his own existence (*Apol.* 46. 5).

Now it seems to me that the basic overall argumentative strategy of those Christian authors who did criticize Socrates was to have the best of both sides. Even those authors who did criticize Socrates did not want to deny that Socrates refused to worship the traditional gods, and perhaps not even that Socrates did believe in one God. This would put them into the position to query why they should be persecuted for atheism, if they just did what Socrates had done, and if educated pagans had seen almost immediately that it had been wrong to condemn Socrates to death. But if one took this line, one ran the risk that Socrates and the Christian martyrs, or even Jesus, might seem to have more in common than one was willing to grant Socrates and thereby pagan philosophy and pagan culture. Hence the effort to undermine the reputation of Socrates and thus to draw a clear line between Socrates and the martyrs. In this way one could use Socrates both (i) to defend Christians against the charge of atheism and thus, moreover, to embarrass educated pagans, and (ii) to attack paganism for adopting as a model a person who was corrupt and corrupted others.

Thus, first appearances to the contrary notwithstanding, I, to my own disappointment, have come to the conclusion that ancient Christian remarks about Socrates for the most part follow a rather transparent pattern of argument which is dictated by their apologetic needs, rather than by some deep understanding of the actual Socrates. Ancient Christians in general, it seems, were interested in Socrates only to the extent that he served their apologetical purposes. They did not have sufficient interest in the actual Socrates to be able from their perspective to say something about him which sheds new light on him.

But if we say this, we should also remember that late antiquity quite generally, in particular once Platonism had become dominant, did not have much interest in the actual Socrates, let alone anything to say about him which seems enlightening. The Platonists' heroes were Pythagoras and Plato. They had great difficulties somehow fitting Socrates into their view of the past. One could talk about the divine Plato or the divine Iamblichus, but Socrates clearly resisted the epithet 'divine'. One could write saints' lives of Pythagoras or Apollonius of Tyana, but nobody would have dreamt of writing a saint's life of Socrates.

It is really very difficult to see what the highly cultured society of the fourth or fifth century, whether Christian or pagan, would have done with an actual Socrates. Although the Athenians sentenced Socrates to death, they also had a much better understanding of him and more real sympathy for him than did late antiquity in general.

Index

Acts of Martyrs 190–1
Adam, J. 76 n 6, 87
Aenesidemus 169 n 2, 170 n 3, 172 n 7
Aeschines the orator 157
Aeschines of Sphettus 159, 164
agreement 72–87
  argument that Socrates made an 79–84
  two kinds of 73–5
akrasia (weakness of the will) 8, 18, 24–6, 29–34, 36, 39, 44, 51–3, 56
Alcibiades 23, 159, 160, 164
Alcinous 197
Alexander of Aphrodisias 18, 63 n 6
Ammonius Sakkas 198
Anaxagoras 173, 175
Anaxarchus 199
Annas, J. 157 n, 158 n 2, 166 n 8
Antiochus 172, 173
Antisthenes 7 n 13, 10, 10 n 24, 11, 188, 194
Antoninus Pius 195
Anytus 196, 199
Apollodorus 160
Apollonius, martyr 191
Apollonius of Tyana 202
apologetics 191–2, 195–6
aporia 88–109
aporia, and speechlessness/inarticulateness 92, 94–7, 99, 102
aporia, articulation of 98, 100
aporia, *catharsis* 88–9, 92–8, 107–9
aporia, solving of 91, 98, 100, 106
aporia, *zētēsis* 89, 97–109
Apuleius 197
Aquinas, T. 68, 68 n 11
Arcesilaus 169–87 *passim*
Aristippus 188
Aristo of Chios 169 n 2
Aristophanes 163
Aristotle 7, 8, 9, 11 & n 29, 13, 15, 18, 19, 23 n 9, 29, 30 n 19, 32, 33

& n 24, 34 n 26, 36, 39, 41, 43 n 47, 44, 50, 51 & n 2, 54 & n 4, 55 n 5, 56, 57, 63, 89, 90 & n 4, 91, 106, 108 & n 23, 109 n 24, 122, 125, 126 n 21, 128, 137, 138 n 33, 153, 154, 173, 194, 200
astheneia 33
Atkins, E. M. 85 n 18, 87
Augustine 67 n 10, 185 n 28, 195

Back, A. 149
Bandini, M. 48
Beere, J. 20 n
belonging to the subject 147–8, 150–2
Benson, H. H. 43 n 48, 48
Bentham, J. 53
Berkeley G. 170
Bett, R. 176 n 16
Beversluis, J. 20 n 2, 42 n 42, 48, 88 n 1, 89 n 2, 96, 102 n 18
Bluck, R. S. 129 nn 1 & 2
Boolos, G. 152, 153 n 6, 156
Bostock, D. 73 n 2, 86 n 19. 87
Brancacci, A. 7 n 13, 10 n 22, 10 n 23, 14 n 35, 17
Brittain, C. 173 n 8, 175 n 12, 176 n 14
Broackes, J. 109 n 25
Brown, L. 1, 128 n 25, 132 n 9, 135 n 22
Burnyeat, M. 88, 104 n 21, 170 n 4

Carneades 169, 170 nn 3 & 4, 171 n 5, 172, 173, 184
cave, image of (in *Republic*) 165 n 7
Celsus 199, 200
Charles, D. 1, 33 n 24, 39, 48, 64 n 7, 109 n 25, 133 n 13, 137 n 26, 140 n 38, 141 n 40, 142 n 1, 149, 155, 156
Christianity 190–202 *passim*
Chroust, A.-H. 20 n 2
Chrysippus 10 n 24

Index

Cicero 84, 85, 85 n 18, 86, 169–84 *passim*
Clarke, S. 58, 70 n 15, 71
Cleanthes 10
Cleary, J. 109 n 25
Clement of Alexandria 194
Clement of Rome 200
Clitomachus 169 n 2, 170 n 3, 184
Cohen, S. M. 59 n 3
collective plural predication 142, 146–51
concept 61–2, 65–6
Connolly, J. 109 n 25
consent, tacit 75, 79–80, 86
consequentialism 43, 107
Continuous Theory of Being of Hippias 144–6
contract, Hume on 72
contradiction 54, 61–2, 69, 90, 93, 98, 106, 164, 166–7
Cooper, J. M. 1, 3 & n 1, 8 n 14, 9 n 19, 20 n 48
Coventry, L. 83 n 15
Crantor 173
Crescens 198
Crison 162
Critias 23, 157
Crito, arguments concerning agreement 73–84
Crombie, I. M. 110 n 1
Cudworth, R. 58, 69, 70 n 14, 71
Cyprianus 200
Cyril of Alexandria 200

Day, J. 110 n 1, 128 n 25
definiens—definiendum 63, 94, 133–5
definition 4–6, 13–15, 17–19, 24, 28–9, 40–4, 46, 53, 58–61, 63–6, 93–8, 101–9, 110–28, 129–41, 144–5, 159–61, 163–6
of shape and colour 123–6, 136–41
Delatte, A. 8 n 15, 8 n 16, 9 n 20, 37, 48
Deman, T. 11 n 29, 13 n 34
Democritus 173, 175
demons 193, 196–7, 200
deontologism 41–7
Descartes, R. 170

dialectic 4–7, 11 n 29, 13–14, 19, 108, 192
dialectic, non-refutative 5
dialectic, protreptical 6
dialectic, Socratic 177–9
Diels, H. 158 n 3
Dillon, J. 109 n 25
Diocletian 195
Diogenes Laertius 169 n 2, 171 n 6, 172 n 7
Diotima 160
distributive predication 142, 144, 146, 149, 151
Dittmar, H. 160 n 4, 164
dokimasia 79, 80 n 12
Dorion, L. A. 3 & n 1, 4 n 3, 5 n 8, 6 n 9, 7 n 13, 21 & n 3, 21 n 4, 35 n 28, 48
Dummett, M. 151, 152 n 5
Dustin, C. 109 n 25

Elements of Geometry 138–9 n 33
elenchus 4, 6, 7, 11, 12, 14, 19, 45, 88–9, 164–5, 167
elenchus, agreement in 73, 83–4
Empedocles 136, 139 n 35, 173, 175
enkrateia 7–9, 12–13, 19, 37
Epictetus 10 n 24, 11, 198
Epicurus 53, 177, 200
Erbse, H. 3 n 1, 10 n 22, 11 n 27
eristic 161–3
Erler, M. 91 n 8, 100 n 17
erōs 160, 165–6
essence 94, 113, 120–8, 130, 133 n 13
Euclid 137, 138 n 33
Euclid of Megara 188
Eudemus 138–9 n 33
Euripides 85, 200
Eusebius 176 n 16, 185 n 28, 191
explanation 26 n 15, 31, 64–6, 68
extention-intention (of a concept) 63–4, 132, 135, 149, 158

Favorinus 171 n 5
Fine, G. 63 n 6, 123 n 19, 128 n 25

Flavius Josephus 197
flux 63–5
Forster, E. S. 138 n 31
Frede, M. 1, 2, 170 n 4
Frege, G. 146, 147 n 3, 151, 152
Friedländer, P. 129 n 2

Gallop, D. 158 n 3
Gauthier, R. A. 8 n 15, 8 n 16
Geach, P. T. 42 n 39, 48
Gellius, Aulus 171 n 5
geometry 104, 136–8, 138 n 33, 140
Giannantoni, G. 5 n 6
Gigon, O. 5 n 6, 5 n 8, 7 n 13
goēs (illusionist, magician) 160, 165–7
Gorgias 136
grasp, cognitive 181–2 n 24
Gray, V. J. 3 n 1, 4 n 3, 5 n 8
Griffin, M. T. 85 n 18, 87 n 20
Grote, G. 78

Hannibal 85
Harte, V. 73, 74 n 4, 87
Hartman, E. 13 n 33
Heath, T. 138 n 32
hedonism 31, 45, 50–7, 200
Heraclitus 117 n 9
Herillus 169 n 2
Hippocrates of Chios 138–9 n 33
Hirsch, E. 153, 156
Hobbes, T. 69, 70, 71
Hoerber, R. 137 n 25
Homer 20
Hossack, K. 152, 156
Hude, C. 8 n 15, 37
Hume, D. 72, 80, 87, 170 n 4
Hutton, S. 69 n 13
hypothesis 100–1, 106, 120

Iamblichus 201
idolatry 190–1, 194–5
Ildefonse, F. 48
intellectualism, Socratic 7, 9, 18–19, 24–30, 38, 44, 47, 52
Irwin, T. H. 1, 33 n 24, 43, 44, 46 n 53, 48, 129 n 2

Joël, K. 5 n 8, 6 n 10, 7 nn 12 & 13, 8 n 17, 10 nn 22, 23, & 24, 11 nn 27 & 29, 12 n 30, 13 n 33
John Chrysostom 200–1
Jolif, J. Y. 8 n 15
Judaism 193–4
Judson, L. 128 n 25
justice 15–16, 62–4, 66, 67–8
Justin the martyr 195–9

Kahn, C. H. 1, 20 n 2, 22 n 5, 22 n 6, 23 n 9, 29 n 17, 31 n 21, 39 n 33, 48, 88 n 1, 89, 95, 118 n 10, 131 nn 6 & 7
Kalligas, P. 157, 166 n 8
Kant, I. 41, 170
Karasmanis, V. 1, 109 n 25, 120 n 12, 122 n 17, 128 n 25, 347, 138 n 32
Kerferd, G. 145
Kidd, I. 91 n 8
Klein, J. 137 n 24
Klosko, G. 48
Kneale, M. 18 n 47
Kneale, W. 18 n 47
knowledge (and ignorance) 88, 97, 99, 104
knowledge (practical) 35, 39–42, 46–7
knowledge, Socratic conception of 178–9
Kraut, R. 48, 78, 80, 81, 82 & n 14, 86 n 19, 87

Lane, M. S. 75 n 5, 76 n 6, 87
law of nature 68, 70
Laws, personified in *Crito* 73–84, 87
legal status of Christians 193–4
Leon 138 n 33
Lesher, J. 42 n 43, 42 n 44, 48
Levine, J. 109 n 25
Lewis, D. 152, 153, 156
Lilla, S. 192
Locke, J. 72, 75, 79, 80, 86, 87
Lorenz, H. 20 n
Lucullus 173, 175, 185 n 28
Lyons, W. 104 n 20, 109 n 25

McKirahan, R. 31 n 21, 48, 141 n 40
Maier, H. 5 n 6, 10 n 22, 11 n 29, 14 n 39
Marchant, E. C. 8 n 15, 8 n 16, 35 n 27, 37
Marcus Aurelius 191, 195, 196, 198
Madigan, A. 109 n 25
Matthews, G. B. 88 n 1, 90 & n 5, 109 n 24
Medea 52
medicine 163, 165
Meletus 38–9, 196, 199
Meno's paradox 117, 125, 131
Minucius Felix 200
monotheism 194
Montaigne, M. de 170
morality, eternal and immutable 69
Morris Cartwright, H. 156
Morrison, D. R. 3 n 1, 18 n 45, 20 n 2
Morton, A. 156

Natali, C. 1, 3 n 1, 17 n 43, 37, 40 n 35, 45, 48
Nehamas, A. 20 n, 22 n 6, 23 n 9, 42, 48, 132 n 9, 167 n 9
Nietzsche F. 127 n 23, 157
Novo, S. 10 n 22, 12 n 30, 13 n 33, 14 n 39, 17, 18 n 44
Numenius 185 n 27, 197

oaths 80 n 12
obligation, political 72–3, 80–1, 84, 86–7
O'Byrne, B. 109 n 25
Oliver, A. 146, 147 n 3, 151, 152, 156
Origen 198, 199, 200
Orpheus 159
Ostwald, M. 50 n 1

paideia 163–4
Parmenides 158 n 3, 162, 175
Patrides, C. A. 70 n 14
Penner, T. 22 n 6, 43, 46 n 54, 48
'persuade or obey' 16–17, 78–9
Phaedra 52
Phileas 191

Philo of Alexandria 172 n 7
Philo of Larissa 169 n 2, 173, 175, 176 nn 15 & 16, 184
Philodemus 194
Photius 170
Piesse, A. 109 n 25
piety 15–16, 58, 60–4, 66–7
Pionius 191
Plotinus 198
plural subjects 151–6
Plutarch 182 n 24
Politis, V. 1, 141 n 40
Polemo 173
polytheism 193–4
Porphyry 195
Powell, J. G. F. 87
Prior, W. J. 49
Proclus 138–9 n 33
Prodicus 164
property(ies) 60–7, 121, 142–3, 147–56
property ownership 142, 148–51, 154–5
propeteia 32–3
Protagoras 159, 161, 162, 164
prudentialism 45–7
purgation 163–4, 166
Pyrrho 169 n 2, 171 n 7, 172 n 7, 176 n 16
Pyrrhoneans 169–86 *passim*
Pythagoras 201–2

Raz, J. 74, 84 n 17, 87
reason as guide to life 181–3
recollection 104, 119 n 11, 122, 126, 129, 167
Rhodes, P. J. 80 nn 11 & 12, 87
Robinson, R. 110 n 1, 129 n 2
Roochnick, D. 97 n 13, 109 n 25
Rossetti, L. 21 n 3, 47 n 55
Rowe, C. J. 162 n 6
Rumfitt, G. 149, 152, 153, 156
Rusticus 198

Santas, G. X. 26 n 15, 31 n 21, 32 n 23, 41 n 37, 49
Santoni, A. 8 n 16
Scaltsas, T. 1, 142 n 1, 156

Scepticism, Academic 169–72, 174–6, 183–7
Scepticism, Philonian, and Ciceronian 173–6
Scepticism, Pyrrhonian 183–7
Schenkl, K. 13 n 33
Schofield, M. 86, 87, 169 n 1, 177 n 16, 180 n 23, 182 n 24
Scotus, D. 68, 69
Sedley, D. N. 184 n 26, 186, 187 n 30
Seel, G. 1
Sextus Empiricus 169, 170 n 3, 171, 172 n 7, 176, 180 n 23, 182 n 24, 183, 184 n 26, 185, n 27, 186 n 29
Sharples, R. W. 18 n 46, 58 n 2, 129 n 2, 130 n 3, 137 nn 24, 27, & 28
Sharvy, R. 59 n 3
signification 112–28
Simmons, A. J. 80, 87
Simonides 52, 56, 162, 179 nn 21 & 22
Simons, P. 151, 152, 153, 156
Smith, B. 156
Socratic problem 20–1
Socratic paradox 8 n 14, 26, 55–6
sophists, sophistry 157–68 *passim*
Sophocles 200
sōphrosynē 7, 27, 37
Storey, D. 102 n 19, 109 n 25
Strauss, L. 4 n 3, 5 n 8, 8 n 16, 9 n 19, 13 n 33, 14 n 39
Striker, G. 170 n 4, 172 n 7, 179–80 n 23, 184 n 26

Tarrant, H. 171 n 5, 172 n 7
Taylor, C. C. W. 1, 66 n 9, 84 n 16, 87, 91 n 7, 100 n 15, 156, 157
Tertullian 192, 200–1
Theudius 138 n 33
Thomas, J. E. 129 n 2, 130 n 5, 137 nn 24 & 27
Thucidides 84

ti-hopoion distinction 130–1, 136
Timarchus 157
Timon of Phlius 172 n 7, 176 n 16
Torquatus 177
Tselemanis, P. 141 n 40

Van der Berg, B. 109 n 25
Vasiliou, I. 90 n 5
Viano, C. 3 n 1
virtue (*aretē*) 5–6, 25–6, 28–9, 34, 41, 43–4, 50, 52–4, 56, 129–35, 161, 163, 165, 167
Vlastos, G. 5 nn 6 & 7, 23 n 9, 29 n 17, 31 n 21, 33 n 25, 34 n 26, 35 n 27, 35 n 28, 42 nn 41 & 44, 49, 50 n 1, 51, 54, 59 n 3, 83, 84 n 16, 87, 127 n 24, 131 n 7
voluntarism 67–70
Von Staden, H. 20 n

Walsh, J. J. 9 n 19
Waterfield, R. 145, 156
Weiss, R. 73, 74 nn 3 & 4, 76 n 7, 77 nn 8 & 9, 87
Wellmann, R. R. 6 n 10, 10 n 23, 14 n 39
Whitehead, A. N. 53
Wiggins, D. 153
Wolter, A. B. 69 n 12
Woodruff, P. 42 nn 43 & 44, 49, 156
Woozley, A. D. 82, 87
Wright, C. 58 n 1

Xenophanes 171 n 7, 172 n 7, 175
Xenophon 3–49 *passim*

Yi, B. 147 n 3, 149, 152, 153, 156

Zeno the Stoic 10, 169 n 2, 173, 182 n 24
Zeyl, D. J. 31 n 21, 49